ENRICO ACERBI

THE AUSTRIAN ARMY 1805-1809
VOL. 1 THE INFANTRY

KAISERLICHE-KÖNIGLICHE HEER

I0568934

SOLDIERS&WEAPONS 029

SOLDIERSHOP PUBLISHING

THE AUTHOR

Dr.Enrico Acerbi born in Valdagno (Vicenza - Italy) on 13.8.1952; graduated in Medicine, expert in Toxicology, worked as Blood Transfusionist in local Hospital, now retired and living in Valdagno (Vicenza), partner of the War Museum of Rovereto, member of the Napoleonic Association of Italy and historiographer of the Great War. Enrico Acerbi developed historical Research during the '90s. For five years he collaborated with the Center for Great War Studies at Asiago. He also collaborated with the "Montane Community" of Arsiero as Teacher at the so called Popular University (historical training courses on the First World War) and with the Montane Community Agno-Chiampo (reconstruction of the fortifications made in the Great War). Partner of the Italian War Museum of Rovereto and founding member of the Great War Historical Research Group of Valdagno, currently entrusted to the study of Napoleonic history in Veneto and Italy. Graphic illustrator of articles on Napoleonic history. He has already published several history subjects.

ACKNOWLEDGMENT

I would particularly like to thank Robert Burnham of http://www.napoleon-series.org and all the friends, who participate in this very interesting website; above all Mr. Robert Ouvrard and Mr. Leopold Kudma. Thanks also to István Nagy for having send me part of his interesting works and articles (also if reading them in Hungarian language it had been an hard task to perform). Many thanks also to Prof. Vladimir Brnardić of Zagreb for having provided considerable assistance with the Croatian sources. Finally thanks to "The 1809 International Research Society" for the Certificate of Honour they gave to m for this work about the "Kaiserlich-königlich Armée". Naturally, a special thanks to Soldiershop for giving me this beautiful opportunity.

ISBN: 978-88-93273695   1st edition September 2018

Title: Soldiers&Weapons 029 - **The Austrian army 1806-1809. Vol 1 The Infantry** by Enrico Acerbi
Editor: Luca Cristini Editore, for the brand: Soldiershop. Cover & Art Design: Luca S. Cristini.

In cover: Imperial infantry 1089. (Ottendeld artwork)

SOLDIERSHOP PUBLISHING

PREFACE

Even when a History writer would have wanted to celebrate, maybe the greatest European power (on land), namely the Austrian Empire, he certainly would not had chosen the terrible year 1809. What for the military apparatus in Vienna could have been a beginning of a Great Military Reform, the triumph of the Generalissimus Archduke Charles, became one of the worst nightmares of Habsburg history.

In short, after a series of unfortunate events and bad military conduct, Austria disappeared from the European scene, losing further important territories but, above all, losing its mighty armies. The author chooses to tell about that period, evaluating the military organization, starting from the recruitment, up to the details of the various units, because that army, was the largest army fielded by Austria before the Great War: man told about 600,000 men, including the Levies of regional volunteers, called Landwehr (in the territories of the Austrian Crown) and Insurrectio (in the territories of the Crown of St. Stephen).

Financial hardship had indicated that the increase in the new military Force had to be conducted in a more inexpensive way. The Generalissimus had found the solution with the creation of the Landwehr, in which, in wartime, we could recruit large masses of Wehrfahigen men (suitable for Duty), without having to sustain substantial expenses during the peacetime. In the first month of this year the field units of the army counted 321.469 men with 36.560 sabres, where Fuhrwesen (Train), garrison artillery, Border Cordon troops and Marines (Marineinfanterie) were not included (a total of 21.320 men and 9.461 horses).

For the supplement of the war force and the formation of replacements were available:

- The first reserve of the German infantry units: 59.800 men

- The second reserve of the German infantry units: 73.600 men.

For the defence of the inner lands of the monarchy, first acted the Depots of the field regiments, were possible, with an average strength, according to the new system, calculated in 54.000 men and 5.000 horses.

In a second time had to act the new-established Landwehr, around 152.219 men, as soon as it would have been better organized. The Hungarian Insurrectio started with 50.000 men and 20.000 horses, while the new formations, mobilized in the Military Border, would have been 44.303 men and 171 horses strong.

So Austria entered into war with the most powerful military force of the whole Napoleonic Period (in numbers of fighters), an effort which hardly seemed possible and which surprised the world. Unfortunately its three armies (and the Landwehr) did not surprised Bonaparte, who kicked off Austria from the battlefields till 1813.

Enrico Acerbi

CONTENTS :

▲ Equestrian portrait of Kaiser Franz I, by P.J.Krafft

THE AUSTRIAN IMPERIAL-ROYAL ARMY
(KAISERLICHE-KÖNIGLICHE HEER) 1805 – 1809

The following table explains why the year 1809 (Anno Neun in Austria) was chosen in order to present one of the most powerful armies of the Napoleonic Era. In that disgraceful year (for Austria) the Habsburg Empire launched a campaign with the greatest military contingent, of about 630.000 men. This powerful army, however, was stopped by one of the more brilliant and hazardous campaign of Napoléon, was battered and weakened till the following years.

Year	Emperor	Event	Contingent (men)
1650		Thirty Years War	150.000
1673	Leopold I		60.000
1690			97.000
1706	Joseph I	Erzherzog Eugen	130.000
1735	Carl III		150.000
	Maria Theresia	Seven Years War	200.000
1777			244.000
1788		Turks War	364.000
1792		Peacetime	290.000
1792-1796	Joseph II	Revolutionary Wars	314.000-500.000
1800			495.000
1802			462.000
1803			310.000
1804			355.000
1806			345.000
1808			390.000
1809			**630.000** [1]
1810	Franz I		290.000
1811			233.000

Source: Neue Statistisch-Geographische Beschreibung des Königreichs Ungarn, Croatien, Slavonien und der ungarischen Militär Grenze, Weygand, Leipzig 1832

THE AUSTRIAN MILITARY REFORMS
Evolution of the Infantry Units 1802-1816 (source Wrede)

Date	Stand	Bat.	n. comp.	Gren. comp.	Reg. Tot. Comp.	German reg comp.		Hungarian reg. comp.		Gren. comp.	Reg. Staff
						line	Res. depot	line	Res. depot		
1802	Peace	3	6	2	20	167	4 comp	207		142	46
1805	War	3	6		24	192	233	212	212	143	53
1805	Peace	4	4	4 *	20	120		129		129	46
1806	War	5	4		24	201	215	201	212	201	51
1807	Peace	2	6	2	18	186	4 comp.	206	4 comp.	136	70
1809	War	3	6		20	198		219		145	75
1809	Peace	3	6	2	20	186	440	206	Res. depot ***	136	70
1816	War				30 (22) **	218	208	238		145	75

* independent battalions - ** included two Landwehr battalions (only for Erbländer or Imperial hereditary provinces) each with 6 companies - *** Hungarian Reserve Depot (one division) had two companies (440 men in peace and 208 in war)

▲ Hungarian infantry, officer and grenadier, 1805. From Ottenfeld artwork

Authorized Strength Numbers for Regiments

Date	Stand	German reg. line	Hungarian reg. line	Grenadier battalions	Landwehr battalions	Grenzer battalions	notes
1802	Peace	3348	4068	852	--	1242	
1805	War	4838	5198	858	--	1272	
1805	Peace	2884	2884	516 *	--	774	
1806	War	4163	4163	804 *	--	1206	
1807	Peace	3318	3638	816	--	1236	After 1809 regiment's Artillery (service or "bedienung" of 97 men) was lost
1809	War	4053	4401	870	--	1314	
1809	Peace	3318	3638	816	--	1236	Hungarian line regiments. Had one Reserve division as Depot
1816	War	5160	5063	870	1308	1428	

With 4 companies each – two veteran, old or Alt-Grenadiere companies (with the fur cap) - two young or Jung Grenadiere companies (with shako).

The nominal number of the Gemeinen (common troopers) of a company was 160. After the 1809 disaster the numbers of the soldiers went down to 60 in the German regiments and 100 in the Hungarian regiments.

The nominal number of the grenadiers of a company was 120 in the German regiments and 150-160 in the Hungarian regiments.

These numbers was not always rigid. In Octobere 1805, for example, in Italy the Austrian army was noticeably reinforced. There, the Infantry regiments had 4 fusiliers battalions plus one Grenadier's battalion, which remained by its regiment. Two Infantry regiments formed a brigade. On October 18, 1805, as regular order of battle, every Infantry brigade had a 3 pdr battery (no artillery for cavalry brigades). The regiments moved with their own artillery and, for this, was formed a special support reserve of 180 2-horse drawn carriages (Karren) and 33 4-horse drawn ammunition wagons (Leiterwagen). The artillery park was, as in the previous campaigns, at Palmanova in Friuli.

Austrian Army 1807-1812 Schemes[3]

After 1800 and the first army reorganization, the Austrian army or K.K. Österreichisches Heer improved its organization with a new recruiting system and the widening of the duty services, created new units and enlarged the Hungarian troops (probably either for having lost a large amount of crown lands, either under the direct French threats). As said, the great test for this new army completely failed in 1809. At the end of 1807 the forces ("Stande") of the Austrian army was the following:

Infantry: 63 Line Infantry regiments -- 1 Jäger Infantry regiment -- 17 National-Grenzregimenter or Military Border regiments.

Cavalry: 8 Cuirassier regiments -- 6 Dragoon regiments -- 6 Chevaulégers regiments -- 12 Hussars regiments -- 3 Uhlans regiments

Artillery: 4 Feldartillerie regiments.

Staff: (see the following dictionary of army ranks for details upon Austrian names)

Engineers: (Geniedirektor or Engineers commander: Archduke John)

Engineers Corps or Ingenieur Korps: 4 FML, 5 GM, 6 colonels, 8 Lieut.colonels, 12 majors, 64 captains, 47 lieutenants

Miners or Mineur Korps: 1 Colonel, 1 Lieut.Colonel, 1 major, 4 captains, 4 lieutenants, 4 Second lieutenant, 1 adjutant, 4 companies of 100 men.

Generalquartiermeister Staff: (GM Mayer), 4 colonels, 6 lieutenant colonels, 14 majors, 23 captains, 13 lieutenants scattered in the territory, fortresses, major cities, the military border, and sometimes named when needed.

Pontooners (Battalion Czaikisten): 1 colonel, 5 captains, 6 lieutenants, 6 second lieutenant, 11 Oberbrückenmeister (a kind of sergeant major), 6 companies each with 100 men.

Military Train (Militärfuhrwesens Korps): 1 colonel, 1 lieutenant colonel, 1 major, 6 Premier-rittmeister (first captain), 9 second-rittmeister (2nd captain), 26 lieutenants, 34 second lieutenant, 11 adjutanten scattered in the train (Fuhrwesens) divisions of the major cities.

Remountierung-Beschälswesens (horse breeding and horse replacements providers): 2 colonels, 2 lieutenant colonels, 2 majors, 3 rittmeister (scattered among the stations of Mezöhegyés, Meskowitz, Brandeis, Olmütz, Kolnitz, Vienna and Wels).

Kriegskommissariat (War Commissioner): 22 Oberkriegskommissäre, 72 Feldkriegskommissäre, 74 Kriegskommissariat officers (scattered in countryland, provinces).

Militär-Ökonomie-Commissionen and Depots (Commissioners for Military Economy and Depots): at Stockerau, Prague, Alt-Ofen (now Budapest), Brünn, Podgorze, Jaroslaw, Marburg, Karlsburg and Vienna (each with 1 Staff officer, 1 captain and 2 lieutenants).

Invalidenhäuser (Hospitals for Invalids): Vienna, Prague, Turnau, Pettau (each with a commander, a Staff officer, 1 Auditor, 1 Rechnungsführer, 1 adjutant, 1 arzt (surgeon), 1 kaplan
(priest), 1 Kriegscommissär).

Military academies: Vienna (Engineers), Wiener-Neustadt (Cadets), Joseph-Akademie of Vienna (medical service), Thierarznei-und Thierspital-Institutof Vienna (veterinary).

Military Police (Wiener Militär-Polizeiwache): at Vienna. Mounted and foot "gendarmes". (2 captains, 1 lieutenant and 1 second lieutenant, 1 adjutant and 300 policemen.

Imperial Guards (Leibgarde):

	Adelige erste Arcieren Leibgarde		
1	Hauptmann (captain)	2	Kapitän-leutnant (lieut.captains)
2	Oberlieutenant	1	Unterlieutenant
1	Premier-Wachtmeister	5	Second-Wachtmeister
3	Vize-Second Wachtmeister	60	Garden (guards)
1	Kaplan (priest)	1	Auditor
1	Kasseverwalter	1	Adjutant
1	Oberarzt		

	Ungarische adelige Leibgarde		
1	Käpitan (captain)	1	Kapitän-leutnant (Lieut.captains)
2	Premier-Wachtmeister	4	Second-Wachtmeister
1	Kaplan (priest)	52	Garden (guards)
1	Rechnungsführer	1	Auditor
1	Arzt	1	Adjutant

	Trabanten Leibgarde		
1	Hauptmann (captain)	1	Kapitän-leutnant (Lieut.captains)
2	Oberlieutenant	1	Premier-Wachtmeister
	Hofburgwache		
1	Hauptmann (captain)	1	Oberlieutenant
1	Unterlieutenant	2	Feldwebel
10	Korporale	154	gemeine

THE GERMAN LINE INFANTRY

Line infantry had regiments with 2 Grenadiers companies and 16 fusiliers companies. The regiment was split in three battalions: the 1st or Leibbattalion, the 2nd or Oberstbattalion (both with 6 companies), the 3rd or Oberstlieutenantsbattalion with 4 companies.

An infantry company had:

Staff	German Regiment Fusilier Company – 186 men		
1	Hauptmann or Capitain-Lieutenant	1	Oberlieutenant
1	Unterlieutenant	1	Fähnrich or Führer (Ensign)
1	Feldwebel	2	Gefreyte
6	Corporalen	1	Fourierschützen
2	Tambouren	1	Zimmermann
3	Privatdiener	160	Gemeine

German Infantry Grenadier Company (end of 1807)

Staff	German Regiment Grenadier Company		
1	Hauptmann or Capitain-Lieutenant	1	Oberlieutenant
1	Unterlieutenant	1	Feldwebel
6	Corporalen	1	Fourierschützen
2	Tambouren	1	Zimmermann
3	Privatdiener	140	Grenadiere

The German regiments or "Deutsch infanterie Regiments"- (those from the Erbländer or hereditary lands and regions) in peacetime: as under August 7, 1810, Emperor Franz Order, diffused by Hofkriegsrat compared with the new layout of August 10, 1811. The German Infantry regiments of the Austrian army had: 2 grenadier companies and 12 fusilier companies. Each fusilier company could have roughly 180 men (160 after 1805 and only 60 after the disaster of 1809).

	Line German Infantry Regiment Staff		
1	Oberst superior and Regiments Inhaber (Owner)	1	Oberst and Regiments Commandant
1	Oberstlieutenant	2	Majors
1	Regiments Caplan (priest)	1	Regiments Auditor
1	Regiments Adjutant (oberlieutenants or Fähnriche)	3	Bataillonsadjutanten (unterlieutenants or Fähnriche)
1	Regiments Rechnungsführer	6	K.k. ordinäre Cadetten
1	Regimentsarzt	1	Profoß
4	Ober-Ärzte	6	Unter-Ärzte
9	Führer	9	Fourieren
4	Fourierschützen	1	Regiments Tambour
5	Privatdienern		

Each battalion had one flag, which remained in the middle or in the wing (first line) of an attacking platoon. It was carried by a Führer, who was at his officers side. Companies had four platoons. (Züge) and no sections. In peacetime there were 7 Vize-Korporalen, who were helped, in campaign, by 1 Feldwebel and 6 Korporalen.

The Hungarian and the Siebenbürgisches (Transylvania) Line Infantry regiments of the Austrian army had: 2 grenadier companies and 16 fusilier companies. Hungarian companies could have around 200 men. The situation of the Hungarian Infantry regiments will be described in the Hungarian section. After the 1809 disaster this was the evolution of the Austrian "German" units:

German Infantry Regiments after 1811

	Line German Infantry Regiment Staff		
1	Oberst superior and Regiments Inhaber	1	Oberst and Regiments Commandant
1	Oberstlieutenant	2	Majore
1	Regiments Caplan	1	Regiments Auditor
1	Regiments Feldarzt	1	Regiments Rechnungsführer
1	Regiments Adjutant	6	K.k. ordn. Cadetten
3	Ober-Ärtze	9	Unter-Arzte
9	Fourieren	1	Regiments Tambour
4	Fourierschützen	8	Hautboisten (Hoboisten)
1	Profoß	5	Privatdienern
	total	56	

	Line German Infantry Regiment		officers and NCOs from the disbanded 3rd battalions
3	Hauptleute	1	Capitan-Lieutenant
4	Oberlieutenants	4	Unterlieutenants
2	Fähnriche	4	Feldwebeln
2	Führern	24	Corporalen
4	Fourierschützen	8	Tambouren
32	Grefreiten	10	Privatdienern
	Total	98	

German Infantry Company after 1811

	German Grenadier Company Staff		
1	Hauptmann	1	Oberlieutenant
1	Unterlieutenant	1	Feldwebel
6	Corporalen	1	Fourierschützen
2	Tambouren	1	Zimmermann (carpenter)
2	Privatdiener	?	Grenadiere (in the stated number)

	German Fusilier Company Staff		
1	Hauptmann or Capitain-Lieutenant	1	Oberlieutenant
1	Unterlieutenant	1	Fähnrich or Führer (Ensign)
1	Feldwebel	8	Gefreyten
6	Corporalen	1	Fourierschützen
2	Tambouren	1	Zimmermann
2	Privatdiener	?	Gemeine (in the stated number)

Wishing to present the Austrian army in detail, I decided to order the various units in branch of services, leaving only Infantry in a recruitment areas form, in an attempt to explain the Austrian system of raising regiments by areas (Werbergänzung) or regions of the same nationality. The following table is a numerical index of the infantry regiments with the appropriate section to look for them. Finally I enclosed a small dictionary of the Austrian ranks, for people who wants to enter more details.

N°	Inhaber (Owner)	Former/situation	Nationality	H=Hun G=Ger	Facings colour	Button
1	Kaiser Franz		Moravia	G	pompadour red	gold
2	Hiller		Hungary-slovak	H	kaiser yellow	gold
3	Archduke Charles		Lower Austria	G	sky blue	white
4	Hoch u.Deutschmeister		Lower Austria (Vienna)	G	sky blue	gold
5	1st Garrison	disb. 1807 into 1st-2nd Batt.			dark blue	white
6	2nd Garrison	disb. 1807 into 3rd-4th Batt.			black	white
7	Schröder		Moravia	G	dark brown	white
8	Arch. Louis		Moravia	G	poppy red	gold
9	Czartoryski	Dutch	Galicia	G	apple green	gold
10	Anton Mittrowski		Moravia	G	bright green	white
11	Erzherzog Rainer		Bohemia	G	rose	white
12	Manfredini		Moravia	G	dark brown	gold
13	Reisky	Italy-Friaul dis.1809	Küstenland	G	grass green	gold
14	Klebeck		Upper Austria	G	black	gold
15	Zach		Moravia	G	madder red	gold
16	Lusignan		Styria	G	violet	gold
17	Reuss-Plauen		Bohemia	G	light brown	white
18	Stuart		Bohemia	G	pompadour red	white
19	Alvinczy		Central Hungary	H	sky blue	white
20	Kaunitz		Moravia	G	crab red	white
21	Rohan		Bohemia	G	sea green	gold
22	Coburg		Moravia	G	kaiser yellow	white
23	Würzburg	disbanded 1809	Poland	G	poppy red	white
24	Strauch		Galicia	G	dark blue	white
25	Zedwitz		Bohemia	G	sea green	white
26	Hohenlohe		Carinthia	G	bright green	gold
27	Strassoldo		Styria	G	kaiser yellow	gold
28	Frelich		Bohemia	G	grass green	white
29	Lindenau		Moravia	G	bleumorant (l.blue)	white
30	De Ligne	Dutch	Galicia	G	light grey	gold
31	Benjowsky		Transylvania	H	kaiser yellow	white
32	Eszterhazy		Central Hungary	H	sky blue	gold
33	Sztáray/Colloredo Mansfeld		Northern Hungary	H	dark blue	white
34	Davidovich		Northern Hungary	H	madder red	white
35	Arch. J.N. Argenteau		Bohemia	G	madder red	gold
36	Kolowrat		Bohemia	G	gris de lin (mauve)	white
37	Weidenfeld		Eastern Hungary	H	poppy red	gold
38	Württemberg	Dutch disb. 1809	Poland	G	rose	gold
39	Duka		Eastern hungary	H	poppy red	white
40	Josef Mittrowsky		Moravia	G	crimson	white
41	Kottulinsky	Vorder Österreich	Galicia	G	yellow	white
42	Erbach		Bohemia	G	orange	white
43	Simbschen	disbanded 1809	Krain	G	yellow	gold
44	Bellegarde	Lombardia - Italy	Galicia	G	madder red	white
45	De Vaux	disbanded 1809	Salzburg	G	crimson	gold
46	Chasteler	Italy- Tyrol disbanded 1809	Galicia	G	dark blue	gold
47	Vogelsang		Bohemia	G	steel green	white
48	Vukassovich	Lombardia - Italy	Southern Hungary	H	steel green	gold
49	Kerpen		Lower Austria	G	pike grey	white
50	Stain	disbanded 1809	Poland	G	violet	white
51	Spleny		Transylvania	H	dark blue	gold
52	Arch. Franz Carl		Southern Hungary	H	pompadour red	gold
53	Jellacic		Croatia	H	pompadour red	white
54	Froon		Bohemia	G	apple green	white
55	Reuss-Greitz	Dutch disb. 1809	Poland	G	bleumorant	gold
56	Wenzel Colloredo		Silesia	G	steel green	gold
57	Josef Colloredo		Moravia	G	grisdelin (mauve)	gold
58	Beaulieu	Dutch	Galicia	G	black	white
59	Jordis		Upper Austria	G	orange	gold
60	Gyulai		Eastern Hungary	H	steel green	white
61	St. Julien		Banat	H	grass green	gold
62	Franz Jellacic		Banat	H	grass green	white
63	Baillet	Dutch - Italy	Galicia	G	light brown	gold

The Austrian Shako

In the k.k. Hofkriegsrat Verordnung August 18, 1806 ."Reintroduction of the Csako in the Army" begun the history of the infantry headgear. In this document it was told that, keeping in account that the legal duration of the infantry helmet was fixed in 12 years, it appears clear, now, that it was a too much long timing. We have to consider that:

1- after 6 years of use, only few models of the original manufacture did exist;

2- furthermore the helmet has given proof to be an expensive headgear;

3- in addition, many helmets were missing due to wounds, prisony etc., before the expiration of their terms of duration.

Besides, among infantry, such helmets were considered as uncomfortable; considering also that many head wounds were of unavoidable ordinariness, considering that the shape of the same helmets was subject to meteorological variations and that their manufacture and reparations caused intolerable expenses for the Companies' commanders "His Majesty has stated to eliminate them, a bit at a time, in order to equip all infantry units with the Czako". However this change would had to happen only after each helmet would had reached its expiration date, first beginning only with the hungarian regiments. Acting in a such way allowed the return of the Hungarian infantry helmets back to the Economy Commission, which would had delivered them to the German infantry units, in order to complete and fulfill stocks and in order to have a number of helmets which could be enough for the whole German force; the Commission would had delivered a congruous number of Czakos to the hungarian units, of course. This caused a delay of many years in the gradually changing of headgears for the German infantry units. Officers retained their helmets till the whole regiment would had been considered ready for the total substitution. Between various units of the German infantry it was exstimeed a legal duration of helmets for an utter 6 years period. This provision did not exempt Hungarian regiment from avoiding heavy expenses.

The "official" (k.k. sources) substitution of Caskets with Shakos began in 1808, after the December 1807 Verordnung (with some exceptions – see after) but went ahead in a very cumbersome way (due of lack of resources and the exaggerated increase in troopers considering the Landwehr units). The first units to receive Shakos were the Hungarians (it was a common hat in Insurrectio units) but, at the beginning of the 1809 Bavarian campaign, several German regiments wore the old helmets.

So, i.e., k.k. IR 54 Morzin (Bohemian) in 1808 "Got the Csako instead of the helmet. Every battalion had its own flag.." And this comes from the official history of the hungarian k.k.IR 34 FZM baron Paul Davidovich – year is 1807: "In September we received the imperial infantry Czakos instead of the helmet, as head protection, the Grenadiers, however, maintained their Bärenmützen."

In the official history of the hungarian k.k.IR 30 De Ligne (Galician) and from k.k. IR62 Jellacich (Hungarian) there were similar notes: " In December 1806 the infantry got the Csako instead of the helmet. This was made of black tissue, reinforced hardly on the top, provided with one neck and two front-back sunshades, decorated frontally with a bar and a brass Cockade, which ended with a yellow-black Rosette. Also the Officers wore the Czako like troopers, but without sunshades and did have bar, cockade, rosette, and Rank Insignia in gold. Corporals had one yellow Arras-Lace "Harrasborte", Führer and Feldwebel had two yellow Arras laces ... the subaltern officers had one, black stripe across, which became a wide, golden band for "Hauptleuten" and, finally, the Officers of the Staff gained an hat with golden stripes but without Plume (Federbusch).

Austrian sources: Adjustierungsvorschrift v.J. 1798, October 26

Notes:

[1] Including Landwehr, Insurrectio (40000) and volunteers.

[2] Wrede Alphons Frhr. von: "Geschichte der K. und K. Wehrmacht", I. Band, Wien 1898.

[3] Source: Carl Edler von Bundschuh bearb.v. „Uibersicht (sic) der bey der k.k. Oesterreichischen Armee bestehenden Milit.r-Oekonomie-Systems und allen dahin Bezug nehmenden Gesetze", Erster Band, Prag 1812. Some numbers are very hard to read in the tables, so my apologies if few mistakes could have occurred.

[4] In addition to what previously explained we can say that, in 1807, the term "german", according to the original language of people, is quite unappropriate. In effect among the so called "german" units (which wore white trousers) there were bohemian, moravian, silesian, galician units. Otherwise among the "hungarian" infantry there were the Transilvanian (Siebenbürgische) and Banater units, some of which actually spoke German.

[5] Soldiers who served as personal waiters (orderly).

[6] Music band NCOs with the Feldwebel's rank.

[7] Three in the case of the presence of a F.hnrich.

[8] Archduke John Nepomuk died on February 19, 1909. The regiment was taken by graf Eugen Argenteau.

Austrian facings colour schemes
1790-1815

Dunkelrot - Dark red -RGB 128-0-0

Pompadour rot - RGB 166-49-90

Krapprot -Madder red -RGB 194-43-41

Violett - violet - RGB 129-41-124

Carmoisin rot - RGB 148-59-91

Ponceau - Poppy red -RGB 255-0-0

Krebsrot- Lobster red -RGB 222-64-93

Gris de Lin - RGB 230-150-197 gray of flax, flax gray. - A color mixed of white,
Rosenrot- pink -RGB 255-98-178

Dunkebraun - Dark brown -RGB 94-56-32

Lichtbraun - hazel -RGB 181-123-65

Weiss - white -RGB 255-255-255

Schwarz - black -RGB 0-0-0

Orangegelb - orange -RGB 250-133-30

Kaisergelb- gambodge -RGB 247-207-5

Schwefelgelb- sulphur -RGB 252-240-10

Stahlgrün- steel green -RGB 9-103-85

Grassgrün - grass green - RGB 122-143-83
Apfelgrün - apple -RGB 70-204-81

Dunkelgrün - Dark green-RGB 7-68-0

Meergrün- sea green -RGB 107-191-155

Paperlgrün - poplar green - RGB 195-235-87

Himmelblau - sky blue - RGB 101-217-235

Bleumorant- RGB 58-141-179 (fr.)"dying Bleu", a shade of light Blue (china-pottery colour)

Franzblau- French blue RGB 28-90-138
Dunkelblau- dark blue RGB 33-52-129
Hechtgrau - pike grey -RGB 99-137-148

Grau - Aschgrau - Feldgrau -grey - RGB 182-196-187

(IN)FELIX AUSTRIA ESSAY ON THE AUSTRIAN ARMY 1805-1809

"A *vant un mois nous serons à Vienne!* " said Napoleon during his proclamation to the army, day of the Regensburg quarters, on April 24. On 13 May 1809, the French entered, for the second time, the Austrian capital city and seized it. Austrian forces were, at the time, considerably weakened; they lost 50.000 men dead, wounded or prisoners; lost also around 100 a large part of their depots and a considerable amount of horse-trained vehicles. Archduke Charles' Army was split in two parts; repulsed inside Bohemia, behind its former line of ope-rations, were the most of that prince's forces. Archduke John's Army's, quickly recalled towards Vienna, left Italy free for the French and Italian troops.

This long article has the target to examine the Austrian army after (during) the attempts of the Archduke Charles reform, from the beginning of 1809 till the end of the various campaigns which caused the collapse of the Austrian military organization. As introduction, however, it could be worthy of attention to examine the way taken by Austrian military apparatus since the first reform that brought directly to the ruinous year 1805. It is a schematic summary useful to understand the following organization decreed in Vienna.

Common Text Abbreviations

Abt.	Abteilung = unit (small unit in fact), detachment	FrK	Freikorps = Volunteers unit
AOK	Armeeoberkommando = general headquarters	GbKan	Gebirgskanone = mountain gun
AR	Artillerieregiment = artillery regiment	GM	General Major = brigadier
Bn.	Bataillon = battalion	Hb	Haubitze = howitzer
Brig	Infanteriebrigade = infantry brigade	HKG	Hofkriegsrat = Imperial War Council
Bt	Batterie = battery	IR	Infanterieregiment
Comm.	commander	Jäg.	Jäger = light infantry
comp	Kompagnie = company	K.K.	Imperial-Royal
Det	Detachement = detachment	Ldwr	Landwehr
Div.	Division = infantry division	Maj.	Major
div.	division = cavalry division	Ob.	Oberst = Colonel
FJB	Feldjägerbataillon = rifle battalion (light infantry)	ObstLt.	Oberstleutnant = Lieutenant Colonel
FM	Feld-Marschall = Field-marshal	ObLt.	Oberlieutnant = 1st Lieutenant
FML	Feld-Marschall Leutnant= Field-marshal lieutenant	Rgt.	Regiment
Frw	Freiwilligen = volunteer	Sqn(s).	cavalry Squadron (s)
Frh.	Freiherr = Baron	Zug	= platoon

The Fatal Destiny of the Austrian Empire till the Horrible "Anno Neun"[1]

Table: All territorial properties, gains and losses are given in "geografischen Quadrat-Meilen" (Q.M.) or Square-Miles, that's around 2,59 km² .

Year	Event	Note	Gains	Losses
1797	Peace of Campo- Formio.	Austria cedes the Austrian Netherlands, Falkenstein, Lombardy, and Modena; gaining Venice, Istria, Dalmatia, and the Gulf of Cattaro.	784.63	843.47
1801	Peace of Luneville.	Austria cedes Toscana, Fristhal, and the Etsch region. In return it gains Salzburg, Berchtesgaden, and part of Passau.	193	392.86
1802	'Entschädigungsreceß'	compensates Austria, which gains Trient and Brixen, the *secundogenitur* part of Eichstädt.	100.80	
1803	Purchase of Lindau and Rothenfels.		9	
1804	Exchange of Blumeneck and other small pieces of ground in Weingarten.		2.50	

1805	Peace of Preßburg.	Austria loses Venice, Istria, Dalmatia, the Gulf of Cattaro, Tyrol with Vorarlberg, Breisgau, and all Swabian manors; gaining Würzburg for the *secundogenitur*, the 'Deutsch-meisterthum' for an Austrian prince, and the guarantee for compensation for the house of Oesterreich-Este.	90	1410.40
1806		Franz II cedes the throne of the German Empire, and accepts the title of Emperor of Austria. Dissolving of Germany. Austrian-Würzburg joins the Confederation of the Rhine and acquires the 'Reichsrittergüter'.	5	
1807	Gränzreceß with Italy.	The Isonzo becomes the Austrian border	3	22.38
1809	Peace of Vienna.	Austria cedes the whole Krain, Friaul, Trieste, part of Croatia and Kärnten, the manor Rezuns, Salzburg, Berchtesgaden, Passau, the Inn quarter, part of the Hausruck, the whole of West Galicia, the Zamosc region, the Krakau region, and to Russia a part of East Galicia, later to decide on.		1846.22

First Archduke Charles Reforms (as president of the Hofkriegsrat[2] : Jan. 9, 1801 – 1805)

Charles, now FM (Field-marshal) and Hofkriegsrat president, in 1801 wrote to the Emperor Franz: "*In the case of an utter war we must purge every interference in the chain of command* " (the Staatsrate or the local states parliaments, various bureaus and so on) . The Emperor followed that suggestions and, on December 1801, created the Ministry of War (Kriegs-und Marine Ministerium) giving it to Charles and relegating the Hofkriegsrat in a second decisional line.

The Ministry concentrated all the financial matters related to the army and the war, in order to increase the investments. On December 5th, 1801 the Emperor Franz ordered a new formation of the Army, which, on February 1st, 1802 began to be reformed, by cavalry and the light troops, with the:

1 --- disbanding of the 1800's Light infantry battalions and raising of the Tiroler-Jäger-Regiment. Also disbanded were two old cavalry regiments, the Jäger zu Pferd and the Slavonische Grenz-Husaren-Regiment. Other cavalry units (3 reg. Cuirassiers, 3 Dragoons reg.; only the Szekler-Husaren-Regiment was retained)

2 --- raising a third Uhlans regiment. then followed other provisions:

3 --- artillery introduced the system of Line and Reserve batteries, now all commanded by artillery officers. Line artillery was formed with the former regiments-battalion guns (regiment = 4 pieces of 6 or 3 pdrs.; Grenadier battalion = 2 pieces of 6; Grenzers or Military Border units= 2 pieces of 6 or 3 pdrs. per battalion). The organisation of the Reserve batteries, however, was not easy (poor finances and lack of horses) and it was mandatory to call civilians fund-raisers to complete the reform.

4 --- the Pontoneers obtained 5 companies, while the Sappers and the Miners were now autonomous Corps; Pioneers, which were under the command of the General-Quartiermeisterstab (General Quartermaster), had to be raised only in the case of a war.

This table presents the new Archduke Charles peacetime army:

N.	Troops	Batt.	Gren. Div.	Companies	Squ.	Men	Total
61	Line infantry regular regiments	3	1			215.028	
1	Jäger regiments (Light infantry)	3				2.586	
17	Border regiments (Grenzer)	2				44.214	261.828
8	Cuirassiers regiments				8	12.256	
6	Dragoons regiments				8	9.192	
6	Chevaulégers regiments				8	10.884	
11	Hussars regiments				8	21.336	
1	Hussars regiment				6		59.110
3	Uhlans regiments				8	5.442	
4	Artillerie Rgt.			16		11.260	12.336
1	Bombardiers corps			5		1.076	
	Total						333.274

In wartime, the total force to be reached was 433.387. Practically these numbers were never reached (lack of finances). So at the beginning of 1805, the number of the retired soldiers was 97.152, that of the not-serving cavalrymen was 37.095 and, in the whole Monarchy lands, there was no single battery ready to operate. Moreover, in January 1809, it lacked still 13.076 men in order to complete the peacetime force. There were 186.446 infantrymen, 37.095 "sabres" and 11.124 artillerymen under the Vienna's Colours.

A New General Staff

The Austrian Army was one of the first military organization to lay down separate orders even for the dressing of its general officers; note that by 1798 regulations (concerning the dress of both general officers and staff) those booklets contained rigid instructions not only for dress uniforms but also for service, court and town dress.

To the Hungarian cavalry generals were given a special uniform based on the hussar dressing style and this was often adopted by other cavalry generals, as they were also the colonels-in-chief of hussar regiments, with colours based on their regimental facings.

During the last half of 18th century and at the beginning of 19th, the Austrian general staff did not correspond to a modern applications of warfare. After the Hubertsburg peace which ended the Seven-Years war, the whole institutions of the army, in a great chaos, were reshaped by marshal Lacy's genius in one more modern appropriate form.

Finally, according to the general views of Charles, the general staff was separated in three sections, namely:
1) the Adjutantur, with the general-quartermaster office as well as the school (as teacher) for future Staff officers;
2) the Mappeurs or, how designated in the French army, "Géographes" engineers;
3) others Officers commanded to the war archives (Kriegsarchiv).

This was the first aim of the reform: education of specialists staff officers.

In autumn 1804 ended the first period of the Charles' Reforms. The Archduke, above all, dedicated his work mainly to administrative matters (lack of money!?) so the army was not ready to mobilize. However there was a Coalition, political heavy interferences, the hope to act with a strong Russian help and so on ....

The General Mack Period

In 1804 disagreements between Emperor Franz and his brother, the Archduke Charles, [3] led to general baron Karl Mack von Leiberich being appointed chief of the quartermaster general Staff and, after Mack's instigation, a number of regimental changes were ordered in preparation for the forthcoming campaign of 1805. Charles however retained his charge as War Ministry and continued his plan to reform the army with:

A New Conscription System

With regard to the soldiers' enrollment, the first reform began in 1802 (Imperial Patent on May 4, 1802), when was firstly stated a new way in timing the military period of duty, with the idea of a different service period from the previous "lifelong" one: some years in active duty, others in Reserve mode.

A consequence of this was the 1804 act (Conscription-Normale Oct. 23, 1804), when army complementary recruitment districts (in Galicia) acted side by side to those of the historical "German" [4] hereditary countries, by which the Levy was put on a wider basis increasing the population suitable to military duty and with the limitation of a too large number of emancipations.

This was the second target of the Reform: every regimental conscription area could have permanent "supporting" districts (Hilfsbezirke) in order to straightforwardly reach the full military strenght of wartime (and peacetime too). Every infantry regiment now recruited no more in a generic administrative province (Kreis) of the Empire, but in a stated District of Levy (Conscriptionsbezirk), which got the same number of its own regiment. This system will last till the Great War 1914-1918, practically unchanged. This made simplier all the conscription operations and faster the operations to mobilize troops. The Conscription director of the Bezirk was a General Staff officer of the same regiment. For the supplement of the military strength, they now needed armies of same forces, in peace as in war, with only a few branches of the suitable armed forces obliged to have still long Duty times, in the interest of the military training. [5] Therefore the widespread lifelong Duty was abolished and began the gradual elimination of the older veteran soldiers. Obviously the new system (like in all Austrian new "adventures") needed a gradual and longtiming way to be mastered. So, in 1805, there was a substantial confusion in all attempts to re-constitute the wartime strenght of infantryunits.

During 1805, the heavy political interferences caused the necessity to act time by time, approximatively, and this utterly weakened the military force of Austria. FML (Field-marshall lieutenant) Mack recognized the extreme need to gather all available resources, but it was hardly enough to make one ready army, however, to be reorganized from its roots. Infantry and cavalry had new arrangements. Only artillery maintained its organisation. The cavalry regiments were to be organized on 4 divisions [6] of 3 squadrons each, but only some had 3 while many had only 2 effective sqns. Probably many thought the next campaign had to be fought mainly with (by) the Russian forces, the British money and the Austrian bravery. But this was not sufficient.

Revolution in Infantry Organization

The number of companies in each line infantry battalion was reduced from six to four with each "German" company established at a strength of 160 other ranks, 180 for the Hungarian companies and 120 for the elite Grenadier companies. This system, during the war, affected directly the army of Italy.

This was the first cause of the 1805 military failure. The need to organize all the line regiments caused: the weakest Austrian battalions of the napoleonic period.

The 'surplus' companies were used to form additional battalions giving the regiment a strength of five field battalions of fusiliers, each of four companies in strength, including the former depot (Kader) battalion and a sixth 'elite' battalion made up of the two Grenadier companies and two fusilier companies, redesignated Velite-Grenadiere; this last battalion was the depot battalion during peace time and had to be detached to the Army Reserve during war time.

The Grenadier divisions of each infantry regiment had been always formed into semi-permanent battalions to act as a tactical Elite reserve, except during the 1805 campaign when each regiment had its own Grenadier battalion. This was the second cause of the 1805 military failure: the extreme weakness of spreading Elite units

Battalions were numbered 1 to 6, with the Grenadier battalion always receiving the number 5 for all regiments, and battalion-divisions and companies numbered consecutively through the regiment. The battalion's artillery, which previously distributed three guns per battalion was now brigaded into a single six gun regimental battery. However the abolition of the battalion-regimental artillery was a reform not applied at all. See after.

At the beginning of the 1805 campaign, this re-organisation was, however, only partially completed and many regiments, particularly those stationed away far from the main field army, retained the former organisation, while many regiments were forced to undertake changes during the mobilisation, with the subsequent ensuing chaos. At this point some questions raise among the researchers:

1- Was it a typical Austrian disposition to have good rules with the quite impossibilty practical application of them? (this happened also in 1809 with the army Corps).

2- Who really was general Mack: a genius who acted in wrong times or a true military donkey?

The Vanguard Duties

With the dissolution of the (poor and somehow unuseful) light infantry battalions, in 1801, was formed a regular Jäger regiment from the cadres of existing troops and titled the "Tyroler-Jäger-Regiment", establishing itself with three battalions each of six companies organised in the same manner as the line infantry fusiliers.

The third Austrian weak-point was the incapacity to answer to the necessity to raise fast and mobile reconnaissance units, tirailleurs like the french Légère.

At beginning the Jägers operated as independent battalions, assigned to different brigades as required, and soon proved their worth in the field. In 1805 the regiment was officially taken into the line, given the number 64 and had an exclusive recruitment inside the Tyrol .

The Greater Mack Mistake

One more dynamic reform was that of the Verpflegsanstalten (supply centers), which FML Mack imagined as reshaped after the French example. As Napoleon did, therefore, Mack applied the requisition system over the seized territory instead of the previous food magazines organization. In few time he decided to shrink the army Train to an half of its force.

The natural consequence of this latter rule was that they anyway raised defective transport units or "Trainwesens", and they also gave to private enterprises not only the management of the army Train, but also the renting of the carriages for line and reserve artillery.

This was the fourth Austrian weak-point : a complete chaos in the Supply lines.

In vain Archduke Charles braced himself, with all his energy, against this pernicious project, which could have been executed in a more favourable moment, anyway not under very unfavourable circumstances, as in mobilization period, when there were a real danger of damaging the whole army within few months. Mack's influ-

▲ Light infantry 1801–1805. From Ottenfeld artwork

ence, however, was already greater; and his suggested army reorganization (Heeresorganisation) became effective thanks the imperial acts (Handbillets) of Persenburg, June 14th, enforced on August 1st, with the new standards which had to be accepted everywhere.

Charles wrote: "In political respect one must suppose once again that, FML Mack, have got data and special instructions, without whose knowledge it will be impossible to judge the eccentric way of his ruling!"

So Mack went to war, Napoleon did the residual tasks at Austerlitz.

This table is a short compendium of the Austrian military Reforms (from 1805) which led till the "Great powerful army" of 1809.

YEAR	Date	Act	Former or detail	New
1805	April	New regulations for cavalry (Graf Grünne)	Deployment in 3 ranks	abolished. Now in 2 ranks.
	Aug 1	Reduction of the infantry and cavalry baggage Train	4-horse drawn Wagen (company/squadron)	4-horse drawn Wagen (inf/cav division)
	Aug 1	Mack Reform	Inf. battalions of 6 comp. + 2 comp. grenadiers	Inf. battalions of 4 comp. Regiment = 5 battalions
1805	Sept	Pioniers Vorschrift	regiment = 20 comp. 3 batt. + Grenadiers div.	20 companies
				Pioniers comp. + 2 men 60 men armed
		infantry in Italy	Regiments	Regiments with 4 batt. + 1 Grenadier battalion with regiments
			Brigades	2 regiments + 1 battery 3 pdr. (Cavalry brig. had no artillery)
		New organization of the Supreme Command	Ministerial Kanzlei (GM graf Grünne)	Correspondance with Hofkriegsrat, private mail of the Supreme Commander, with Allies, with Enemies, management of the common funding
			Operationskanzlei (FML Zach)	Registrations of operations, Military Diaries, military acts.
			Detailkanzlei (ObstLt Piccard)	Army lists, task tables, Army/divisions orders.
			Armee-Generalkommando (FML baron Skal)	Supplies (food, uniforms, Train, medical, territorial service etc.)
1806	Febr 10	Supreme Command	New rank ?	Archduke Charles as Generalissimus
	Oct 20	Wiener Neustadt Academy		new organization
1807	September 1		Regulations	New Dienstreglement for infantry
	end of the year	New organization in field	Regiments in 5 batt.	3 battalions (I and II with 6 coys, III with 4), 2 grenadiers comp. – 1-2 depot comp.
		New artillery system	regimental	batteries (brigade, position and reserve)
		Light infantry	disbanding the light batt.	raising the Jäger (Feldjäger) batt.
		Uniform	cask helmets for infantry	substitution with Shakos
1808		Remounts for cavalry	various places	all to Wiener-Neustadt Central Armee Equitation Institut
		Militär-Grenze	Recruitment	new Confinien-Werbung Act
		Kadeten-kompanien		new raising of Academy cadets coys
	May 12	Reserve-Anstalt Act		extension of the military service duty. Men in Reserve status.
	June 9	Imperial Patent		Formation of the Landwehr force
1809	Febr	New organization in field	Armies split in Treffen, Wings, divisions and brigades	Army Corps (2 inf. Div. + 3rd Div. with Light cavalry and 2-3 batt. of light troops)
		Hungarian recruitment		new rules (Werb-Instruction)

The Generalissimus Period

In 1806 Archduke Charles regained control of the army administration and promptly began to push through his reforms in an attempt to bring some degree of modernisation to the K.K.[7] Armee. On February 10, 1806, Charles wrote to his brother, the Emperor Franz:

"After the last unhappy events and a peace gained with so big sacrifices, it is necessary, with the highest urgency, to bring the war power of the Monarchy in such a condition that it could become a reliable protection for my hereditary country, after measuring the resources in men and finances, distinguished by order and training. The first step for reaching this purpose I think, Yours Grace, I have to act in the quality of a Generalissimus,[8] at the top of my complete army."

This was a steady Charles' idea, that of concentrating the Supreme Command in a single hand. Charles was aware that the French victories had been gained as France had one chief and one commander (not Coalitions, not Hofkriegsrat, no politics).

Charles choose three men in order to upgrade his "1805 battered" army: a political and military Adjutant, the FML Earl Philipp Grünne, the general quartermaster Mayer and his personal generaladjutant baron Wimpffen. They put in forced retirement not less than 25 high generals, in the first month of 1806; the substitutes were younger and more ready to learn new ways of warfare. They organized a new Hofkriegsrat which could manage military matters in a very fast way. The whole army received a fixed deployment or "Ordre de Bataille" also for peacetime, gradually raising new "Corps" staffs, which had to recruit troops in their areas and which could swiftly activate (mobilize) units in early wartime.

In 1807 and 1808 were published the new "Reglements" for the troop-training and finally Austria had also its "légère" with the raising of the Feldjäger battalions. The serious problem of lack of horses was managed creating the Equitationsinstitut and the system of the Pferde-depots (horses depots), which had to gather and keep all kind of cavalry equipments. As for infantry, Charles created also the Landwehr (territorial) army, a "shield" against invaders (Schutze des Landes gegen Invasionen) and other.

The Charles Conscription System improved

When, in 1806, the Emperor Franz abdicated his title of Holy Roman Empire Emperor, Austria suspended the recruitments from the historical electoral (German) areas. In order to enroll again the "now foreign" citizens in its army, in 1807, they created the "Borders Levy" (Confinen-Werbung, instead of the former Reichs-Werbung), but the support of this additional Levy was unsatisfactory and unuseful. [9] Austria had to recruit soldiers mainly in its national lands, but volunteers were always welcome (from Netherlands, Rhinelands, Bavaria, Saxony, Italy and from all the previous lost territories.). So, in order to reach the stated military strength, a Supreme Resolution Act (June 12, 1806) created the Reserve (Reserve-Anstalt). Its organization was strictly tracked by Charles himself, ending in 1808 with the creation of the Landwehr.

Every regiment had to maintain a force of 2 battalions as Reserve-Mannschaft (each with 600-700 men), which could have been asked to enroll again in the case of war. Every man of the Reserve had his Legitimationskarte and the Reserve Duty period now lasted from 17 till 40 years. [10]

This Reform, in 1809, was extended also into Hungary (neue Werbe-Instruction für Ungarn), where the recruitment was still free (voluntary). Now the Magyars were enrolled in the Counties areas, numbered with the same regiment numbers as in the hereditary lands. Insurrectio national units (a sort of Hungarian Landwehr already present since the end of the 18th Century) and the Grenzregiments of the Military Border maintained their own historical systems.

Charles then passed to his old project: the "shield against invaders". But it was more probable that he would try to turn round the French prohibition to the Austrian rearmament by exploiting the territorial areas as the already existing Hungarian model. Basing on his personal experience in raising an own Legion (thanks to his faithful Bohemians) Charles suggested to raise a national defensive army force, similar to the Magyar Insurrectio army. This was the first step along the stairway which would have had to bring to the rebirth of the imperial army. The provision for the Landwehr caused minimal alarm in France, as the system was structured as defensive. In addition, the new territorial army would have had to regulate the control and the command over the volunteers units (Freiwillige), which were various and numerous in the Austrian tradition.

The orders to establish the raising of the Landwehr were issued with the Imperial Patent of 9th June 1808. This act made compulsory the service in the militia, for all males of the hereditary lands (Austria, Moravia, Bohemia,

Silesia and Galicia) aged between 18 and 45, unless exempted or already serving with the reserve units. In four provinces, Upper and Lower Austria, Bohemia and Inner Austria, were planned 170 battalions, however, actually, only around 70 battalions took the field. Each province was subdivided into districts, each required to raise between one and five battalions of six companies, organised as the line infantry and under the command of retired officers of the regular army or "self-commissioned" nobles and landowners.

Although some "Freikorps", or volunteer battalions, were initially a military element completely separate from the Landwehr, being recruited from willing volunteers who signed only for the duration of the war, these units soon began to give the best recruits to the Landwehr, which, in fact, became the Cadre corps, around which the whole system operated. Napoleon strongly disagreed with this "secondary" army system and one of the clauses of the Vienna Treaty was the total Abolition of the Landwehr armies.

A New (or Maybe a Reverse Thread) Infantry

Considering the persistent lack of resources the Generalissimus did not think anyway to increase the standing army by the creation of new troops units. His first (tactical) provision was to change the structure of the infantry regiments back to that formally used before Mack's reforms. Regiments now consisted of two field battalions each of six-companies and a depot battalion of two companies, increased to four in 1808.

This was the second step towards rearmament: Austrian battalions retook their former fire power.

The two elite Grenadier companies of each regiment were again brigaded together and combined with Grenadier divisions of other regiments to form Grenadier battalions, during war time. The third step for the effectiveness: return of the Elite reserve (similar to the French Guards units)

Whenever called to war standing, the regiment raised four additional companies, two being drafted into the third battalion, giving the unit three full field battalions and the remaining two forming the cadre of a new depot battalion, the fourth. However, during the 1809 campaign, several regiments augmented this fourth battalions and a few even had five field battalions serving in different armies. Battalions were numbered 1 to 3, divisions 1 to 9 and companies 1 to 18 consecutively through the regiment and was introduced a new administrative unit, the zug (similar to the modern platoon) which was a quarter-company, or the half of an half-company.

This was the fourth trial to reach the best efficiency in campaign: the target to create small detachments with "smart" NCOs (Zugsführern, which actually wasn't yet a regular army rank) able to act by own initiative. ("à la prussienne" or as Prussian did).

A New Artillery and a New Mobility

In 1807 Archduke Charles withdrew definitively the regimental and battalion guns from infantry to form brigade batteries, except for the Grenzer regiments which continued to maintain two light artillery pieces per battalion. This was the fifth goal to reach: a new artillery system able to concentrate pieces forming Grand Batteries (as French did). The historical two Garrison regiments (5th and 6th) were disbanded in 1807; the 1st Garrison regiment (Nr. 5) forming the 1st and 2nd Garrison battalions and the 2nd Garrison regiment (Nr. 6), forming the 3rd and 4th. [11] Charles, in 1808, continued with his light infantry's reform by raising seven new battalions, formed by experienced officers and N.C.O.s coming from existing regular battalions and from recruits found in Tyrol, among the skilled marksmen taken from other infantry regiments and the various estates throughout the Bohemian, Galician and Moravian regions; this virtually eradicating the skilled hunters from the countryside, as some prominent landowners complained. In 1809 was raised an eleventh Jäger battalion. However, in order to fill the companies to full strength, only nine battalions were in the field that year. In order to emphasize their battle mission, rather than their wood hunters origin, they were called as Field (Feld) hunters (Jäger).

The sixth Charles' original provision, made to create a fast moving infantry, capable of cover and support tasks so was: the raising of the Feldjäger battalions (bataillons de Tirailleurs) assigned to Vanguard units as very mobile units.

Imperial Austrian Cavalry

It is universally known that Austria had a famous (and expensive) cavalry, master of acting as support, escort, reconnaissance branch. They were the core of the vanguard units. But that wonderful and skilled cavalry was completely unable to maneuver and perform in great masses (cavalry brigades, even divisions), unlike the French cavalry, which trained itself to learn this.

In the far 1792, at the beginning of the French revolutionary wars, the cavalry of the K.K. Armee consisted of thirty-five regiments: two carabiniers, nine cuirassiers, six dragoons, seven chevauleger, nine hussars, one uhlan regiment and a halfregiment of Stabs-dragoner (General Staff dragoons). It was an heritage of the Maria-There-sia's cavalry; the branch had a lot of historical regiments, which did the same things in battle.

It became essential to reform and to gather together the units, and the first simplification was the reorganisation of 1798. Then the carabinier regiments were absorbed into the cuirassiers, while a further "armored" regiment born, bringing the total to twelve. Dragoons and chevaulegers were combined into a single branch and two new regiments formed. The hussars were brought up to twelve regiments, a new uhlan regiment raised and a single regiment of "Chasseurs à cheval" (Jäger-zu-Pferde) brought into being.

Even if Archduke Charles was not a cavalry specialist, he agreed to modernize the noble branch of the army. First of all it was necessary to eliminate the "afoot cavalry" (Dragoons), which often had acted like a sort of "light infantry" moving fastly with horses. In 1798 Austria organized its first true light cavalry (the Light dragoons), which comprised the former Chevaulégers regiments. However that early experience led under poor training (lack of time for the 1799 and 1800 campaigns) did not prove to be worthy.

A second simplification happened in 1801, under some crisis in the imperial finances. Cavalry was again re-organised, the cuirassier regiments reduced to eight, whilst the dragoons regiments were again divided into dragoons and chevaulegers; the mounted Jäger regiment was disbanded, as was also one hussars regiment. The Stabs-dragoner regiment was reduced to a single division (2 squadrons). After that provisions Austria waited till 1809 to see the birth of a third uhlan regiment. Gradually the Austrians became to consider to train the Dragoons as heavy cavalry mounted with firearms, leaving to Chevaulegers (hussars and uhlans too) the light cavalry tasks. Unluckily, after the 1805 "fiasco", lacking horses (remounts) Vienna was forced, in 1806, to reduce heavy cavalry, cuirassiers and dragoons, to "ghost" regiments each with only two divisions (two-squadrons each), with other two Depot-divisions in wartime. Chevaulegers, hussars and uhlans (which all maneuvered in the same way, differentiating themselves only for their own ethnic and traditional composition, as per recruitment) had eight squadrons in four divisions, with the exception of the Grenz-Husaren-Regiment "Szekler" Nr. 11, which maintained only six squadrons. The depot squadrons remained as in the previous times. The heavy cavalry squadrons now consisted of 135 men (they were 150) and the light cavalry squadrons of 150 troopers (they were 180).

Probably one of the several causes of the 1809 failures was the presence of weaker cavalry units (with few reserve horses available), which dramatically increased the difficulty to train and to manoeuver as large (brigade) masses. This will be primarily manifest at the great cavalry battle of the Bavarian 1809 campaign: Alt-Eglofsheim.

Each cavalry squadron was now divided into two Flügels (wings), or half-squadrons, and each "Flügel" in turn into two "züge" (platoons). The cavalry divisions were numbered 1 to 4 consecutively and the squadrons 1 to 8 consecutively, with each "Flügel" numbered 1 and 2 within its own squadron. The "züge", however, were numbered by their rank in the line. Therefore the 1st Squadron had "züge" 1, 3, 5 and 7, the 2nd Squadron the "züge" 2, 4, 6, and 8, and accordingly through the whole regiment. As in infantry, the regiments were named after their Proprietors commanders (Inhaber) and each division and squadron therein named after their commanding officer.

The "Guns" and Charles Reforms

The organization of the Austrian artillery underwent very few changes, since the Seven Years War, and was a so intricate branch to even reach a point similar to a complete disorder. In 1792 there existed three Feld-Artillerie-Regimenten (artillery regiments), a Bombardier Corps (bombers), an Artillerie-Fusilier-Bataillon, the Artillerie-Feldzeugamt (ordnance workshops) and the Garnison-Artillerie-Districten Batteries (fortress artillery).

The Field Artillery Regiments were purely administrative bodies, the personnel and ordnance being split into non- permanent companies, assigned to the infantry as battalion's artillery and to the cavalry as brigade's batteries, with the surplus guns assigned to the Artillery Reserve.

The Bombardier-Corps and Artillerie-Fusilier-Bataillon, with certain elements of the Garrison Artillery, provided the men and guns for the Artillery Reserve, and the Feldzeugamt was responsible for the maintenance of the ordnance. Archduke Charles had got firsthand experience of the more efficient artillery system of the French army and in 1806 started to reorganize and modernise the Austrian artillery administration using his experience. So he considered necessary a totally new a modern system, "à la Française", which involved transports.

First, in 1806, regimental artillery companies were withdrawn and the various artillery units reorganised to form four regiments (each of four battalions). Each artillery battalion consisted of four companies or batteries. The more skilled gunners from the Bombardier-Corps were reorganised into five companies and distributed throughout the artillery to manage and supervise the howitzers workings.

The Artillerie-Feldzeugamt was retained, but its personnel was distributed as required and the Garrison artillery was redesignated the Gewehr-Fabrique-Corps, responsible for all garrison artillery and fortifications.

A new Handlanger-Corps (workers) was formed into eight companies or four divisions, to provide labour for the gun placements, formerly provided by infantry or extra artillery personnel. These companies were distributed throughout the batteries as required. In 1808 was adopted also the British Congreve Rocket System and each of the four artillery regiments formed its Feuerwerkscompagnie.

The Pieces

Prior to 1807 the regimental artillery contingents usually consisted of 3 pdr light field guns, assigned to line infantry regiments serving in Italy and in the Military Border, the 6 pdr field guns were assigned to the remaining line regiments and a mix of 6 pdr, 12 pdr field guns and 7 pdr howitzers assigned to the artillery Reserve, which was an unofficial formation distributed at the discretion of the field commanders. Cavalry had its Kavallerie-Batterien, usually made of four 3 pdr field guns, distributed on a regimental basis when in campaign.

In 1807 artillery was reorganised into:
- the Brigade batteries, assigned one to each infantry brigade, (3 pdr or 6 pdr field guns)
- the Position batteries (heavier guns) which were distributed to Divisions, whilst each cavalry brigade was assigned a Kavallerie-Batterie.

Battery Composition 1807-13

Type	Field Guns	Howitzers
3 pdr Brigade Batterie	8 x 3 pdr	---
6 pdr Brigade Batterie	8 x 6 pdr	---
6 pdr Positions-Batterie	4 x 6 pdr	2 x 7 pdr
12 pdr Positions-Batterie	4 x 12 pdr	2 x 7 pdr
3 pdr Kavallerie-Batterie	4 x 3 pdr	2 x 7 pdr
6 pdr Kavallerie-Batterie	4 x 6 pdr	2 x 7 pdr

Artillery Military Train

The reform of the military transports (Train) was probably the most important reform of Archduke Charles. It was a totally new system were the former civil Train, became militarized. All transports, draft horses and drivers for artillery were now provided by the new Militar-Fuhrwesens-Korps, where most of the draft animals and personnel were recruited on a civilian contract basis for each campaign.

In 1808 the Fuhrwesen were officially taken into the army with an established strength and were organised on a regimental basis around the park division. Then, for the first time, the officers received rank as commissioned officers. The corps was divided into small divisions of around 80 - 200 men and horses, dependant on their duties, and distributed throughout the artillery. The Fuhrwesenkorps-Artillerie-Bespannungsdivisionen attached to each battery of foot artillery were commanded by a Rittmeister (captain) or Oberleutnant (1st lieutenant), assisted by an Unterleutnant (2nd lieutenant), two Wachtmeisters (sergeants), and a Corporal with 80 drivers. The Fuhrwesenkorps-Artillerie- Reitendedivisionen, attached to the cavalry batteries, had a similar command staff but with 200 drivers. The 3 pdr and 6 pdr field guns and the smaller ammunition wagons required four draft horses, while the larger pieces and wagons, along with the cavalry guns, needed six to mobilize. However, by 1809, most guns were served by six- horse teams, for greater speed and mobility.

The "Minds" (Technical Troops)

The technical corps of the Austrian Army was divided into two sections: the Engineer Corps, consisting of engineers, sappers and miners under the General Director of Engineers, and the Pioneer Corps, made up of the pioneers and pontooners under the jurisdiction of the General Quartermaster's Department.

Because of the eight-year training period required, and the reluctance of educated young noblemen to enlist with the technical corps, the Engineer Corps was always maintained at full strength and consisted of ten general officers, General-Directeurs, Pro-Directeurs, Inspecteurs and Genie-Generals, six Ingenieurs-Obersten, twelve Ingenieurs- Oberstleutnants, ten Ingenieursmajors, thirty Ingenieurshauptmann and 106 Ingenieurs-Hauptleutnants and Oberleutnants. These officers were distributed as commanders and advisory officers to the Sappeurs-Korps (sappers) and Mineurs-Korps (miners), the former consisting of three companies and the latter of four companies, (each corps being under the command of a Sappeur/Mineurmajor with a captain commanding each company assisted by a lieutenant).

Companies consisted of about 120 men directed by two Sappeur/Mineurfeldwebel, two Sappeur/Minenmeister, two Sappeur/Minenführer with the equivalent ranks of corporal, lance-corporal and gefreiter. The troopers were called Ober-, Alt, and Jungsappeur/Mineur (1st, senior and junior sappers). Recruits for the engineer departments had previously been drawn from the infantry. However, after 1798, they were carefully selected from civilian craftsmen and the better infantry volunteers and had to pass intelligence tests and examinations, be physically fit and able to read and write German fluently before they were allowed to join the corps.

The Pioneers (Pionniers-Korps) and Pontoons (Pontoniers-Korps) had previously been raised only in the event of war, but in 1792 were established two battalions of pioneers and one battalion of pontoniers, each with six companies of 120 men.

In addition to the above there existed a single battalion of 'boat-handlers', the Czaikisten-bataillon (in German Tschaikisten or Titler), a "Grenzer" unit responsible for patrolling and maintaining security of the river Danube near the Turkish border, which, in war time, were assigned to assist the pontooner units.

The name was taken from the 'Tschaike', a type of small, swift, shallow-draft sailing boat, armed with heavy cannon and ideal for river patrol duties. In 1809 the battalion consisted of three divisions, each of two companies of about 180 all ranks.

Charles Reforms

In 1807 the Engineer and Quartermasters' Department technical units were combined to form a single administrative block under the Director General of Engineers, although each corps remained separate with its own specific duties. The engineers (Ingenieur-Korps) continued to supply the experienced and technically trained officers to all departments; the sappers (Sappeur-Korps) were responsible for fortifications, and the miners (Mineur-Korps) for defensive and offensive works. The pioneers' duties generally overlapped the latter, but continued to have special responsibility for the construction of artillery sites and field works, whereas the Pontonier Korps was responsible for the pontoon trains and all bridging works.

By 1809 each of the Sappeur and Mineur Korps were fielding five, and later six, companies of 120 men, and the Pontonier battalion had six companies each of 125 men serving 300 pontoon wagons. The Pioneer Korps, requiring less training than the sappers, had been increased to nine divisions, each of two companies, with about 200 men per company.

Peacetime force of the Austrian Army (1802-1809)

N.	Troops (March 1809)	Batt	Gren. Div.	Comp.	Sq.	Manpowwer	Total
61	line infantry regiments	3	2	2 dep		237.820	323.837
	Fekd jager	9		1		9.756	
	Garrison battalions	4				4.456	261.828)
17	Military Border regiments (Grenzer)	2 + 1				71.805	
8	Cuirassiers				7 *	8.248	45.510
6	Dragoons				7	6.186	
6	Chevaulégers				9	8.874	(end 1802
11	Hussars				9	17.769	59.110)
1	Hussars				9		
3	Uhlans				9	4.433	
4	Artillery			16		11.246	14.100
1	Bombardier Corps			5		1.075	
1	Handlanger battalion	1				1.779	(12.336)
	TOTAL						383.447 (333.274)

* (6 plus 1 Reserve [Depot] squadron)

Wartime Force of the Austrian Army 1805 (Coalition)

Troops (Oct. 9, 1805)	Tyrol	Italy	others	Germany	Total
Infantry	53.440	142.840	29.500	89.280	315.060
Cavalry	2.240	13.440	1.500	22.682	39.862
TOTAL					354.922 [12]

The Army of 1809

Therefore, the operation of raising the new military force had to be aimed towards another, less expensive, way. The Generalissimus found his goal in the establishment of the Landwehr, with which, in wartime, it could be used large masses of Wehrfahigen (fit to Duty) men, without arising substantial expenses during peacetime. Generally supported by the Archdukes John and Maximilian, Charles created this quite new institution, which probably did not correspond fully to his hopes, during the 1809 war, needing only a little bit longer time of preparation. So Austria entered into war with one of the most powerful military force (in numbers of fighters), an effort which hardly seemed possible and which surprised the world. In the first month of this year the field units of the army counted 321.469 men with 36.560 sabres,[13] where Fuhrwesen, garrison artillery, Border Cordon troops and Marines (Marineinfanterie) were not included.[14]

For the supplement of the war force and the formation of replacements were available:
- The first reserve of the German infantry units: 59.800 men
- The second reserve of the German infantry units: 73.600 men

For self-replacement of the Hungarian regiments, the Landstag of Bratislava (Pressburg) had granted on August 31, 1808, 20.000 recruits by whom 11.000 were committed for immediate employment. The first 12.000 men were actived and put in march columns, with the Order of February 2, 1809. Cavalry had a Reserve of 2.760 horses.

If one deducts roughly 8.000 soldiers serving the depots, remained available, for offensive operations, 360.000 men and 39.000 horses [15], whereas 109.280 men, the remainder of the Reserves and of the Hungarian recruits, were retained part in the depots, part still in the homeland eventually to replace troops in campaign.

Charles' Second Army

For the defence of the inner lands of the monarchy, first acted the Depots of the field regiments, were possible, with an average strength, according to the new system, calculated in 54.000 men and 5.000 horses.

In a second time acted the new-established Landwehr, around 152.219 man, as soon as organized. The Hungarian Insurrectio started with 50.000 men and 20.000 horses, while the new formations mobilized in the Military Border should have been 44.303 men and 171 horses strong. This improved a second line army, actually called the "Sedentärtruppen", around 300.522 men and 25.171 horses (maybe ?). In effect reliable data about the rough number of the not-organized reserves, Landwehr and Hungarian Insurrectio are currently still lacking.

The Emperor had to procure, obviously, weapons, clothes and pieces of equipment for these large masses of soldiers. If one considers that the army of 1805 had been poor in supplies, in every moment of that war, it must astonish that few years of peacetime could have succeeded in equipping, at least, the troops ready for the campaign. Supplies were accumulated even for the Sedentärformationen, but they were not sufficient for activate such large masses; particularly there existed a perceptible lack of rifles and ammunition.

A "Conscriptionsgesetz" of 1807 had regulated the gathering of the horses needed by the army. Certainly, the horses amounts present in the countrylands was right abundant, but there were lot of difficulties to "enroll" the carriage animals and, in general, even more for the train and for the cavalry remounts. The money for purchasing them abroad was absent (by this reason several cavalry regiments had been dissolved in the time) and the low number of riders, at the time, was a sensitive disadvantage towards the probably future French opponent In any case Austria entered the war with the most powerful army of all its times, but with a lethal disorganization in its services.

A Lost opportunity. Why Archduke Charles Lost the 1809 War.

Out of the numerous arrangements which were early studied in 1808, with few exceptions, in this period there happened also another important attempt to improve the tactical arrangements and training of the whole army, indirectly revising the Mack "mistakes of the past".

It was the introduction of the Corps-System by which Archduke Charles entirely erased the old traditions of Treffen (battlelines), Wings, Reserve Corps and so on. He wanted to give to the army this tactically deployment modelling it on what was applied in France. The aim was also the complete remake of the 1798 system of the large Legions, a primitive form of dividing armies in group of Divisions.

The new Corps were formed by 28 battalions, 16 squadrons, 10 artillery batteries and 2 companies of pioneers. As for infantry 2 or 3 regiments (each with 3 battalions) formed a brigade and two brigades (generally) formed a Line Division under a Feldmarschalleutnant. With light infantry and light cavalry it was usually formed the Light brigade or Avant- garde brigade (generally with 2-3 battalions and 1 light cavalry regiment), while two

Light brigades formed a Light Division. So the army Corps were composed by 2 Line Divisions and one Light Division, ... in theory.

The Corps commander, so, could have had at disposition a small linear army to be led under the tactical old and well- known principles; the Line Divisions represented the "corps de bataille" (or the old Treffen) while the Light Division was employed for service of vanguard; there were also special "Corps de Réserve", acting as strategical reserve force.

This rigid Ordre de Bataille put into evidence that Austrian Staff had not comprised the real nature of the new French Corps-system, having almost abandoned the aim to eventually create operative divisions capable to act as independent bodies, as the French did in campaign.

As an other proof of weakness subsequently appeared that the army commanders put nearly no value on the preservation of the Corps structure. The column formation, practiced in the former wars, emerged again without particular consideration for the new deployment in field. Also within the Corps the originally settled "Ordre de bataille" changed time by time, in spite of the Generalissimus orders, who forbade this arbitrary actions.

It was a problem of a new system with old Generals.

But the decisive characteristic, which stressed the Archduke, was the necessity to model the Order of battle according to the topographic characteristic of the battlefields (mostly hills and rough terrains in Bavaria as in Italy). So Charles early granted, grunting, his permission to some free arrangements, protected by sufficient cavalry and artillery mass batteries, while in Bohemia, in late April, he turned back on his steps.

However the whole Reform was not born to let generals play with their little armies. The main idea was to have large autonomous Corps, each with their own train, artillery and engineers parks following the troops. Forced to manoeuver those Corps in narrow areas, forced to use the few roads and trails available (under heavy rains in Bavaria), trains and parks often crossed together on the roads, produced traffic jams and, when they were forced to withdraw, they lost huge quantities of materials along the retreat's ways.

Deepening more the evaluation of the military train problems can be observed that if, in 1805, supplies arrived chaotically or did not arrive at all, in 1809 the early defeats caused the lost of large quantities of materials in the jammed roads and caused also the necessity to split the army of Germany in two groups, also because there was no space to allow all to move in order.

The experience had clearly shown that French troops knew how to manage days of campaigning without depots and supplies; it can be overlooked and admired their art to live by requisitions from the countryside. They, however, not only managed the food requisition, but even knew how stock unnecessary supplies to make Center of Operations, limiting to the minimum the food usage. Austrian did not so.

The army arrangement in large operative independent unities required a new organization with moving depots; each independent Corps had its own carriage park with bread, rusk, oat and hay, and, as permanently subordinates, some supply columns. The Corps commanders now had to be familiar with the Supply chains, had to dispose the daily transports (Tagesstaffeln) of the supply trains. The bad communications demanded the accumulation of several depots behind the lines, and the utter changes in the operative plans caused deadly confusion. Under these circumstances it would have been better if the Army command had reserved itself the leading of the depots, occasionally sending separate columns to supply the corps.

This was a major fault in the Charles Army reorganization, which probably led directly to the campaigns' defeats. Charles had reformed the old stationary Austrian supply system raising a new, reasonably mobile structure, smaller than the old one and split among the Corps. But Napoléon (and Eugène) were still faster in moving, manoeuvering and supplying and Charles did not have any hope to beat the French other than in immobile field deployment or by exploiting some exceptional leaks in the enemy logistic system (remember the bridges at Aspern). So he won Napoléon when the "Empereur" was unable to maneuver, having the wide Danube on his back, but failed to win the final decisive static battle at Wagram. This was the sunset of the Austrian military star, a great mind (maybe a lesser commander in field) and the Generalissimus went back to his estates.

SOURCES

Angeli Moriz, Von, *Erzherzog Carl von Österreich als Feldherr und Heeresorganisator*: Im Auftrage seiner Söhne, der Herren Erzherzoge Albrecht und Wilhelm, dann seiner Enkel, der Herren Erzherzoge Friedrich und Eugen; nach österreichischen Original-acten dargestellt, 5 vol., W. Braumüller, 1897.

Bancalari G., *Beiträge zur Geschichte des österreichischen Heerwesens*, 2 vol., L.W. Seidel, 1872

Charles, Erzherzog Karl von Österreich, *Ausgewählte Schriften Weiland seiner kaiserlichen Hoheit des Erzherzogs Carl von Oesterreich*, Braumüller, 1894.

Czoernig Karl, *Ethnographie der oesterreichischen Monarchie*, kaiserlich-koeniglichen Hof- und Staatsdruckerei, Vienne 1857

Gallina Josef Freiherr von, *Die Armee in der Bewegung*: Mit 8 Tafeln und Plänen, Verlag des Militär- wissen-schaftlichen Vereins in commission bei C. Gerold's Sohn, 1872

Gallina. Joseph Freiherr von, *Beiträge zur Geschichte des Österreichischen Heerwesens, Erstes Heft: Der Zeitraum von 1757 bis 1814,* Mit besonderer Rücksichtnahme auf Organisation, Verpflegung und Taktik, Seidel & Sohn, Vienne 1872

Heller von Hellewald Friedrich Anton, Der Feldzug des Jahres 1809 in Süddeutschland, II Band, Vienne 1864
– Hornthal edler von, Horsetzky Adolf von, Gallina Josef Freiherr von, *Beiträge zum Studium des Feldzuges 1805: Nach einem Aufsatze des F.-m.-LT. Gallina*, K.k. Kriegsschule, 1885

Lordick Heiner *Der Feldzug 1809 : Truppen und Verbände unter Österreichs Fahnen* ; [Elektronische Ressource] CD des Heeresgeschichtlichen Museums / Wien : Heeresgeschichtl. Museum, 2001. - 1 CD-ROM ; in four parts
1- *Namensliste der wichtigsten auf österreichischer Seite beteiligten Personen im Feldzug 1809 unter besonderer Berück-sichtigung Tirols*
2- *Verzeichnis der k. k. Armeen, Armeekorps, Brigaden, selbständigen Abteilungen im Feldzug 1809*
3- *Verzeichnis der k. k. Regimenter, Bataillone, selbständigen Formationen (bis Kompaniestärke) im Feldzug 1809 4- Verzeichnis der Schützen- und Landsturmeinheiten Österreichs im Jahr 1809*

Mayerhoffer von Vedropolje Eberhard, Criste Oskar, Regensburg. vol 1 de "Krieg 1809", Kriegsgeschichtlichen Abt. k.u.k. Kriegsarchiv Vienne 1907.

Meynert Hermann Günther Von, *Geschichte der K.k. Österreichischen Armee: Ihrer Heranbildung und organisation, so wie ihrer Schicksale, thaten und Feldzüge*, C. Gerold & sohn, Vienne 1852.

Rauchensteiner Manfried, *Kaiser Franz und Erzherzog Carl: Dynastie und Heerwesen in Österreich 1796-1809*, Verlag für Geschichte und Politik, 1972

Regele Oskar, *Generalstabschefs aus vier Jahrhunderten das Amt des Chefs des Generalstabes in der Donaumonarchie, seine Träger und Organe von 1529 bis 1918: Das Amt des Chefs des Generalstabes in der Donaumonarchie. Seine Träger und Organe von 1529 bis 1918*, Herold, 1966.

Rothenberg Gunther E., *Napoleon's Great Adversaries: The Archduke Charles and the Austrian Army, 1792-1814*, Batsford, 1982
Saski Commandant, *Campagne de 1809 en Allemagne et en Autriche*. 2e vol. Paris / Nancy 1899 - 1902 – Vanicek Fr. , *Specialgeschichte der Militärgrenze*, 4 volumes. , Wien 1875.

Wrede Alfons Frhr von, Semek Anton, *Geschichte der K. und K. Wehrmacht: Die Regimenter, Corps, Branchen und Anstalten von 1618 bis Ende des XIX. Jahrhunderts*, 5 vol., Austro-Hungarian Monarchy, Kriegsarchiv Mittheilungen, L.   W. Seidel, 1901

Notes

[1]   Source: Franz Müller *"Die kaiserl. königl. österreichische Armee, seit Errichtung der stehenden Kriegsheere bis auf die neueste Zeit"* 2. Band (Prag,1845) pp. 399-402

[2]   The *Hofkriegsrat* was the Court Council of War of the Habsburg Monarchy, which had a Chief and other higher generals.

[3]   From England encouraged and from Russia pushed ahead, with the Präliminarvertrag of November 4, 1804, Emperor Franz, as well as the chancellor count Ludwig Cobenzl, wished a new war, while Archduke Charles tried to soften the Diplomats by taking all opportunities to explain, more and more, that a well-being Monarchy demanded only one good peace system, basing on Diplomacy.

[4]   When speaking upon the Austrian empire, treat the term "German" referring to imperial citizens resident in the Cisleithanian countries, mostly of German languages (such as Rhinelands, Bohemia, Austria, Tyrol and Styria, but also Moravia, Silesia and Galicia). The Transleithanian countries, Hungary and the Military border (i.e. Croatia) used the word "hungarian" .

[5]   However there was also a lifetime Duty reserved to vagabonds.

[6]   Maybe it's important to remember that a division was also a small units of two squadrons (cavalry).

[7]   K.K. (Kaiserliche-königliche) or better K.k. (since the second k was less important) meant Imperial-royal and was the official prefix for all the Imperial organizations (military included). Note the difference with the late K.u.K. (after the Ausgleich Act of 1867) which meant Kaiserliche-und-Königliche (Imperial and Royal)

when the king of Hungary charge (König) was separated from the Emperor's charge (Kaiser) and when the second letter K became a capital letter. The use of the K.K. caused also the nickname "Kaiserlichs" which italians and french troops gave to Austrians from 1794.

[8]   A new rank ? Not at all. This was the supreme commander rank of prince Suvorov in 1799 when led an Austro- russian coalition in Italy.

[9]   The mercenary nature of these soldiers and the promise of a less severe treatment (maybe corporal punishments) if they should had entered the Austrian ranks, in addition with a more lax discipline made the "foreigners" (Ausländer) very poor soldiers. During the campaign in Bavaria in 1809, whenever an opportunity arose, indeed, a lot of foreigners deserted.

[10]   Note the 40 German and galizian regiments had to keep Reserve men not only for their own use, but also for the rest of the military branches, whenever needed.

[11]   In 1809, following the loss of territories following Bonaparte's victory, eight line regiments were disbanded Nrs. 13, 23, 38, 43, 45, 46, 50 and 55, these numbers remaining vacant until Nrs. 13, 23, 38, and 43 were reformed with recruitments in the new Italian territorial gains of 1814.

[12]   Note the number is lower than the peacetime force value of 1809 - also if adding a total of around 13.000 artillerymen not present in the table. This could be a sign of the Austrian military weakness under general Mack leadership.

[13]   The source of these numbers (a bit different from the above table) is K. A. F. A. 1809, Hauptarmee, 1, 41, 47. in Krieg 1809 – band I – Regensburg. The Grenzregimenter are counted into the infantry total. The starting force of the Army was 244.259 men with 32.145 horses. The number of the Absenten available for the war was 57.818 men and 1700 horses.

[14]   For a total of 21.320 men and 9.461 horses.

[15]   Active 313.469 men, 36.560 horses. Recruitment of the German infantry 33.120 men, Recruitment of the Hungarian infantry 11.000 men. Cavalry Reserve 2760 men and 2760 horses. In total 360.349 men, 39.320 horses.

▲ Austrian officers and drummer Infantry 1798-1805. From Ottenfeld artwork

▲ Austrian Infantry 1798-1805. From Ottenfeld artwork

THE REGULAR INFANTRY

ORDERED BY RECRUITMENT DISTRICT: UPPER AND LOWER AUSTRIA AND SALZBURG

Lower Austria : (German: Niederösterreich) is currently one of the nine states or Bundesländer in Austria. The capital of Lower Austria was Vienna, but the main town was St. Polten. It was divided into four Cantons or Vierteln. The "Viertel unter dem Wienerwald" – today called Industrieviertel in Niederösterreich – The "Viertel ober dem Wienerwald" (today Mostviertel in Niederösterreich) - The Untermannhartsberg - today Weinviertel in Niederösterreich and the Obermanhartsberg (today Waldwiertel in Niederösterreich.

Upper Austria (German: Oberösterreich) had its capital at Linz. Upper Austria was (and is) traditionally divided into four cantons: Hausrückviertel - the central part of Oberösterreich, Innviertel - (or Innkreis), is the northwestern Viertel, Mühlviertel - the northern Viertel at the borders of Bohemia and Niederösterreich., Traunviertel - the southeastern Viertel of the four regions.

Salzburg. The Archbishopric of Salzburg was secularized in 1803 as the Electorate of Salzburg, but the shortlived principality was annexed by the Austrian Empire in 1805. After the Napoleonic Wars, the Salzburg territory was administered from Linz as the department of Salzach within the Archduchy of Upper Austria.

This was strictly the "Austria" territory, the only province populated entirely by Germans; who, therefore, populated also other areas of the Empire and mainly in the Länder which bordered Austria such as Styria, Carinthia and Bohemia, wher a Circle was completely dwelt by Germans: Elbogen.

Vienna. It was the capital city of the Austrian Empire. At the time Vienna was really two cities in one: the city inside the walls and the suburbs. The city had narrow streets and high building giving the impression that people dwelt a very narrow space. The prominence of its monuments contrasted with the simplicity and the conviviality of its inhabitants, which, however, mostly lived at home, populating the streets only during the good seasons. Opposing to this impression was the suburbs area with large streets, gardens and estates of the noblemen. Vienna was split in four cantons: Stuben, Carinthian, Wiedden and the Scotch. Streets and houses were numbered with the Canton name. In 1812 Vienna had around 7600 houses and 224.092 inhabitants (106269 males, 117823 females). Only 46437 souls lived inside the walls (garrisons apart) and the rest in the suburbs. Another source referred 6935 houses and 222000 inhabitants, among which were 12000 soldiers. The most important suburbs were Leopoldstadt, Mariahilfe, Rossau and Wieden. [1]

RECRUITMENT
DISTRICTS (KREISE)
1805~1809

The Danube right bank Districts

The under the Vienna Forest Circle (unter der Wiener Wald)

Wiener Neustadt. The main town after Vienna had 5000 – 6000 souls. Neustadt was founded in 1192, and was a favourite residence of numerous Austrian sovereigns, acquiring the title of the "ever-faithful town" (die allzeit getreue Stadt) from its unfailing loyalty. Other important towns of the Circle were Baden, Hainburg, Bruck an der Leitha and Klosterneuburg.

The over the Vienna Forest Circle (ober der Wiener Wald)

St. Polten. The name Sankt Pölten is derived from Hippolytus of Rome. The city was renamed to Sankt Hippolyt, then Sankt Polyt and finally Sankt Pölten. The town had 4500 inhabitants in 1814. Other important towns of the Circle were Tülln, Ips (Ybbs), Waidhofen (a.d Ips river), Mautern, Mölk (Melk), Scheibbs, Amstätten.

The Danube left bank Districts

The over the mount Mannhart (St.Medard) Circle (ober der Mannhartsberg)

Mannhartsberg is a low, flat-lying mountain ridge in Lower Austria. It rises to a maximum height of 537 m northeast of Krems. **Krems**. During the 11th and 12th centuries, Chremis, as it was then called, was almost as large as Vienna. Krems is located at the confluence of the Krems and Danube Rivers at the eastern end of Wachau valley.It had around 6000 souls. Other important towns of the Circle were Zwettl, Böhmisch-Waidhofen, Horn, Gmund.

The under the mount Mannhart (St.Medard) Circle (unter der Mannhartsberg)

Korneuburg. Korneuburg was originally a bank settlement associated with Klosterneuburg under the name Nivenburg. It was first mentioned in 1136, and in 1298 received the right to formal separation from Klosterneuburg. In 1814 it had 3000 inhabitants. Other important towns of the Circle were Laa (or Laha), Marchegg, Enzersdorf, Hollabrunn.

The Upper Austria

Canton Hausrück (Hausrück Viertel) At the Bavarian border north of the Danube.

Linz. Is the chief town of the Canton with 1243 houses and 16476 inhabitants. It had two Major suburbs: Margarethen and Kalvarienwand. The suburb of Urfahr was at the opposite side of the Danube bridge, but technically it was in the Mühlviertel. The city was founded by the Romans, who called it Lentia. The name Linz was first recorded in 799 AD, after Bavarians expanded south and Linz became a center of trade. Other important towns of the Circle were Wels, Efferding, Lambach on river Traun.

Canton Traun (Traun Viertel)

Steyr. Around 980, at the confluence of the rivers Enns and Steyr, it was erected by the Otakars, margraves and later Dukes of Styria, as the Styraburg, today Lamberg Castle. It had two suburbs Steyersdorf and Ennsdorf (the two rivers). In 1814 it had 800 houses and 10000 souls. Other important towns of the Circle were Enns (4400 souls), Gmund, Ebersberg (58 houses and a castle).

Canton Mühl (Mühl Viertel)

The area between the Danube and the Bavaria (north).

Freystadt. The dukes of Babenberg recognized the economic and strategic importance of this place and founded in 1220, a free commercial city named Freistadt (Frienstatt = free city). By putting no taxes along its roads the merchants did prefer that way towards Bavaria. Other important towns of the Circle were Grein and Steyereck.

Canton Inn (Inn Viertel)

It was lost in 1809 after the treaty and given to Bavaria.

Braunau. On river Inn the town was first mentioned around 810 and received the city statute in 1260, which made it one of the oldest cities in Austria. It became a fortress city and important trading route junction, dealing with the salt trade and with ship traffic on the River Inn. Throughout its history it changed hands four times. It was Bavarian until 1779 and became an Austrian town under the terms of the treaty of Teschen, which settled the War of the Bavarian Succession. Under the terms of the treaty of Pressburg, Braunau became Bavarian again in 1809. In 1816, during reorganisation of Europe after the Napoleonic Wars, Bavaria ceded the town to Austria and was compensated by the gain of Aschaffenburg. Other important towns of the Circle were Ried and Schärding.

Circle of Salzburg

Salzburg (Grand Duchy) In 1803 the Archdiocese of Salzburg, along with Eichstätt, Berchtesgaden and part of Passau, were secularized and granted to the Duke Ferdinand of Austria, Grand Duke of Tuscany as a reward for the loss of Tuscany, then French. After the Treaty of Pressburg of 1805 it went to Austria and Ferdinand was rewarded with the Grand Duchy of Würzburg, while Eichstätt and Passau passed to Bavaria. With the Treaty of Vienna of 1809 it went to France and from 1810 to Bavaria. Fianally after the Peace of Paris of 1814 , the city and the area of the former archbishopric returned to Austria, except Rupertwinkel , who remained in Bavaria.

GENERAL ORGANIZATION OF BORDER CORDON TROOPS

(Militärgrenzkordonstruppen)

Hungary – none – see under Military Border Troops
Bohemia (6 companies) - Commander: Major Baron Josef Moskopp
Moravia and Silesia (4 companies) - Commander: Oberstleutnant Count Johann Orlik Lower Austria (2 companies) - Commander: Captain Alois von Klein
Upper Austria (5 companies) - Commander: Oberstleutnant Baron Joseph Stockard von Bernkopf Salzburg (3 companies) - Commander: Captain Thaddäus von Grosser
Illyria and Innerösterreich (3 companies) - Commander: Oberstleutnant Schwandtner
Krain, Friuli and Litorale (6 companies) - Commander: Major Sigmund Teutschenbach von Ehrenruh
Before Aspern: the Cordon companies of Istria, Trieste, Krain etc went to war with Brigade Stojcevich, IX. Corps
Galicia (only detachments = abteilungen)
1st Abteilung Commander: Major Wilhelm von Kukcz –
2nd Abteilung Commander: Oberst Carl Starznisky von Pittkau (in campaign with Brigade Kesslern, Division Hohenlohe Ingelfingen, then Corps Meerveldt, in Reserve) –
3rd Abteilung Commander: Major Baron Carl Wunsch –
4th Abteilung (better known as Company of galizisches Cordonbataillon) Commander: Major Johann Kreyssern then MajorCarl von Feeder.
Cordon Troops named in various Order of battles
Before Aspern: 4 Companies with the Brigade Gyurkovich, in the left Hauptkolonne Knesevich, IX Corps also other 3 companies in the Reserve Truppen Lippa
6 companies with Brigade Khevenhüller, Southern Reserve Truppen finally 3 companies with Brigade Vogl in Klagenfurt.

GARNISONS BATAILLONE (Garrison or Fortress Battalions)

1st Battalion Czernowitz (Duchy of Bukowina) - Commander: Oberstleutnant Count Carl Vignolles. Depot at Czernowitz. Raised from one Battalion of the former 1st Garrison Regiment.
2nd Battalion Peterwardein - Commander: Oberstleutnant Franz Weber von Treuenfels . Depot at Peterwardein. Raised from one Battalion of the former 1st Garrison Regiment.
3rd Battalion Komorn - Commander: Oberstleutnant Baron Dominik Cazzan. Raised from part of the former 2nd Garrison Regiment. Depot at fortress Komorn. **4th Battalion Leopoldstadt** - Commander: Major Franz Bibicz de Deva .
Raised from one Battalion of the former 2nd Garrison Regiment. Depot at fortress Leopoldstadt. Their employment in campaign:
Before Aspern: 1 Battalion with the Brigade Stojcevich, Division Knesevich, IX Corps then 2 Battalions Brigade Stojcevich, IX Corps - 1 Battalion was with the Armée of Innerösterreich with the detached Landwehr Brigade Tommasich. Another Battalion was with Brigade Gavassini, left Hauptkolonne Knesevich.
Between Aspern and Wagram: all with IX Corps
Pest garrison: 2 Battalions were with the Brig./Division Weidenfeld in Ofen under Alvinczy

AUSTRIAN REGIMENTS

Ergänzungsbezirks Kom. HQ Recruiting District	2nd Depot	Werb-bezirk Recruitment Area (Kreis)	Regular Army Inf.Regiment	Landwehr Batt.
Salzburg		Salzburg	45	4
Vienna		Vienna city		2
Vienna	Wiener	Unter Wienerwald (east)	4	2
	Neustadt	Unter Wienerwald (west)	49	2
St. Polten	Vienna	Ober Wienerwald		4
	Krems	Unter Mannhartsberg	3	4
		Ober Mannhartsberg		5
Linz	Horn	Marchland -Mühlviertel	14	4
		Innviertel		3
	Enns	Hausruck Viertel	59	4
	Linz	Traun Viertel		4

K.K. IR 3 – Generalissimus Archduke Carl Ludwig – 3 Battalions[2]

Recruitment: unter dem Manhartsberg, probably part in Galicia. 2 Depot company Brigade Ulbrecht in Krems, Division Mittrowsky under O'Reilly and the Recruitments' transport of the regiment followed the Division Jellachich before Aspern.

Circle	Lower Austria	3 - Unter Mannhartsberg
Depot Kadre:	Vienna - Krems	
Commander: Oberst	Joseph Fölseis	

Before Aspern: enclosed in the Brigade GM Josef von Mayer, Division FML Baron Carl von Lindenau, V Corps Archduke Ludwig. On April 16 it supported the Radetzky attack at the Landshut bridges. On April 18 Division Lindenau was attached to the 1st Reserve Corps and reached Rohr. It marched with the left column towards Schierling and was involved in a counterattack during the days of Teugen and Abensberg (Ober Santing and Leuchling) . On April 22 (Eggmühl) the regiment defended the road to Ratisbon at Lukepoint. The day after the regiment was employed to defend Ratisbon and its bridge; it had severe losses and many prisoners, while few reached the opposite Danube bank with Mayer. A whole Battalion which defended Burg-Weinting was destroyed. During the retreat in Bohemia the brigade Mayer, separated from the V Corps, was enclosed in the III Corps, Brigade Mayer, Division

Vukassovich. Later the regiment was attached to the avant-garde Division FML Count Johann Klenau, Brigade Oberst Count Johann Ignaz Franz von Hardegg auf Glatz und im Marchlande (or simply Hardegg) and was, consequently, with the I Corps. At Aspern: before the battle the avant-garde Klenau became an avant-garde Division for the IV and V columns (Mainly the IV Corps Rosenberg) and the regiment, detached from 3rd column, was in the brigade Oberst Baron Franz von Frehlich (or Fröhlich, who will be generalMajor after May 24) with a strength of 1130 in 3 weak Battalions. [3] During the first battleday the regiment was not engaged (only skirmish fire), but o the second day IR 3 was sent to assault Essling. The losses were: 57 dead, 578 wounded, 2 prisoners for a total of 637 men. Colonel Fölseis and Oberstleutnant Watzel were both wounded. Between Aspern and Wagram: on June 5 the regiment (with IR 50 Stain and Landwehr Battalions Obergfell and Fuchs) was detached in the Brigade Weiss sent between Pressburg and Theben. At the June's end the Archduke Carl regiment was with the Brigade Weiss, Division Radetzky, IV Corps Rosenberg. At Wagram: with Brigade Weiss, Division Radetzky, IV Corps. The two Battalions and the 3rd Stain occupied important positions at Markgraft-Neusiedl. In the second battle day the regiment was enclosed in the new avant-garde of the 1st Rosenberg column, Brigade Provenchères with the Wattrich Jäger Battalion, two Landwehr Battalions of the Ober Mannshartberg and 4 Hussars Sqns. They reached and engaged the French af Grosshofens, but soon came the retreat's order. The losses at Wagram were: 53 dead, 497 wounded, 107 prisoners, 316 missing for a total of 973 men. The regiment followed as rear guard the VI Corps Klenau. After Wagram: the regiment, with the IV Corps, was, under provisional command of Major Veyder, at Unter Wisternitz and did not take part to the Znaim battle. During the bridge defense at Unter-Wisternitz (July 10) the regiment supported by the Wattrich Jäger Battalion and by the 4th Landwehr Ober Mannhartsberg repulsed a violent French attack with many losses: 10 dead, 43 wounded, 58 prisoners (a total of 112 men). Then came the armistice.

K.K. IR 4 - Hoch and Deutschmeister and Generalissimus Archduke Carl - 3 Battalions[4]

Recruitment: in 1808 the Staff and the companies 1-2-3-4 were at Wiener-Neustadt, the companies 5-15-16 were at Mödling, the 6th at Brunn, the 7th at Leobersdorf, 8 and 12 at Neustadt, the 9th at Vöslau, 10th at Gainfarn, 11th at Weigelsdorf, 13 and 14 at Laxenburg. Many officers and NCO had been assigned to organize the Landwehr and 300 men were at Ofen (Budapest) to help the building of the fortress. In August 1808 colonel Philipp von Faber became the commander of the Neustadt Military Academy and the command went to Baron Engelhardt. Recruitment in Unter Wiener Wald - initially: 1 Depot company Brigade Keller in Vienna, Division Mittrowsky under O'Reilly . Raised a DepotDivision and also companies 17 and 18.

Circle	Lower Austria	4 - Vienna and Unter Wienerwald
Depot Kadre:	Wiener Neustadt	
Owner (Inhaber)	FZM Archduke Anton Deutschmeister	
Commander: Oberst	Baron Franz Xaver Engelhardt	interim : Joseph von Klopstein

IR 1 Kaiser Franz

IR 2 FZM baron Johann Hiller

IR 3 Erzherzog Carl

IR 4 Hoch- und Deutschmeister

IR 5 I Garnison Rgt.

IR II Garnison Rgt.

▲ Austrian Infantry uniforms regiments nr. 1,2,3, 4, 5 and Garrison regiment

Before Aspern: was with Hiller's VI Corps, Division GM Baron Carl Vincent, Brigade GM comte Nikolaus Weissenwolf (with IR 49 Wilhelm Baron von Kerpen) with an initial force of 4405 men (118 at Depot). At Abensberg the brigade was under the "Hauptkolonne" Division FML comte Friedrich Baron von Kottulinsky. The first clash came on April 20 when FML Hiller sent colonel Csollich, from his staff, with orders for Weissenwolf to attack the French in the Mostanerhofe forest near Rottenburg. On April 20 at Rottenburg losses: 36 dead, 247 wounded. During the Hiller's southern retreat the Division Vincent was ordered to stop the French between Ergolding and Altdorf, close to the two important Landshut bridges. The regiment suffered the pursuit effects of the Nansouty Cuirassiers Charge against Vincent cavalry, their breakthrough till the bridge. Many were able to reach the river Isar, but not all. On 21 April at Landshut losses: 38 dead, 126 wounded, 1147 prisoners. Without resting, the regiment fought in the avant- garde at Neumarkt and lost utter: 5 dead, 37 wounded, 12 missing. Then came the Ebelsberg day. Weissenwolf deployed his brigade behind some hills, close (800 m) to the road to Enns. At the battle's end the brigade was ordered to grant the withdrawal of the Austrians and to watch the roads. Here came a violent struggle by rifles fire. The colonel commander was severely wounded and gave the command to the Oberstleutnant Joseph von Klopstein. On May 3 at Ebelsberg the losses were: 33 dead, 140 wounded, 186 prisoners and 52 missing. During the further retreat 300 Deutschmeister (the 3rd Battalion) were detached in order to defend the river Enns banks at Ennsdorf, other 29 were wounded there. On may 13, with the capitulation of Vienna part (one third) of the Depot Division (around 2050 recruits trained for 3 to 9 days) was taken prisoner by the French (that's 11 officers and 640 men). During the same day the rest of the regiment had a skirmish fire at Schwarze Laken losing 2 dead and 5 wounded. Before the Aspern battle the Brigade Weissenwolf had been attached to the III Corps Division Schustekh or to the Danube watch corps. The brigade was reinforced by the 5th Battalion Salis-Gigers, Vienna volunteers and by the 3rd Jäger Battalion Baroni. At Aspern: it did not participate at the battle remaining on Danube watch duties. On May 29 von Klopstein became the new regiment's commander. Weissenwolf got the Division command and the regiment went in the Brigade Mayer, V Corps Reuss-Plauen. At Wagram: the Avant-garde of the left Wing or Division Nordmann was formed with troop of the former V and VI Corps. The regiment, with the twin Kerpen was in the Brigade Mayer of the Nordmann Division (which will be again attached to the IV Corps Rosenberg by July 6). The regiment was deployed and attacked along the Russbach. During the second day of the battle the regiment (and its brigade) formed a weak flank near Neusiedl, but was overwhelmed. The rests of the regiment (with the IR 44, 46, 49, 58, one Jäger Battalion, 1st Battalion Znaim, three Hussars regiments) were gathered under FML Radetzky Division and ordered to cover the retreat. After the battle they lost 45 dead, 689 wounded but no more prisoners. After Wagram: the regiment followed the retreat of the IV Corps.

K.K. IR 14 – FZM Baron Wilhelm Klebek – 3 Battalions (the "Schwarze Regiment", the Black Reg., the Blacks) Recruitment: Mühl- and Innviertel. - initially: 2 Depot company Brigade Sinzendorf in Linz, Division Mittrowsky under O' Reilly. DepotDivision Brigade Rüffer, Garrison Linz. The regiment would have had from 1807 a Galician Circle for recruiting, but that Circle was instead assigne to regiment 50 Stain.

Circle	Oberösterreich	Innviertel - Mühlviertel
Depot Kadre:	Horn - Linz	
Commander: Oberst	Albert De Best	Martin von Steinmann

Before Aspern: it began in the Division FML Friedrich Baron von Kottulinsky, Brigade GM Count Otto Hohenfeld, VI Corps FML Baron Hiller. On April 19 the 2nd Battalion (Major Scheibler) fought at Pfaffenhofen. On April 21 it was at the battle of Landshut with heavy losses (237 dead, 723 wounded and many prisoners/missing). On April 24 it fought at Neumarkt attacking the village. On May 1 it had a clash at Riedau, by May 2 between Riedau and Neumarkt and on May 3 at Ebelsberg in the rear guard of the Division FML Emmanuel Schustekh, where the large part of the 2nd Battalion was taken prisoner. In May it lost around 400 men and was reduced to two Battalions.

At Aspern: it was again with the Brigade Hohenfeld, Division Kottulinsky, VI Corps or First column Hiller. It attacked for five times the Aspern cemetery and lost around 300 men.

At Wagram: in the Brigade Adler, Division Hohenfeld, in the Klenau VI Corps together with the attached Combined Innviertel Landwehr Battalion Straka.

After Wagram: at Znaim with Brigade Adler, Division Hohenfeld, VI Corps it was deployed at Wolframitzkirchen and did not take part to the battle

K.K. IR 45 – GM-FML Baron Thierry De Vaux – 3 Battalions[5]

Recruitment: Lower Austria - Styria then Salzburg, Styria (Judenburg District) - initially: 1 Depot company Brigade Legisfeld in Salzburg, Division Mittrowsky unter O' Reilly, 2 companies with Division Lippa in Graz under Kerpen.

Before Aspern: Reserve Depot Companies (2) with the ReserveCorps Lippa. One reserve company raised at Salzburg. Two utter Reserve company will be raised in Graz. Between Aspern and Wagram till Wagram: Depot and Reserve Companies transferred to Graz.

Circle[6]	45 Salzburg	45 Judenburg (Styria)
Depot Kadre:	Salzburg	
Commander: Oberst	Baron Johann Nepomuk von Bach	Samuel von Reissenfels

Before Aspern: in the Division FML Franz Jellachich de Buzim in the Brigade GM Constantin von Ettingshausen (at Munich), VI Corps. In May sent to protect the Lueg Pass, and on May 19 the Division received from Archduke Johann to march towards Styria. During the march 4 companies led by Oberstleutnant Reissenfels were detached to the Chasteler Corps in Tyrol. They will never join the De Vaux.

Between Aspern and Wagram: On May 25 it fought at St.Michael against Division Serras, and there it suffered so many losses which it was allowed only to deploy a combined Battalion of around 1500 men. The Battalion reached Graz and then Körmend where it was attached to the IX Corps FM Gyulai and camped at Lendva.

After Wagram: Von Bach was now generalMajor and Reissenfels became the new commander bringing back the "own" 4 companies in Tirol of his Gruppe "Reissenfels". Finally reaching the strength of 2 Battalions it was enclosed in the Brigade Bach, Division Frimont, Army of Inner Austria. The regiment had incorporated also the 3 reserve companies and then finally marched to Vienna. However, having lost its Circle after the Treaty, the regiment was disbanded.

Disbanding a regiment: on November 13 it came the "Disbanding Order" from the Emperor Franz. Regiments 13, 23, 38, 43, 45, 46, 50 and 55 were fired off. The disbanding station for De Vaux was Wiener-Neustadt. It came to the last flag-raising with: 66 Staff, one combined fusilier Battalion of 1690 men, one grenadier Division of 296 men, one depot Division of 308 men. The flag was assigned to the Church of St.Michael (in memoriam).

K.K. IR 49 – FML-FZM Baron Wilhelm Kerpen – 3 Battalions[7]

Recruitment: Viertel Ober dem Wiener Wald - Initially 1 Depot company in Krems, Division Mittrowsky under O'Reilly and, before Aspern, Reserve Division in Wien then in garrison at St.Polten (Hauptmann Paul Mayer).

Circle	Niederösterreich	49 Ober-Unter Wienerwald (west)
Depot Kadre:	St. Pölten	
Commander: Oberst	Lang von Langenau	Major von Bubna (interim)

Before Aspern: as for IR 4 in the Brigade Weissenwolf, Division Vincent, VI Corps . At Abensberg the brigade was under the "Hauptkolonne" Division FML comte Friedrich Baron von Kottulinsky. Till April 20 it was in Reserve at Pfaffenhausen.

During the Hiller's southern retreat the Division Vincent was ordered to stop the French between Ergolding and Altdorf, close to the two important Landshut bridges. The 1st Battalion was committed on the left Isar bank with orders to cover the retreat, the other two Battalions went on the hills south of Landshut. The 3rd Battalion commander Major O'Brien opened the way with bayonets and saved part of his men marching with Jordis regiment and reaching his own at Vilsbiburg. The Landshut losses were: 34 dead, 122 wounded, 900 missing; many were prisoners. The regiment fought in the avant-garde at Neumarkt only with one company having 15 men wounded. On May 2 Major O'Brien gathered 500 volunteers of the regiment and marched back towards Efferding, in order to hit the French on their rear front. They marched all the night under heavy rain but were forced to abandon the attempt, since the main French columns were too advanced. O'Brien then joined the Kerpen at Ebelsberg the next day. At Ebelsberg, Weissenwolf deployed his brigade behind some hills, close (800 m) to the road to Enns. The 1st Battalion and the 1st Deutschmeister were odered to watch the road on the left bank of the Traun, with an half artillery battery. When the large part of the Corps had passed (8 AM) the bridge the detachment was retreated on the right Traun's bank. One company remained inside the town. The 2nd Battalion (Major von Bubna) and the 3rd (Major Baron Weweld) were deployed in line south of Ebelsberg. They engaged the French stopping their advance. The losses at Ebelsberg were: 42 dead, 166 wounded, 220 missing. At the battle's end the brigade was ordered to grant the withdrawal of the Austrians and to watch the roads. The regiment was at St.Polten, where it learnt the DepotDivision had been transferred to Vienna (it will be taken prisoner). On May 11 the Kerpen reached Lang-Enzersdorf and the following day they fought at Schwarze Laken.

The 1st Battalion and O'Brien formed the first line, the others the second. The Kerpen there lost: 65 dead and 296 wounded (they otherwise captured 370 Oudinot's grenadiers and 15 officers, with a Chef-de-brigade, while around 300 other French went out of combat). O'Brien got command of the Schwarze-Laken island.

Before the Aspern battle the Brigade Weissenwolf had been attached to the III Corps Division Schustekh, the Danube watching corps. The brigade was reinforced by the 5th Battalion Salis-Gigers, Vienna volunteers and by the 3rd Jäger Battalion Baroni. Then Weissenwolf went to the V Corps Reuss-Plauen and the regiment in the Brigade Mayer.

At Aspern: it did not participate at the battle remaining on Schwarze-Laken sector. The regiment camped at Strebersdorf and there received the new attachment to Brigade Mayer, Division Nordmann, IV Corps Rosenberg. At Wagram: the Avant-garde of the left Wing or Division Nordmann was then formed with troop of the former V and VI Corps. The regiment, with the twin Deutschmeister, was in the Brigade Mayer of the Nordmann Division On July 1, the Kerpen were at Stadtl- Enzersdorf. After a shot fire combat it was retreated at Markgraft-Neusiedl where it fought in the second line. Under the heavy artillery bombardment fell Nordmann, dead, Mayer and colonel Langenau, severely wounded. Major von Bubna (1st Battalion) got the provisional command, Major von Taintinière got the command of the 2nd Battalion (in place of Major Callot severely wounded on the first day of the battle) and the, now, Oberstlieutenant O'Brien led again is 3rd Battalion. With the Kerpen fought also the 5th Landwehr Battalion of the Major Count Cavriani, led by the Hauptmann Passon (Cavriani was also wounded). The regiment lost 197 men dead, 611 wounded. The 5th Landwehr Battalion lost 40 men, 203 wounded and 84 missing.

The rests of the regiment (with the IR 4, 44, 46, 58, one Jäger Battalion, 1st Battalion Znaim, three Hussars regiments) were gathered under FML Radetzky Division and ordered to cover the retreat.

After Wagram: the regiment followed the retreat of the IV Corps.

K.K. IR 59 – GM-FML Alexander von Jordis – 3 Battalions[8]

Recruitment: Upper Austria Salzburg - initially 2 Depot company Brigade Sinzendorf in Linz, Division Anton Mittrowsky under O'Reilly then 1 Depot company Brigade Ritter, Garrison Linz. Part detached to the Brigade Hardegg before Aspern.

Circle	Oberösterreich	59 Traunviertel Hausrückviertel
Depot Kadre:	(Salzburg) – Linz - Enns	
Commander: Oberst	Christoph Adler	Baron Georg Weveld

It began the campaign with the "Linz" Division FML comte Friedrich Baron von Kottulinsky in the Brigade GM comte Otto Hohenfeld, VI Corps Hiller. It was always in reserve till the April 21, when it was committed at Landshut and had orders to cover the bridge passages. The regiment deployed on the hills behind the town, left of the main road to Vilsbiburg. Two companies stood inside the town. The counterattack of the regiment caused the following losses: 72 dead, 131 wounded, who mainly were made prisoners. Three companies did fight at Neumarkt losing 18 men, dead, and 34 wounded. The 3rd Battalion was attacked near Riedau during the march and suffered heavy losses practically disappearing from the battlefields. At Ebelsberg the Jordis was not attacked and retreated till Stammersdorf finding part of its Depot Division on the left Danube bank with Brigade Hardegg. Since Ebelsberg the Hohenfeld brigade had been attached to Division Schustekh and the regiment had two Battalions.

At Aspern: the VI Corps became the 1st column under FML Johann Freiherr von Hiller, and the Jordis was in the Brigade Hohenfeld, Division Kottulinsky. The regiment attacked in the first afternoon the village of Aspern. On the second day the attacks were renewed. In the battle they lost: 21 dead, 145 wounded. On May 24, colonel Adler became brigadier and the regiment's command was taken by Baron Georg Weveld. The regiment garrisoned Aspern and the redoubt.

At Wagram: in the Brigade Adler, Division Hohenfeld, VI Corps, it defended Aspern without being able to resist. It then retreated fighting till Korneuburg (July 7), Stockerau (8), Hollabrunn (9).

After Wagram: always in the Brigade Adler, but with Division Schustekh, VI Corps. The 3rd Battalion received another flag in January 1810 in place of that lost at Riedau.

IR 7 FML baron Carl Friedrich Schröder   **IR 8 FZM Archduke Ludwig Joseph**   **IR 9 FML Czartoryski**

IR 10 FML Anton Mittrowsky   **IR 11 Erzherzog Rainer**   **IR 12 Manfredini then Liechtenstein**

▲ Austrian Infantry uniforms regiments nr. 7,8,9,10,11 and 12

IR 13 Reisky

IR 14 Klebek

IR 15 FZM Anton Zach

IR 16 FZM Marquis Franz Lusignan

IR 17 Reuss Plauen

IR 18 FML Stuart then FML Baron D'Aspre

▲ Austrian Infantry uniforms regiments nr. 13, 14, 15, 16, 17 & 18

RECRUITMENT DISTRICT: INNER AUSTRIA (STYRIA, CARINTHIA, KUNSTENLAND)

Inner Österreich or Inner Austria was a term commonly utilized at the times when it existed the VORDER (Outer) ÖSTERREICH, territories in the current Germany and the Vorarlberg. The term was used from the late 14th to the 16th century referring to Styria, Carinthia, Carniola and the Windisch March, the County of Gorizia, Trieste and assorted smaller Habsburg possessions bordering the area (Pazin, Rijeka, Liburnia, Duino). The Slovenian and Croatian part of the territory (i.e. Istria) had also the name of Illyria.

Carinthia : The Duchy of Carinthia (German: Herzogtum Kärnten; Slovene: Vojvodina Koroška) was a duchy located in southern Austria and parts of northern Slovenia. It was part of the Holy Roman Empire from 976 until the dissolution of the Empire in 1806, and a crownland of Austria-Hungary until its dissolution in 1918. The capital city is Klagenfurt, which in Slovenian language is

called Celovec. The next important town is Villach (Beljak). **Styria**. The Duchy of Styria (German: Herzogtum Steiermark; Slovene: Vojvodina Štajerska; Hungarian: Stájerország) was a duchy located in modern-day southern Austria and northern Slovenia. It was a part of the Holy Roman Empire until its dissolution in 1806 and a crownland of Austria-Hungary until its dissolution in 1918. The capital city was and is Graz.

Carniola (Slovenian: Kranjska; German: Krain) is a traditional and historical region of Slovenia. As part of Austria-Hungary, the region was a crown land officially known as the Duchy of Carniola (Vojvodina Kranjska, Herzogtum Krain) until 1918. Its capital was Ljubljana.

Küstenland (Litorale od Coastland)

The **County of Gorizia and Gradisca** (German: Grafschaft Görz; Italian: Contea di Gorizia; Slovenian: Goriška grofija) was a County based around Gorizia in Friuli-Venezia Giulia, current north-eastern Italy.

Imperial free town of Trieste (Italian: Trieste; Slovene and Croatian: Trst) is a city and port in northeastern Italy very near to the Slovenian border, to the North, East and South. Trieste is located at the head of the Gulf of Trieste on the Adriatic Sea.

Istria (Croatian, Slovene: Istra, Italian: Istria), formerly Histria (Latin), is the largest peninsula in the Adriatic Sea. The peninsula is located at the head of the Adriatic between the Gulf of Trieste and the Bay of Kvarner.

Fiume is the Italian and Hungarian name for the city of Rijeka. However, Rijeka was not part of the County Modruš-Rijeka, but under the direct administration of Hungary. It was proposed to recruite for the K.K. Marine.

Dalmatia (Spalato-Split) was the main recruitment area for the K.K. Marine After the loss of the Venetian Litorale.

STYRIA

CARINTHIA

KÜSTENLAND

KRAIN

RECRUITMENT DISTRICTS (KREISE) 1805-1809

▲ Austrian mounted officers of Infantry 1809. From Ottenfeld artwork

AUSTRIAN REGULAR INFANTRY REGIMENTS

Ergänzungsbezirks Kom.		Werb-bezirk	Regular Army	
HQ Recruiting District	Slovenian	Recruitment Area (Kreis)	Infantry Reg.	
Graz		Judenburg	**45**	Aushilfs-Kreis of Salzburg Regiment
		Bruck a.d. Mur		
		Graz	27	
	Maribor	Marburg		
Cilli	Celje	Cilli	16	
Klagenfurt	Celovec	Klagenfurt	26	
	Beljak	Villach		
Laibach	Ljubljana	Ober-Krain	43	
		Unter-Krain		
Trieste	Postojna	Adelsberg	13	also infantry from Istria and Trieste Landwehr
		Görz und Gradisca		
	Trst	Stadt Triest		
Mitterburg	Pažin	Istria	none	K.K. Marine
Fiume	Rijeka	Fiume		

Numbers in bold mean a temporary area of recruitment in order to help the main District to reach the stated strength.

Inner Österreicher Regiment IR 13 - IR 16 - IR 26 - IR 27 - IR 43
K.K. IR 13 - GM-FML Baron Franz Wenzel Reisky von Dubnitz - 3 battalions
Recruitment: Lower Carniola, Görz. – Depot Company: 2 Brigade Khevenhüller in Laibach, Division Lippa under Kerpen.

Krain	Adelsberg	13
Küstenland	Görz-Trieste-Istria	
Depot Kader	Trieste – Görz - Monfalcone	
Commander: oberst	Carl von Fölseis	Count Weichard Gallenberg

- Before Aspern: with 3465 men and 73 in 3 battalions it was in the Brigade Kleinmayr, Div Gorupp, IX Corps FML Ignaz Graf Gyulai. In February von Fölseis became generalMajor and Gallenberg was the new commander. In April the Staff gathered in Trieste and the Regiment was assigned to the Brigade Gavassini, left Hauptkolonne Knesevich. At Sacile the Regiment and the Simbschen infantry were in the Brigade Kálnássy, IX Corps. [2]. At 5 PM hours Gyulai sent ahead the Reisky with the Oguliner, under GM Marziani [3], to attack Sacile and Vigonovo. On May 1 it received the general retreat order. After a week the Brigade Kalnássy deployed behind the Piave (Simbschen at S.Michele and Reisky at Tezze). The Regiment received the attack of the French Brigade Abbé, but resisted till at the moment of the general retreat. They lost the rest of the Brigade following the main column of Archduke Johann. The Regiment lost 40 men dead, 205 missing and 506 prisoners mainly wounded. On May 11 it came to a violent skirmish at San Daniele. There 1000 men and the colonel Gallenberg were made prisoners. The remnants of the Regiment, under the provisional command of Oberstleutnant Andreas Kurz, marched to Ospedaletto. On May 12 the fought at Venzone (other 66 men missing). On May 14 they took position at Tarvis, in the Division Albert Gyulai and Brigade GM Gajoli. During the resistance at the Tarvis pass they lost other 500 men. The Reisky continued to retreat till Graz (May 20) and Papa near Raab.
- After Wagram: The exhausted Regiment was sent to Carlstädt in order to be reorganized, Brigade Khevenhüller, Res. Troops im the South. When the FML Knezevich deployed his Division at Gospic, the Reisky (July 13) moved south and marched to Grašac, After reaching the main column. During these moves it integrated squads of dalmatian volunteers. On July 20 it attacked Ostrovica by night and at the month's end the Regiment was employed in the blockade of Zara (today Zadar) and San Nicolò. Then came the armistice. Total losses were scary : 2261 men (184 dead, 180 missing and 1897 prisoners). The so called "Friuli Regiment" was disbanded at Messendorf by Graz, in February 1810 After the peace.

K.K. IR 16 – FML-FZM Marquis Franz Lusignan – 3 Battalions
Recruitment: Styria, Cillier District
Before Aspern: Reserve Division Lippa and Reserve Companies in Graz. [4]

Styria	Cilli	16
Depot Kader	Leoben, Marburg	
Commander: oberst	Joseph Ruiz de Rosas	Oberstleutnant Hermann Dominik Ertel, ritter von Krelau

- Before Aspern: Brigade Marchal, Division Albert Gyulai, VIII Corps, then Brigade Buol (2 Companies Corps Chasteler). On April 24 the Regiment fought at Volano and Murazzo.
Later 3 battalions Brigade Marchal, Corps Chasteler, detached Gruppe Leiningen (2 Companies of 3rd battalion). The 2nd Battalion was engaged severely at Wörgl and Söll, near Kufstein, by the Bavarians and was then surrounded and taken prisoner. The 1st and the 3rd Battalions were attached to the Brigade Marchal, Division Albert Gyulai, VIII Corps; some companies were also with Brigade Fenner Corps Chasteler then, Gruppe Ertel, Corps Chasteler and Brigade Schmidt, Corps Chasteler (3 Companies)
- Between Aspern and Wagram: 2 companies with Gruppe Ertel, also in the Gruppe Reissenfels, and in the detached Brigade Buol with 1 more battalion detached to the Division Jellačić. At Raab it was in the Jellačić Reserve, Brigade GM Gajoli, with the two Battalions ordered to defend Szabadhégy. Later 10 Companies with the Brigade Lutz, Division Colloredo, Army of Inner Austria, sent to defend the Pressburg bridgehead.
- After Wagram: at Pressburg with the detached Brigade Bianchi then 1 battalion Brigade Buol and 1 battalion Division Jellačić.

K.K. IR 26 – FML Fürst Ludwig Hohenlohe Bartenstein – 3 battalions
Recruitment: Carinthia, Galicia ?? - 2 depot companies Brigade Vogl in Klagenfurt, Division Lippa under Kerpen. depot companies Brigade de Best, Division Colloredo, Army of Inner Austria.

Carinthia	Klagenfurt	26
Depot Kader	Klagenfurt	
Commander: oberst	Franz von Mumb	Count Christian Leiningen Westerburg

- Before Aspern: 3 Battalions Brigade Marchal, Division Albert Gyulai, VIII Corps later Brigade Marchal – always in Tyrol, temporarily also in battalion detachments (Brigade Buol, Fenner, detached Gruppe Leiningen or Regiment's avant-garde), but always under Corps Chasteler, 2 Companies Brigade Vogl in Klagenfurt (Depot). On 21 April Oberstleutnant Leiningen passed the Adige fighting at Lavis, near Trento,which he reached the followinf day. At Volano, April 24, FML Chasteler attacked at the head of one of its Battalions.

- Between Aspern and Wagram: Brigade Buol, Corps Chasteler while 1 battalion was detached with the Gruppe Leiningen. By June 9 the remnant 1 ½ Battalions led by Chasteler reached at Gonobitz the IX Corps Gyulai and fought at Klagenfurt where three companies were taken prisoner. [5] In the meanwhile Leiningen, with his battalion (2nd), wathed the South Tyrol and marched to Bassano (June 3), then returning to Trento where, After the French attack of June 6, recovered his troops in the Trento's castle (the Buon Consiglio). Rescue by the Tyrol's insurgents, Leiningen left Trent and battered the Italians (French) at Rovereto and Ala (June 9).

- After Wagram: 1 battalion had been detached with Brigade Buol in order to defend the Inn valley.

K.K. IR 27 – FML Count Leopold Strassoldo – 3 Battalions

Recruitment: Styria. - Initially: 2 depot companies Brigade and Division Lippa in Graz under Kerpen - Before Aspern: Reserve Division in Graz Corps Kerpen, or Corps Lippa - Between Aspern and Wagram: in Graz garrison of the Schlossberg

Styria	Graz - Marburg Bruck - Judenburg	27 - 45
Depot Kader	Graz	
Commander: oberst	Peter (Ignaz) Marchal de Perclat	from February Count Anton Lamezan-Salins

- Before Aspern: 3 Battalions Brigade Colloredo, Division Albert Gyulai, VIII Corps then Brigade and Division Colloredo, VIII Corps. Colonel Marchal becom a GM left the Regiment giving the command to colonel Lamezan-Salins, which now led 72 officer and 3202 men.

April 16 battle of Fontanafredda (Sacile): the Colloredo Brigade was sent to support Frimont at Porcia. The battle was bloody and the Regiment lost: 258 dead, 599 wounded, 51 missing.

April 28 battle for the Alpone bridge: the Regiment gathered at Soave and a large patrol was attacked near a bridge on the stream Alpone. The 3rd Battalion (Oberstlieutenant Riebenfeld) made some actions and reconnaissances towards Costegiola, Cazzano and Illasi (12 dead and 25 wounded on April 29). The same day the 1st and 2nd Battalions took position at Soave where they were attacked by French: losses 46 dead, 65 wounded, 6 made prisoners and 11 missing.

On April 30 the 3rd Battalion together with the 2nd Banal attacked monte Bastia and skirmish at Montecchio minore losing 12 dead and 27 wounded. The following attack against the castle of Illasi, near Verona, was repulsed by the Bonfanti Brigade ; the Battalions lost 29 dead, 115 wounded and 117 were made prisoners. Then came the general retreat order.

On May 8 it defended the Piave crossing fighting at La Priula and, then, it marched with the army rear guard. On May 11 fought at San Daniele and the following day at Venzone where it lost 11 dead and 49 wounded. After the wounds suffered by GM Colloredo the Brigade was now led by Lamezan-Salins. The Regiment reached Tarvis and deployed at the left wing towards Flitsch (Plezzo) where, on May 17, it was attacked. The losse were heavy: 144 dead, 236 wounded, 141 missing and 164 prisoners. During the following retreat the 3rd Battalion (Major Schlitter) lost the contact and marched separately.

- Between Aspern and Wagram: On May 24 they gathered again together at Radkersburg. On June 1 the Depot Division left Graz and joined the Regiment in order to reinforce the 1st battalion. The day 12 it marched to St. Martin near Raab with Brigade GM Lutz, Division FML Colloredo-Mannsfeld. They deployed left of Szabadhégy in battle order. On June 14 the French attacked the

Regiment's line. At Raab, later during the battle, the first 3 companies were detached with the 2nd Graz Landwehr Battalion Hummel in order to defend the Estate at Kis-Megyer. The losses were: 161 dead, 277 wounded, 197 prisoners, 131 missing.

The Regiment recovered to the Komorn fortress and bridgehead. From the former three Battalions they were be able to raise only a single unit plus a Division from the 3rd battalion. The strength of the Strassoldo was now 33 officers, 803 men. By June 23 they were assigned to the defense of the Pressburg bridgehead, which was attacked by the French from June 30 till 7 July.

- After Wagram: On day 11 they had to leave the bridgehead but a renewed French attack blocked the 2nd company of the combined Strassoldo battalion (Brigade Bianchi). The Depot Division defended the Graz castle's hill. On August 18 died the Owner Count Leopold Strassoldo (in December the Regiment will be assigned to Marquis Chasteler de Courcelles).

K.K. IR 43 – FML-FZM Baron Joseph Simbschen – 3 battalions

Recruitment: Krain – Depot Company: 2 Brigade Khevenhüller in Laibach, Division Lippa under Kerpen. After the peace it was disbanded at Vordernberg on February 1810.

Krain	Oberkrain	43
	Unterkrain	
Depot Kader	Laibach	
Commander: oberst	Franz Bardarini von Kieselstein	

- Before Aspern: considered the „National" Regiment of Carniola (today Slovenia) it began the campaign with the Brigade Kleinmayr, Division Gorupp, IX Corps Ignaz Gyulai. Later was enclosed in the Brigade Kálnássy, IX Corps . On May 8 it did fight at the Piave battle in the Brigade Kálnássy, IX Corps (see also above IR 13 for details). On May 10 it defended the river Tagliamento passage. Later 2 Companies were assigned to the Gruppe Dumontet (Ljubljana), IX Corps,[6] and other 2 Companies to the Brigade Khevenhüller, Reserve Troops in the South .
- Between Aspern and Wagram: fought at Graz with 1 and ½ Battalions with the Brigade Kálnássy, IX Corps. Later it was reorganized in the Brigade Bardarini (its commander), IX Corps.

AUSTRIAN ADRIATIC SEA FLEET - TRIEST, APRIL 23, 1809

GeneralMajor Count Josef L'Espine
Fleet I – Vs. Dalmatia under command of the Oberstleutnant Nepomuk Maidich
Brig "Dolfino"
Schooner "Indagatore"
Trabaccolo (Trabakel) "Dromedario"
Felucca "Mora"
12 Gunboats and Sloops
Fleet 2 – Vs. Venice under command of the Oberstleutnants Matthias Flanagan
Corvette „Armonia" (rented by private owners)
Brig "Eolo"
Brig "Pilade" sent on April 22 in an expedition to Sicily
Brig "Oreste"
Trabaccolo "Bravo"
Trabaccolo "Cammello"
Large tartane "Isabella"
8 Gunboats and Sloops

▲ Austrian Infantry tunic during the Napoleonic wars. From Ottenfeld artwork

IR 19 FZM Joszef Alvinczy   **IR 20 FZM count Wenzel Kaunitz**   **IR 21 FML Viktor Prinz Rohan**

IR 22 FM Prince Sachsen-Coburg   **IR 23 Ferdinand Kurfürst von Würzburg**   **IR 24 FZM Baron Strauch**

▲ Austrian Infantry uniforms regiments nr. 19, 20, 21, 22, 23 & 24

RECRUITMENT DISTRICT: KREISE (SILESIA & MORAVIA) 1805-1809

Moravia (Czech: *Morava*; German: *Mähren*) is a historical region in central Europe in the east of the Czech Republic, one of the former Czech lands. It takes its name from the Morava River which rises in the northwest of the region. Until 1641 Moravia's capital was the centrally-located Olomouc, but after its capture by the Swedes it moved to the larger city of Brno (Brünn) which resisted the invaders successfully. The Moravians are a Slavic ethnic group who speak various dialects of Czech.

Silesia was the former Duchy of Upper and Lower Silesia (German: *Herzogtum Ober- und Niederschlesien*) an autonomous region of the Austrian Empire. It is also known as **Austrian Silesia** (German: *Österreichisch Schlesien*; Czech: *Rakouské Slezsko*; Polish: *Śląsk Austriacki*), and despite the official name it only included parts of Upper Silesia, while none of Lower Silesia was within its borders. It is largely coterminous with - and somehow currently identified as - the region of Czech Silesia. As part of the Kingdom of Bohemia, Silesia was inherited by the House of Habsburg in 1526 after the death of the Bohemian king, Louis II The two main cities were Teschen and Troppau (Opava).

Circles (Districts) see map-image above (datas from a 1814 gazeteer)

Moravia

Brünn (Czech: Brno). Is the capital city of the Margravate of Moravia, a land which was administrated by Prague but having its representatives at Vienna.

It was surrounded with bastions, and with a wide ditch. The most important building of the city was the parochial Church, dedicated to Saint Jakob, all covered in brass. The population was around 16000 inh., and it had 1946 houses in 1814. The town is at the confluence of the rivers Schwartschawa and Switawa and was protected (westwards) by the strong fortress of the Spielberg castle.

Iglau (Czech: Jihlava) a Royal fortified town of 10000 inhabitants (1270 houses) is the main town of that mountain Circle at the bohemian border. The city's German name, Iglau, is derived from the German word for hedgehog, Igel (hence the hedgehog on the coat of arms). An old Slavic settlement upon a ford was moved on a nearby hill where the mining town was founded (ca. 1240) by king Václav I, in the Middle Ages inhabited mostly by Germans (coming mostly from Northern Bavaria and Upper Saxony). Important settlements were:

Gross-Meseritsch (1100 inh.), Trebitsch (3672 inh.), Slawonitz and Stannern (a smal town in effects but renowned for an aerolite fall, the previous year 1808).

Olmütz or Holomauz (Czech: Olomouc) was a fortress surrounded by a marshy land and the river Morava, and former Moravia capital city. In 1814 had over 1000 houses and around 11000 inhabitants. Its Circle had some large towns like Sternberg (3908 inh.), Boskowitz (3519 inh.), Mährisch-Neustadt or Unitschau (3012 inh.), Kogetin (2754 inh.), Zwittau (2520 inh.), Littau or Littowle (2162 inh.). This district periodically split in two parts: the Upper or properly Olmütz and the Lower named as:

Mährische Schönberg (Czech: Šumperk) founded by German colonists in 1269. The German name Schönberg means "beautiful hill", and the name Šumperk is a Czech garbling of the original German name. The town of Šumperk became the center of the area. It was located on a trade route, and the town profited from the copper mines. Its area was close to the Silesian border.

Kremsier (Czech: Kroměříž) with the territories of:

Prerau or Prseron (Czech: Prerov) It was one of the oldest towns in Moravia, withs a Gothic town-hall and an old castle, once occupied by Matthias Corvinus. The Circle had not a large amount of inhabitants but some important towns like Bodenstadt or Podstata (1100 inh.) and, above all, Kremsier (Cremsier or Kromeritz) which was the summer siege (castle) of the Bishop of Olmütz and the District siege. Town of Fulnek had around 5000 inhabitants. Then were also Freyberg (Prsibor) had 261 houses and 3500 inh., Leipnik (3498 inh.), Meseritsch (3357 inh.), Weisskirchen (3272 inh.).

Ungarische Hradische (Czech: Uherské Hradiště) was the earliest known Jewish community dated from 1592. It was founded in 1257 by the Czech king Otakar II Important towns of the Circle were: Bissenz (2477 inh.), Hungarisch Brod (2912 inh.) and Ostrau. The surname Ungarische (hungarian) here means merely slovakian.

Znaim (Czech: Znoymo) or Znaym, Znogma. A Royal town settled on the top of a rough hill over the river Thaya. It will be the final topic of the whole 1809 campaign (battle and armistice). It had 800 houses and 7000 inhabitants.

Silesia

Teschen (Czech: Těšín) also Telling (latin Tessinum), a former Principality of Albert the duke of Saxony had around 5000 inh. (600 houses). In this Circle there were many Poles and that language was mostly spoken. Teschen Circle was formed by the Principalities of Teschen and Bielitz, and the dominions of the families Freystadt, Friedeck, Deutsch-Leuther, Reichwald, Roy and Halb-Oderberg. **Troppau** (Czech: Opava) also Oppain (latin Oppavia or Troppavia) on the river Opa. It was the capital of the Silesian Principality and was surrounded by a tall wall. In it was an ancient castle. It had around 5000 inhabitants and more than 500 houses. Its Circle was formed by the bohemian mountain lands of Troppau, Jägerndorf and Neisse and by the dominions of the Freudenthal and Olbersdorf families. Town of Jägerndorf (Czech: Krnov fron latin Carnovia) had 4650 inh.

MORAVIAN-SILESIAN REGIMENTS

Erganzungsbezirks Kom.		Werb-bezirk	Regular army	Landwehr
HQ Recruiting District	Czech	recruitment area (Kreis)	IR	other
Iglau	Jihlava	Iglau	8	
Znaym	Znojmo	Znaym	22	
Brünn	Brno	Brünn I stadt	29	
		Brünn II	10	
Olmütz	Olomouc	Olmütz (upper)	12	3rd Fortress artillery Rgt.
Mährische Schönberg	Šumperk	Olmütz (lower)	15	6th Feldjäger bn
	Kroměříž	Hradisch	40 - **10**	
Kremsier	Werbbezirk HQ at Olmütz for IR 1	Prerau	1 - **7**	
Troppau	Opava	Troppau	57 - **20**	
Teschen	Těšín	Teschen	56	

Numbers in bold mean a temporary area of recruitment in order to help the main District to reach the stated strength.

K.K. IR 1 - Kaiser Franz Joseph I – 3 battalions
Recruitment: Moravia, Galicia. 1 Depot Company BrigadeBojakowski in Olmütz, Division St.Julien under Argenteau. 1 Depot Company BrigadeEgermann in Sándomierz, Division Meerveldt under Hohenlohe- Ingelfingen.

Moravia	Prerau	01	
Galicia	Sandec	01	
Depot Kader:	Prossnitz (Olmütz). Sandec		
Commander: oberst	Johann von Gredler	after Wagram Gustav Prinz Hohenlohe-Langenburg,	

- before Aspern: many sources refer it began the campaign with III Corps Hohenzollern, Division FML baron Franz von Lusignan, brig. GM Ludwig Thierry. However the "Ersters" were attached to the V Corps column marching towards Landshut and Siegenburg. At Teugen it was committed with the Reserve Corps Liechtenstein (?) [1] forming a rear guard with the Brigade GM Thierry and 10 companies and with the Detachment Oberst Hammer, other 6 companies. In effect it had the task to maintain the link between the III Corps and the V in a dangerous central position.

With the same deployment it was at Abensberg (see details after, under IR 29 Lindenau). It was involved in the unlucky Thierry affair at Offenstetten, where the regiment was almost destroyed (many prisoners). Remnants remained with III corps and the unit was reorganized shortly before Aspern. The commander Gredler died, together with 173 men, other 319 were wounded, the rests were almost all prisoners.[2]

- after Aspern and at Wagram: on June 4, the regiment, now reorganizing in two Battalions, was commanded by Oberstleutnant prince Hohenzollern. It had 1726 men, 850 of which were recruits, and it was attached to BrigadeLilienberg, Division St.Julien, III Corps. The two battalions were not in the battle, but under heavy bombardment (they lost 36 dead and 107 wounded).

- after Wagram: during the Znaim battle it was with the BrigadeReinhardt, Division St.Julien, III Corps Kollowrat.

K.K. IR 7 – GM-FML baron Carl Friedrich Schröder von Lilienhof – 3 battalions

Recruitment: Moravia, West Galicia-Poland. 1 Depot Company BrigadeWodniansky in Olmütz, Division St.Julien under Argenteau. 1 Depot Company BrigadeEgermann in Sándomierz, Division Meerveldt under Hohenlohe- Ingelfingen.

Moravia	Prerau	07	
Galicia	Sanok	07	
Depot Kader:	Nikolsburg, then Leipnik. Sánok		
Commander: Oberst	Anton Drechsel	Johann Mayer von Heldensfeld	

- before Aspern: Brigade GM Nikolaus von Kaiser, Division FML baron Franz von Lusignan, III Corps Hohenzollern . At Teugen it was with the BrigadeKaiser in the avantguard division Vukassovich, III Corps where its commander, colonel Drechsel and the Oberstlieutnant Peccaduc were wounded. Regiment lost 45 dead, 164 wounded, 304 taken prisoner by the French. Major Stark (from grenadiers) took the command and the regiment was in the Vukassovich now rear guard, which took position on the Laaber banks. At Eggmühl it was sent as reinforcement behind the attacked IV Corps and fought the Bavarians at Schierling having 21 wounded. During the first operations in order to organize the retreat towards Ratisbon, the brigade Kaiser was ordered to cover the right. The regiment was indirectly involved in the French breakthrough at Alt-Egglofsheim which happened at dusk and was attacked by French cavalry. 324 men were taken prisoner on April 22 but the Flag was saved. [3] On April 23 the regiment was the first unit, together with Archduke Charles, to cross the Danube bridge and then it was order to cover the passage. 123 men were left behind with that cover mission; also they were taken prisoner by French. The day after colonel Drechsel was promoted to generalmajor and the regiment had a new commander: colonel Johann Mayer von Heldensfeld from the General Staff.

Part of the battered regiment was attached to the River Inn defense (Division Dedovich, VI Corps) : two companies (the 427 men of the training division of the officers Caspary and Siegler) with the Brigade GM comte Rudolf von Sinzendorff, the rest of the regiment in reorganization. The detachment was heavily involved during the French attack at castle Ebelsberg (9 dead and 111 wounded). Captain Heinrich von Siegler had the "Hero of Ebelsberg" mention and (1810) the Maria Theresia Cross.

The 2nd Battalion was later with the Détachement oberst Ignaz von Leuthner (div. Sommariva, III Corps Kollowrat) at Urfahr (May 17), the rest of the Schröder with Division baron Philipp Vukassovich in the Brigade GM Josef von Mayer. At Linz-Urfahr they lost 7 dead, 71 wounded comprising the hero of the day, major von Marinowsky, commander of the 1st Battalion , who died the day after, and 159 taken prisoners. In the meanwhile Siegler detachment had reached Vienna with Dedovich while the rest of the regiment was with Sommariva division, BrigadeSamuel von Giffling, III corps. The Schröder units gathered together on the left Danube bank before Aspern. It did not participated at the battle.

- after Aspern and at Wagram: the regiment re-united with the BrigadeGrill, Division Vukassovich, III Corps. On June 20 arrived also the Train transports of the regiment from Leipnik with 498 men. The companies now were raised to 190 men again. During the French occupation of Vienna, on May 28, died the regiment's Owner at the age of 89 years.

At Wagram the 1st and 2nd Battalions (Colonel Mayer) took place at Stammersdorf while the 3rd Battalion (now under captain Siegler) supported the Grenadiers between Breitenlee and Süssenbrunn. The losses were 11 dead, 38 wounded and 12 missing men.

- after Wagram: at Znaim it took place between Brenditz and Winau with the Brigade von Giffling, Division FML von Schneller, III Corps. After the battle they lost 42 men wounded and 60 taken prisoners.

K.K. IR 8 – FZM Archduke Ludwig Joseph – 3 battalions

Recruitment: Moravia, Galicia. 1 Depotcomp. 1 BrigadeRamberg in Znaim, Div St.Julien under Argenteau. 1 Depot comp BrigadeStarczinsky in Krakow, Division Meerveldt under Hohenlohe- Ingelfingen.

Moravia	Iglau	08	
Galicia	Rzeszów	08	
Depot Kader:	Iglau - Krakow		
Commander: Oberst	Baron Albert Swinburne	after Wagram baron Carl Fürstenwärther	

- before Aspern: Division FML prince Ludwig Hohenlohe-Wartenburg-Bartenstein with the Brigade GM Josef von Grill (IV Corps Rosenberg).On April 10 it crossed the Inn at Schärding being part of the avantgarde Stutterheim, IV Corps. At Teugen it was with the BrigadeRiese, Division prince Hohenlohe- Bartenstein and at Abensberg it was in reserve under Corps direct command, while the 1st Battalion (major baron Biala) distinguished itself during the combats. The right wing of the div. Hohenlohe-Bartenstein was formed also by the "Achter" which engaged a stout resistance among the woods of Ober-Laichling, fighting as skirmishers. There fell the brave major Biala, substituted by the 2nd major Bossmann.[4]

After the retreat in Bohemia the regiment was with the Division Dedovich, BrigadeVon Grill again.

- at Aspern: colonel Swinburne took provisional command of the brigade, always with Division Dedovich. Regiment losses were: 134 dead and 334 wounded. On May 24 Swinburne was promoted to generalmajor and baron Carl Fürstenwärther became the new commander.

- between Aspern and Wagram: on June 14 the regiment (now under Division Rohan, IV Corps) was merged with the 1st Landwehr Battalion of major Nesselrode. The regiment now had 4 battalions.

- at Wagram: with Division FML prince Victor de Rohan and Brigade GM Earl Swimburne, baron von Fürstenwärther led his 3 battalions and the 1st Landwehr Battalion Iglau (major count Nesselrode), IV Corps. It had tasks of supporting and covering the retreat, which it made in the column of IV Corps directed towards Brünn.

K.K. IR 10 – FML baron Anton Mittrowsky – 3 battalions |5|

Recruitment: Moravia, Galicia. 1 Depot Company 1 Brig, Pöck (Boeck?) in Brünn, Division St.Julien under Argenteau. 1 Depot Company BrigadeStarczinsky in Krakau, Division Meerveldt under Hohenlohe-Ingelfingen.

Moravia	Hradisch	10	
	Brünn II		
Galicia	Tarnów	10	
Depot Kader:	Neuhaus then Kremsier. Tarnów		
Commander: Oberst	Domitian De Vaux	Josef Weigl von Löwenwarth	

- before Aspern: it began the campaign with the I Corps GdK count Heinrich Bellegarde first with BrigadeWacquant, div. Ulm then in the reserve corps or Brigade GM count Johann Nostitz. In March the third Battalion was sent at Lobositz with the Am Ende special corps. So the regiment remained with 1st and 2nd Battalion only. Till Aspern they did not fight.

In May it was with the division FML Ludwig Vogelsang, Brigade GM baron Ferdinand Wintzingerode-Ohmfeld (later Division Fresnel) I Corps .

- at Aspern: the I Corps Bellegarde formed the 2nd column. The regiment was in the Brigade Wintzingerode (under GM count Ferdinand von Wartensleben), division FML count Johann Fresnel von Hennequin in the second line. They attacked Aspern in the afternoon. Losses: 55 dead, 611 wounded with the commander De Vaux, 70 taken prisoners. Being a regiment of only two battalions they lost around 50% of their strength. Colonel Domitian De Vaux was promoted and the regiment commander became Josef Weigl von Löwenwarth. The regiment camper at Deutsch-Wagram now deployed with the brigade baron Greth (from June 1 BrigadeClary), Division Fresnel, I Corps. There arrived the 1st Hradischer Landwehr Battalion, which was attached to the regiment. On July 2 the regiment was deployed with the brigade Henneberg.

- at Wagram: the BrigadeClary, Division Fresnel, I Corps was in the right wing of the second line formations. [6] Oberst Weigl led the regiment while the battalions were under Oberstlieutenant O'Daly (1st) and Hauptmann Mazzetti then Hauptmann Koss (2nd). The regiment began to fight in the second battle day near Aderklaa. It lost 50 men dead, 105 wounded, 201 taken prisoners with the commander Weigl himself.

- after Wagram: the regiment was always in the second line of the I Corps deployed from Leschna till Kukrowitz. At the Znaim battle it lost 16 men dead, 919 wounded (taking account also of the wounded at Wagram, who were trasported till Znaim) and 79 prisoners. (note the III Battalion was always with BrigadeAm Ende in Saxony).

K.K. IR 12 – GM-FML Marquis Friedrich (Federico) Manfredini – 3 battalions

Recruitment: Moravia, Galicia. 1 Depot Company BrigadeBojakowski in Olmütz, Division St.Julien under Argenteau. 1 Depot Company Statczinsky in Krakow under Hohenlohe-Ingelfingen.

Moravia	Olmütz (upper)	12
Galicia	Tarnów	12
	Bochnia	
Depot Kader:	Olmütz. Bochnia (Krakow)	
Commander: Oberst	Timotheus von Winzian	Oberstlieutenant Lass

- before Aspern: Brigadeprince Alois Liechtenstein, Division St.Julien, III Corps Hohenzollern with 2678 men. At Teugen-Hausen the division was sent on the left wing of the Lusignan division, which had orders to advance. The two Liechtenstein brothers (Alois and Moritz with the Würzburg unit) led the battle among the woods. There the regiment lost 1/3 of its strength (25 officers and 850 men). The heavy wounded prince was carried to Vienna, leaving the battlefields. The regiment was attached to the BrigadePfanzelter, Division St.Julien, III Corps, participating at Abensberg. At Eggmühl the regiment was in reserve with the twin unit Würzburg (a brigade which continued to be called as Alois Liechtenstein). After the battle they (47 officer and 1757 men) withdrew towards Bohemia with the rear guard division Vukassovich, III Corps. [7]
Manfredini regiment remained in the ranks of the III Corps, now under Kollowrat. The third Battalion in the former Brigade GM Josef von Pfanzelter, Division baron Philipp Vukassovich, then in the avant-garde column (Avant-garde brigade GM count Carl Crenneville), the 1st and the 2nd battalions detached with their colonel brigade Timotheus von Winzian (taken prisoner by a württemberg's chasseur à cheval, after the Urfahr battle). After the battle of Linz-Urfahr (May 17) the two battalions had the task to cover the retreat till Gallneukirchen. There the regiment lost three companies of the III Battalion , taken prisoner with the two colonels Winzian and Diemar.

- at Aspern: the regiment did not take part at the battle, it was reorganizing under the provisional commander Oberstlieutenant Lass.

- at Wagram: was with the BrigadeLilienberg, Division St.Julien, III Corps. The regiment defended itself in mass formation against French cavalry, losing 313 dead or wounded, 171 missing. After the battle the regiment was the reserve of the VI Corps.

- after Wagram: it fought at Znaim detached to the BrigadeRheinhardt, Division St.Julien, III Corps Kollowrat between Brenditz, Kukrowitz and Winau.

K.K. IR 15 – FML-FZM baron Anton Zach – 3 battalions [8]

Recruitment: Bohemia (?), Silesia - Moravia – Galicia. 1 Depot Company BrigadeBojakowski, Division St.Julien under Argenteau. 1 Depot Company BrigadeStarczinsky in Krakow, Division Meerveldt under Hohenlohe-Ingelfingen.

Moravia	Olmütz (unter)	15
Galicia	Myslenice	15
Depot Kader:	Myslenice and Hohenstadt	
	Mährische Schönberg, Chrudim (?) - Bohemia [9]	
Commander: Oberst	Ludwig Carpé von Carpenstein	

-        before Aspern: the regiment had these Staff officers – Carpé, colonel commander, Oschée Oberst-leutnant, majors Mohr, Niessel and Bourguignon. The two additional companies of the 3rd Battalion were raised at Hohenstadt in Moravia and at Calvaria, near Wadowice in Myslenice province. There were also raised the two Kader. The regiment was assigned to the division FML baron Thomas von Brady in the Brigade GM Wenzel Buresch von Greifenbach, II Corps. On April 1 the regiment gathered all its companies for a total strength of 3719 men in 18 companies. After the battle of Eggmühl the regiment was ordered to watch the right Danube bank and to cover the evacuation of Ratisbon. It was with Brigade GM Carl von Fölseis (Division FML Franz Weber von Treuenfels) in the western part of the city together with Zettwitz regiment. The two regiments organized a firm defense between the houses and blocking the bridge but the losses were vey heavy: 34 officers and 1980 men. After the retreat it returned in the ranks of the BrigadeBuresch, II Corps but for the heavy losses practically disappeared the third Battalion .

-        at Aspern: still with the BrigadeBuresch, Division Brady, II Corps. After the hard battle the regiment lost 90 dead and 378 wounded. During the month of June the regiment restored its strength up to 2777 men.

-        at Wagram: still with the BrigadeBuresch, Division Brady, II Corps Hohenzollern. It was detached with other 3 battalions to Pillichsdorf, losing the contact with the Corps and linking only with the IV Corps. During the two days battle the regiment lost 65 men dead and 282 wounded.

-        after Wagram: still in the BrigadeBuresch, interim Division Buresch, II Corps with a strength of 1454 men (while other 773 men were ill in hospitals). During the battle of Znaim the regiment was deployed behind the cavalry and did not take part to the fights (two companies apart).

K.K. IR 20 – FML-FZM count Wenzel Kaunitz Rietberg – 3 battalions

Recruitment: Moravia, Silesia and Galicia. At beginning of war: 1 Depot Company BrigadeWodniansky in Olmütz, Division St.Julien under Argenteau. 1 Depot Company BrigadeEgermann in Sándomierz, Division Meerveldt under Hohenlohe-Ingelfingen. Before Aspern: 2. Depot Company with the VII Corps in Saxony.

Silesia	Troppau	20	
	Tarnów		
Galicia	Sandec	20	
	Jaslo		
Depot Kader:	Neustadt (Moravia) then Troppau.		
Commander: Oberst	count Albert Murray de Melgum	Joseph Bresslern von Sternau [10]	Jakob von Luxem

-        before Aspern: it was in the Brigade GM Josef von Bieber, Division count Franz Saint Julien-Waldsee, III Corps. The regiment was at Teugen deployed in the village of Hausen.
Losses at: Teugen-Hausen (19 dead, 12 prisoners, 173 missing), On April 21 it was in brigade with IR 38 Württemberg, under Bieber. On the late afternoon the regiment was overrun by a French cavalry charge; its losses at Eggmühl (6 dead, 14 wounded, 74 prisoners, 860 missing). After the retreat in Bohemia the regiment followed St.Julien division the third column (left wing) in the area Neumarkt-Mauthausen of the Urfahr battle, but it had no clashes there. It did not take part at the Aspern battle.[11]

-        at Wagram: The regiment took parte at the defense organized by III Corps and suffered heavy losses: lost at Wagram (328 dead or wounded, 6 prisoners, 2 missing) .

-        after Wagram: the regiment was with the III Corps deployed from Brenditz till Winau without taking any part in the battle.
Note: the 2nd Depot company distinguished itself during the defence of Sandomierz in Galicia under commando of capitän- lieutenant Laux.

K.K. IR 22 – FM Prince Friedrich Josias Sachsen-Coburg-Saalfeld (Coburg Rgt.) 3 battalions

Recruitment: Moravia, Galicia. 1 Depot Company BrigadeRamberg in Znaim, Division St.Julien under Argenteau. 1 Depot Company BrigadeEgermann in Sándomierz, Division Meerveldt under Hohenlohe- Ingelfingen.

Moravia	Znaim	22	
Galicia	Sanok	22	
Depot Kader:	Znaim. Sanok		
Commander: Oberst	baron Wenzel Vettel von Lilienberg	Josef von Watzel	

▲ Austrian and Hungarian Infantry 1809. From Ottenfeld artwork

- before Aspern: they left Znaim with a force of 4792 m. (3 battalions) with the BrigadeRiese, Division Hohenlohe Bartenstein, IV Corps Rosenberg. On April 21 the regiment was on the Schneidart Hills when the French began the advance. Being shot by enemy artillery the regiment changed its position and General Staff Lieut. Col. Quosdanovich ordered to the II Battalion (major Nennel) a counterattack. The bad news from Landshut forced the regiment to withdraw till Laichling. At Thann it was under its colonel Vettel von Lilienberg (as new brigadier under Division Sommariva, IV Corps). At Abensberg it returned under BrigadeRiese, Division Hohenlohe Bartenstein, IV Corps Rosenberg and fought at Eggmühl at the right austrian wing, under direct command of prince Ludwig Hohenlohe-Wartenburg-Bartenstein. [12] Then the Coburger followed the Archduke Charles retreat in Bohemia meeting the Hiller's units at Korneuburg, by May 16. There the regiment was deployed with the BrigadeGrill, Division Dedovich, VI Corps.

- at Aspern: the same baron Martin von Dedovich led the 4th column during the battle of Aspern. The avantgarde of the column was the III Battalion (Oberstleutnant von Kornritter). The first Battalion (major Kolb) defended itself in square formations during the French cuirassier charge. Kornritter took the command as Vettel was wounded and during the 2nd day the command passed to major von Nennel. The regiment at Aspern lost: (423 men dead, 388 wounded, 143 prisoners, 155 missing for a total of 1109 men.) [13] Oberstlieutnant Kornritter von Ehrenhalm died after his severe wounds.

- between Aspern and Wagram: On June 4, the Coburg was reached by 4 Moravian Landwehr Battalions, of which the 1st Znaim Battalion (major Haugwitz) was attached to the regiment. On June 7 colonel Vettel von Lilienberg became a major general. The regiments command was taken by Oberst Josef von Watzel (of IR 3) and the regiment was brigaded with GM Earl of Swinburne brigade, Division FML prince Viktor Rohan, IV Corps.

- at Wagram: it was in the BrigadeSwinburne, Division Rohan, IV Corps. The regiment after the battle lost 34 dead and 165 wounded; the side 1st Moravian Battalion (Znaimer) lost 28 dead, 82 wounded and 440 taken prisoners.

- after Wagram: the regiment was attached to the Division FML Radetzky of VI Corps (prince Rohan had been wounded) and withdrew toward Olmütz.

K.K. IR 29 – FML-FZM Karl von Lindenau – 3 battalions [14]

Recruitment: Moravia, Galicia. 1 Depot Company BrigadePöck in Brünn, Division St.Julien under Argenteau. 1 Depot Company BrigadeBicking in Lemberg, Division Meerveldt under Hohenlohe- Ingelfingen.

Moravia	Brünn I	29
Galicia	Rzeszów	29
Depot Kader:	Brünn. Rzeszów	
Commander: Oberst	Anton von Hammer	Philipp Pflüger von Lilienfels

- before Aspern:
Before the opening of the hostilities the Lindenau waited for the two companies of the third Battalion which were completed in Galicia. In their place were organized two new companies so-called "Augmentierungskompagnien". The regiment Depotdivision (other two companies) were at Brünn in Moravia. The battalions of the Lindenau were in the Division FML Emmanuel von Schustekh (V Corps under Archduke Ludwig), and then with Division FML. prince Reuss-Plauen. The regiment's commander, Oberst von Hammer, became generalmajor and the new colonel commander was the former Oberstleutnant Philipp Pflüger von Lindenfels. Originally the Lindenau was assigned to the bohemian III Corps, but before the invasion of Bavaria it went with the V. Marched towards Landshut arriving near Siegenburg (April 19). During the Abensberg battle the corps commander Archduke Ludwig disposed the division of FML Schustekh to the "control of the withdrawing troops". At Abensberg the regiment lost 6 men dead, 206 wounded then prisoners and 312 prisoners.
On April 21 it was at the Landshut battle without fighting an reached, retreating, the river Inn at Mühldorf on April 23. During the retreat it lost other 2 men dead and 212 taken prisoners. This is was the regiment's history tells. But the whole story was rather different. [15]
The column march order (V Corps) was the following:
the Avant-garde brigade GM Ludwig Thierry with the regiments
IR 1 Kaiser Franz – 10 companies, IR 29 FML Carl von Lindenau – 6 companies, Dragoons n. 4 baron Franz von Levenehr – 4 ¾ sqns., ½ brigade battery (4 pieces - 6 pdr);
the Détachement oberst Anton von Hammer with
IR 1 Kaiser Franz – 6 companies, IR 29 FML Carl von Lindenau – 10 companies, Dragoons n°4 baron Franz von Levenehr – 1 ¼ sqns., ½ brigade battery (4 pieces - 6 pdr).

The two units (brigades) took position linking the V Corps column and the III Corps, a delicate location for a direct strong hit there could have compromised the front splitting in two the Austrian army. Thierry was in front of Offenstetten and Hammer on the Kirchdorf hill. The command of the sector was taken by FML Schustekh and FML Lusignan of the III Corps. There Thierry was overrun by a joint attack of Bavarian and Württemberg troops, which surrounded him giving an awful defeat and surrounding also GM Hammer detachment at Kirchdorf. The remnants two battalions remained in the avant-garde Division Reuss Plauen, V Corps.

On April 24 the column pointed towards Neumarkt clashing with the French vanguards. Lindenau took part to that battle losing 2 men dead and 36 wounded and taken prisoners. During the following retreat the Division Schustekh was ordered to act as the rear guard of the march to Vienna. At May 3, three companies of the 2nd Battalion took position in the Ebelsberg castle (detachment Pflüger) with the troops of the VI Corps, while the rest of the 2nd and the 1st Battalion were with the BrigadeHammer, Division and Corps Reuss-Plauen (V). The regiment lost 15 dead, 242 wounded and then prisoners and 9 missing. A renewed 3rd Battalion was attached to the autonomous Brigade (left Danube bank) oberst count Johann Ignaz Franz von Hardegg while the rest of the Schustekh division stopped its march at Krems, watching the bridge on Danube (BrigadeHammer then Rheinwaldt).

- at Aspern and after: the regiment, which had now again 3 Battalions controlled the Danube area called Schwarze Laken near Nußdorf.

- at Wagram: was in the BrigadePflüger, autonomous, then BrigadePflüger, Division Weissenwolf, V Corps watching the northern Danube banks.

- after Wagram: The regiment fought in the Znaim battle with the Brigade Pflüger von Lindenfels, V Corps deployed between the two Thaya bridges, from the Klosterbruck till Alt-Shallersdorf (the so called Chaussée-bruck) together with the 5th Battalion volunteers of Vienna. The 1st Battalion under Hauptmann baron Hauer was at Brenditz, two divisions of the 2nd Battalion were in the Weingärten in front of Znaim, while the 6th division was on the right, on the road to the Weingärten. [16] The third Battalion was split between the bridges. The regiment's losses were all from 2nd and 3rd battalions: 22 dead, 206 wounded, 181 taken prisoners.

K.K. IR 40 – FZM count Joseph Mittrowsky (vacant)[17] – 3 battalions

Recruitment: Moravia, Galicia. 1 Depot Company BrigadeDu Noyer in Ung. Hradisch, Division St.Julien under Argenteau . 1 Depot Company BrigadeStarczinsky in Crakow, Division Meerveldt under Hohenlohe- Ingelfingen.

Moravia	Ungarische Hradisch	40
Galicia	Jaslo	40
Depot Kader:	Kremsier. Jaslo.	
Commander: Oberst	Chevalier Thomas Rheinbach	then Count Joseph Lamezan-Salins

- before Aspern: it was with the Brigade GM ritter Adrian Joseph Rheinwaldt von Waldegg, Division Hohenlohe-Bartenstein, IV Corps Rosenberg. Marched with the VI Corps not taking part at the Landshut clash. Participated at the clashes of Dinzling (April 19), Oberleuchling, and marginally at Eggmühl (was practically attached to the V Corps of Archduke Ludwig).

- After the retreat it was attached to the Division FML Henry XV prince Reuss-Plauen (interim commander of the V Corps) with its BrigadeRheinwaldt. In the battle of Ebelsberg the third Battalion (Oberstleutnant count Lamezan-Salins) distinguished itself when supported the defense at the castle. Then the first Battalion (major count Anton Kinsky) covered the retreat fighting at Asten.

Having organized a so called "System of protection for the upper – Linz - and lower – Vienna – Austria" the brigade Rheinwaldt was again attached to IV Corps, with Division Dedovich and, for few time, with the rear guard of Radetzky. Its train was at the complete disposition of the BrigadeHardegg on the right Danube bank. The regiment took position at the centre (Schwanenstadt) of the left Danube bank defense and had the task to watch the Danube from Linz till Neu-Aigen, a front of 20 miles (always with the BrigadeRheinwaldt, now Division Emmanuel von Schustekh, IV Corps). During this period the regiment was split in divisions or single companies.

- between Aspern and Wagram: On May 31 one company made a fake-attack against Mautern.

- at Wagram: two companies (Oberlieutenant baron Scheibler) made a Streif-Kommando with some Vincent Chevaulégers and tried a night attack (4-5 July) against the Tabor island near Mauthausen.

K.K. IR 56 – FML-FM count Wenzel Colloredo-Waldsee – 3 battalions [18]

Recruitment: Moravia, Silesia, Galicia. 1 Depot Company BrigadePietsch in Troppau, Division St.Julien under Argenteau - 1 Depot Company BrigadeStarczinsky in Krakow, Division Meerveldt under Hohenlohe- Ingelfingen.

Silesia	Teschen	56
Galicia	Myslenice	56
Depot Kader:	Teschen, Myslenice	
Commander: Oberst	Benedikt von Giffing	

- before Aspern: during mid March the three battalions (3060 men) gathered themselves under the Brigade GM Nikolaus von Kaiser, Division FML baron Franz von Lusignan, III Corps Hohenzollern. It fought at Teugen-Hausen and then (on April 20) retreated covering the Division Vukassovich beyond the Laaber on the hills of Dietenhofen. After the Abensberg battle the regiment (autonomous BrigadeKaiser) was sent behind the retreating IV Corps with orders to cover their movements. The regiment stopped at Schierling where it was attacked by the Bavarians. That battle lasted till night. During the days of the Eggmühl battle the Daun had only defensive orders and retreated with the corps to Ratisbon and then to Bohemia. In May the regiment was in the BrigadeGiffing (its commander) under the division FML Vukassovich.

On May 17 the III Corps now under FML count Carl Kollowrath-Krakowsky formed several attack columns in oder to seize Linz. The 1st Column, Division marquis Hannibal Sommariva, marched from Neu-Helmonsödt till the Pöstlingberg and had ½ 2nd Battalion IR 56 with the Staff, while the 1st and the other ½ 2nd Battalion were with the Détachement Oberstlieutenant baron Georg von Süden(on Pöstlingberg).

The 3rd Battalion was with the Avant-garde brigade GM count Carl Crenneville of the II Column Vukassovich (centre) marching from Gallneukirchen. The losses at the Linz-Urfahr battle were 3 men dead, 51 wounded, 112 wounded and made prisoners, 80 prisoners and 17 missing.

In June the regiment had reinforcements reaching a force of 2140 men and was assigned to the BrigadeGrill, Division Vukassovich, III Corps

- at Wagram: during the first day of battle the regiment was with the III Corps at Hagenbrunn with the BrigadeGrill. In the second day the Daun occupied Breitenlee. It resisted to the last French counterattacks and retreated during the incoming night. Its losses were: 26 men dead, 95 wounded, prisoners and missing 195 men.

- after Wagram: after the death of Vukassovich the regiment was assigned to the BrigadeGiffing, Division Schneller, III Corps and went not in battle at Znaim.

K.K. IR 57 – GM-FM count Joseph Colloredo-Waldsee – 3 battalions

Recruitment: Moravia, Galicia. Also Bohemia (Leitomishl till 1808). 1 Depot Company BrigadeWodniansky in Olmütz, Division St.Julien under Argenteau. 1 Depot Company BrigadeStarczinsky in Krakow, Division Meerveldt under Hohenlohe- Ingelfingen .

Silesia	Troppau	57
Galicia	Bochnia	57
Depot Kader:	Olmütz, Leitomischl, Bochnia (Krakow)	
Commander: Oberst	Carl Heinrich Ellger	

- before Aspern: the first two battalions were organized in Moravia, while the third in Galicia.

1st and 2nd Battalions with Brigade GM Wenzel Buresch von Greifenbach, Division FML baron Thomas von Brady, II Corps Kollowrath. They began the campaign with 44 officers, 162 NCOs, 23 Musikanten, 24 Zimmerleuten and 2019 men. [19]

The third Battalion remained under the bohemian general HQ. The regiment was in the main column of the II Corps when it seized Ratisbon. It took part at the Eggmühl battle but without strong committment. After the retreat in Bohemia the 3rd Battalion was attached to the Brigade GM Andreas von Schneller, Division comte Franz Saint Julien-Waldsee (III Corps now Kollowrat) while the other two battalions remained with Buresch under the II Corps (now Hohenzollern).

- at Aspern: the Josef Colloredo Rgt. was in the 3rd Column Hohenzollern with BrigadeBuresch, Division Brady. The regiment lost 422 men in the battle (92 dead, 305 wounded and 25 missing). On June 26 the 3rd Battalion merged with the regiment.

- at Wagram: Colloredo had finally 3 Battalions and 3146 men. The regiment lost 37 dead, 183 wounded, 85 taken prisoner, 247 missing. The regiment was also at Znaim with Hohenzollern.

RECRUITMENT DISTRICT: KREISE (GALICIA & LITTLE POLAND) 1805-1809

Galicia (Ukrainian: Halychyna, Polish: Galicja, German: Galizien) is a historical region in East Central Europe, currently divided between Poland and Ukraine, named after Ukrainian city of Halych. In 1772, Galicia was the largest part of the area annexed by Austria in the First Partition of Poland. As such, the Austrian region of Poland and what was later to become Ukraine was known as the Kingdom of Galicia and Lodomeria to underline the Hungarian claims to the country. To the first partition of Poland was added the district of New or West Galicia in 1795; but at the peace of Vienna in 1809 West Galicia and Cracow were surrendered to the grand-duchy of Warsaw, and in 1810 part of East Galicia, including Tarnopol, was made over to Russia.

However, a large portion of ethnically Polish lands to the west was also added to the province, which changed the geographical reference of the term, Galicia. Lviv (Lemberg, Lwów) served as capital of Austrian Galicia, which was dominated by the Polish aristocracy, despite the fact that the population of the eastern half of the province was mostly Ukrainian, or "Ruthenian", as they were known at the time..

Western Galicia Lesser Poland (also "Little Poland", Polish: Małopolska) is one of the historical regions of Poland. It forms the southernmost part of the country. Actually it was known as New Galicia or Western Galicia (Polish: Nowa Galicja or Galicja Zachodnia, German: West-Galizien) and was an administrative region of the Habsburg Monarchy, created after the Third Partition of Poland in 1795. In 1803 it was merged with Kingdom of Galicia and Lodomeria, but retained some autonomy. It existed until the Austrian defeat by Napoleon in 1809, when the region was attached to the Duchy of Warsaw by the Treaty of Schönbrunn.

Circles (Districts) see map-image above (data from a 1814 gazeteer)

Galicia

Berezhany (Polish/Ruthenian :Brzeżany) - recruitment area (Kreis) Brzeżany. Touched by the D'nestr the Circle was crossed by the rivers Lipa and Zlota-Lipa. It had 3 towns, 16 large villages, 324 villages, 33904 houses, 43370 dwellings and 192452 souls.

Brzeżany First written record about the town dates to 1375. First it was a normal village, which by the privilege of the prince Wladislaw Opolski (Vladyslav Opolsky). Ukrainians (or Ruthenians/Rusyns as they were called then), who comprised the most part

of Berezhany population, were undergoing the the greatest social and national oppression. They were excluded from the town administration institutions, suffered the violences, they were not even allowed to liver in town center. In the end of 16th century, Berezhany numbered 413 courtyards, where 2.000 people lived.

Czernowitz (Polish/Ruthenian :Chernivtsi)- recruitment area (Kreis) Duchy of Bukowina. Bukovina or Austrian Moldavia took the name from Stephan V called the Great, prince of Moldavia, who having defeated the Poles there, forced the people to an eternal cultivation of oaks in order to remember his victory. Bukow, in the local language, meant oak. It had 3 towns, 3 large villages, 267 villages, 38890 houses, 223139 souls.

Czernowitz was at the time of the Austrian Occupation (1775) an unimportant village. It was created a town in 1786, and at the beginning of the 19th century it numbered only 5000 inhabitants. In 1777 the Porte, under whose ruleship Moldavia was, ceded Bukowina to Austria. It was incorporated with Galicia in a single province in 1786.

Czortków (Polish/Ruthenian :Chortkiv) - recruitment area (Kreis) Zaleszczyki (Czortków). The old Zaleszczyki district was split in two parts, where Czortków became the northern and Kolomea the southern.

First mentioned in documents dating back to 1522. Chortkiv was founded in 1522 by J. Czortkowski with the right of Magdeburg law. During the uprisings of 1648 Czortkow was one of the bases of the peasant rebels. From 1672 to 1683 the city was under Turkish rule then under Polish rule from 1699 and under Austrian rule from 1772. Until 1779. Czortkow castle was the residence of the Potocki magnates. The town declined in the second half of the 17th century, during the Polish-Turkish wars. Under Austrian rule it was the center of the Chortkiv district; later it became a county center.

Gródek – Horodok (Polish/Ruthenian :Gródek Jagielloński) - recruitment area (Kreis) Zolkiew. It was one of the northern districts and had 4 towns, 18 large villages, 264 villages, 35434 houses, 48590 dwellings and one population of 198313 inhabitants.

Horodok Already in XIII century town started to play an important role in the political and economical life of principality of Halychyna and Volyn. Horodok lied on an important trade route, connecting East and West, North and South. Town was a famous salt trade center. In XIV century it was annexed to Poland. Polish famous lord and king Vladyslav the II Yahailo lived in the town for a long time. In 1389 Horodok got the right of Magdebourg. In XV and XVI centuries town suffered destruction from Tatar troops. In 1591 Ukrainians of Horodok created a public organization that defended national rights.

Zólkiew Zhovkva (Zolkiewka)The Ukrainian for Zolkiew would be Zhovkva, the Russian Zholkva. The first mention refers to 1368 as WinnikI Untill 1556 belongs to familly WysockI After being bought by S. Zolkiewskiego it's name was change to Zolkiew in 1598. From 1620 till 1629 did belong to Danilowich fammily and from 1629 to royal familly SobieskI From 1740 was a property of Count Radziwill's family . Magdeburg Right was given in 1663. In 16th century it was a largest congregation of jewis population in Poland and Ormian in 17th . In 1772 was anexed by Austrian Empire .

Kolomea (Polish/Ruthenian :Kolomyja)- recruitment area (Kreis) Kolomea. This Circle matched the ancient Podolia (capital Zniatyn which will be the future siege of the circle) and was raised from the southern part of the former large Zaleszczyki district (see above). It was crossed by the large D'nestr river and by the Pruth at south. It had 1 main town, 7 large villages, 107 villages, 16126 houses and 19035 dwellings. It was one of the less populated: 84929 souls.

Kolomea is a very old town and is mentioned already in 1240, but the assertion that it was a Roman settlement under the name of Colonia is not proved. It was the principal town of the Polish province of Pokutia, and it suffered severely during the 15th and 16th centuries from the attacks of the Moldavians and the Tatars.

Jassel (Polish/Ruthenian :Jaslo) - recruitment area (Kreis) Jaslo. At the hungarian border, this Circle was of the smallest of Galicia. It was crossed by two main rivers, the Wisloka, at east, and the Jasiel. However an intricate web of smaller streams and channel croosed its territory. It had 5 towns, 11 large villages, 370 villages, 28523 houses and around 193857 inhabitants.

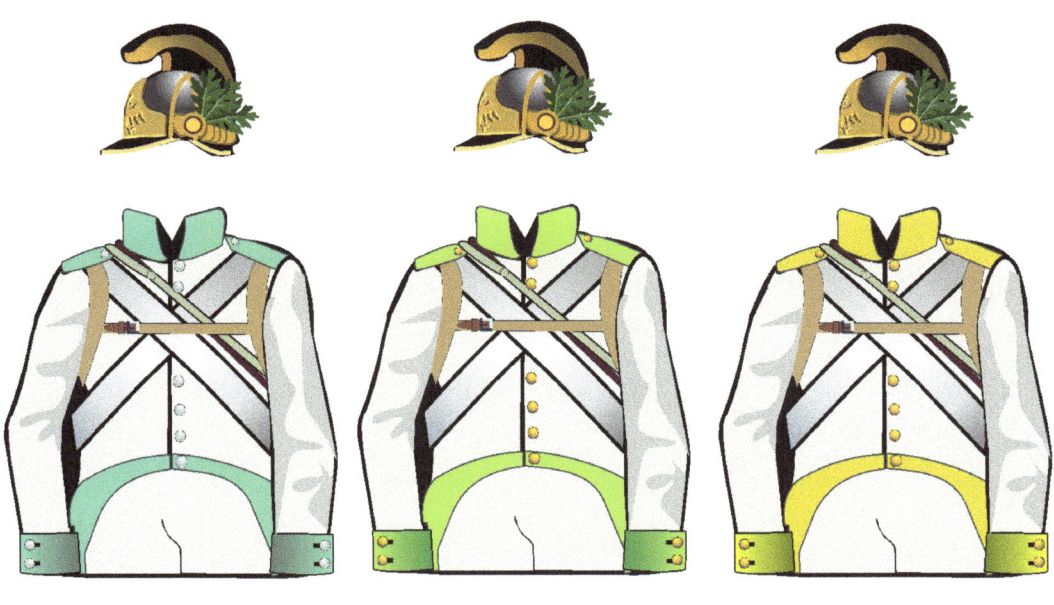

IR 25 FML Zedtwitz   **IR 26 FML Ludwig Hohenlohe–Bartestein**   **IR 27 Strassoldo then Chasteler**

IR 28 FML Michael Fröhlich   **IR 29 FZM Karl von Lindenau**   **IR 30 FM prince De Ligne**

▲ Austrian Infantry uniforms regiments nr. 25, 26, 27, 28, 29 & 30

Jaslo The name derives from Old Polish common word for the "manger" or "trough [trof]" which sounded "jasło". In 1772, following the initial partition of Poland, Jasło region came under the rule of Austria. From 1780 years Lviv became the capital of Galicia and the siege of the governor. At that time Jaslo and adjacent areas were part of the Dukla Circle, which was one of the 18 new administrative units of Galicia. In 1790 Jaslo became the main administrative district and this fact positively influenced the development of the city. Jaslo at that time consisted of only 1500 inhabitants.

Lemberg (Polish/Ruthenian: Lwów/L'viv, latin Leopolis) - recruitment area (Kreis) Lemberg. A Circle of flatlands crossed by the Wereszyca rivers. It had 4 towns, 2 large villages, 148 villages, 18279 houses and 31463 dwellings with a populace of 134656 inhabitants.

Lemberg The inner town was formerly fortified, but the fortifications were transformed into pleasure grounds in 1811. L'viv was first mentioned in 1256 in connection with the fire of Kholm. but the first settlement appeared here in the 6th century. L'viv became the center of trade and commerce of the region. The city's location on the crossroads of trade routs led to its rapid economic development. It had 24000 souls in 1814.

Przemysl (Polish/Ruthenian :Peremyshl) - recruitment area (Kreis) Przemysl. A widely flat Circle, crossed by the San river. It had 5 towns, 12 large villages, 372 villages, 37008 houses, 51289 dwellings, and 210649 souls.

Przemysl Its location 12 km from the Polish-Ukrainian border-crossing Medyka, at the gateway to the Bieszczady Mountains, has directed its development strategy towards the town becoming a trade centre and an important transport junction

Reichshof (Polish/Ruthenian :Rzeszów) - recruitment area (Kreis) Rzeszów. This Circle had heavy forests in the northern part and was crossed by many rivers, of whom the most important were the San and the Wisloka. It had 4 towns, 12 large villages, 331 villages, 36804 houses and 52307 dwellings, with a population of 222669 souls.

Rzeszów A city of southeast Poland east of Crakow. Chartered in the 14th century, it passed to Austria in 1772. Its close proximity to Slovakia and Ukraine, crossings of major transportation routes leading from the north to the south and from the west to the east, made Rzeszów an important transportation hub

Saanig (Polish/Ruthenian :Sánok) - recruitment area (Kreis) Sanok. The Circle was crossed from north to south by the large river San and by the Wisloka. It had 10 towns, 10 large villages, 426 villages, 33148 houses, 51472 dwellings and 208472 souls.

Sánok was founded in 1339, and, in the same year, it obtained the Status of City. It is on the southern edge of its region, around half way between Rzeszów and Przemyśl. It is 45 km far from Jezioro Solińskie, on the river San banks and not far from its estuary.

Salzberg (Polish/Ruthenian :Bochnia) - recruitment area (Kreis) Bochnia. The smallest Circle in Galicia and one of the westernmost, Bochnia was crossed by the Vistula river (east-west) and by Raba river (north-south). It had 3 major towns, 9 large villages, 349 villages, 24219 houses, 37219 dwellings an a population of 160870 inhabitants.

Bochnia. The city of Bochnia lies 45 km east of Crakow, almost midway between Crakow and Tarnow. The city was established around 1200 CE and was closely linked to the discovery of salt deposits in the area (from which the name Salzberg : mountain of salt).

Sambir (Polish/Ruthenian :Sambor)- recruitment area (Kreis) Sambor. One of the larger Galician Circles, it was crossed (east-west) by the river Dn'estr and by the river Stry in the south. In the Circle existed 7 towns, 3 large villages and 353 villages, 49715 houses and 59896 dwellings, with a populace of 237362 souls.

Sambor It was founded in the 12th century and served as an important center of the Halich princedom. In the 13th century, the Tatars destroyed it, and in the year 1241 it was burnt down. According to the calculations, there were 3486 inhabitants in 1760. The number was smaller in the 18th century than it had been in the 16th and 17th , due to the diminution of the population in 1705 as a result of the cholera epidemic. Official statistics came in the 19th, according to which Sambor had, in 1828, 1281 houses and 8616 inhabitants.

Sandec a Circle with an irregular shape and crossed by large rivers like the Dunajec and the Poprad. This Circle had 8 towns, 5 large villages, 386 villages, 28128 houses, 42919 dwellings and 186554 inhabitants.

Neusandez (Polish/Ruthenian :Nowy Sącz) - recruitment area (Kreis) Sandec. By far the largest town of the region is Nowy Sacz (Sonch), which lies above the confluence of the Dunajec (Dunayets) and Poprad, 25 miles (40 km) west of Gorlice. Despite its name, it had already celebrated its 800th anniversary. Chartered in 1298, it passed to Austria in 1772.

Stanislau (Polish/Ruthenian :Stanisławów) - recruitment area (Kreis) Stanislau. This was a Circle with large rivers crossing: the D'nestr, the Pruth and the Bistrica. Its southern part was mountainous in the hungarian border. It had 6 towns, 18 large villages, 319 villages, 40414 houses and 52691 dwellings, with a population of 230122 inhabitants.

Stanislau Because of the large ethnic Polish population, the Polish town name, Stanislawow, was colloquially used by many people, in its shortened version of Stanislaw (pronounced Stanislav). Stanislau was founded by Stanislav Potocki (y. 1683).

Stryi (Polish/Ruthenian :Stryi) - recruitment area (Kreis) StryI The Circle, one of the largest in Galicia, is rather montainous and had 3 towns, 8 large villages, 289 villages, 30284 houses and 41551 dwellings with 171719 inhabitants.

Stryl The town, on the road from Russia to Hungary, located on the Stryj riverside, falling into the Dniestr river, was settled in the valley, at the foot of East Bieszczady Mountains, part of Karpaty mountain chain. This is the same road that was chosen by Swietoslaw, the son-in-law of the Polish King Boleslaw Chrobry, Prince of Kijev and his large family to escape from his brother. According to old stories, here, not far from Stryj, in what is presently the large village of Siemiginow, Swietoslaw's seven sons were killed. Stryy was first populated by Jews in the late 1500's. The first synagogue was built in 1660. After Poland was partitioned, Stryy became part of the Austrian Empire in 1772

Tarnau (Polish/Ruthenian :Tarnów) - recruitment area (Kreis) Tarnów.This Circle was mountainous in its southern part with mosly hills than mountains. It had 5 towns, 9 large villages, 461 villages, 30773 houses, 47747 dwellings and 205244 souls.

Tarnow The first recorded mention of Tarnów was in 1125. In 1264 Daniel of Galicia and Bolesław V the Chaste met in the town to establish the borders of their domains. It was granted city rights on March 7, 1330 by Władysław I the Elbow-high. It was annexed by Habsburg Austria in 1772 during the First Partition of Poland. The Diocese of Tarnów was formed in1785.

Ternopil (Polish/Ruthenian :Tarnopol) - recruitment area (Kreis) Tarnopol. Ternopil' was founded as a fortress in 1540. Despite frequent raids by the Tatars in the 16th and 17th centuries, it developed into a trade center. In 1772 it passed to Austria, and grew in the 19th century. The town came into being around the Polish castle-fortress. The locality where the town was founded was called "arnopil" - "the black-thorn field" may be because of the Polish "tarn" (thorn).

Zolochiv (Polish/Ruthenian :Złoczów/Zolochiv) - recruitment area (Kreis) Zloczów. One of the nothern Circles of Galicia crossed by many rivers among which the main were the Bug and the StryI It had 6 towns, 19 large villages, 299 villages, 32910 houses and 45779 dwellings with 191432 souls.

Zloczów The first mention refers to the town in 1483. In 1520 the town was given the Magdeburg Right. Zloczow was mentioned as a town in the fifteenth century, but gained the status of a city in 1523. It held two trade fairs a year and a weekly market day. During the sixteenth century the town was damaged heavily by the invasions of the Tartars. The Sobieski family became the owners in 1598. A citadel was built to guard the town from enemies and invasions, and in 1649 the Cossacks captured the town. In that year there was a plague that badly injured those who survived the war. From
1687 until the end of the eighteenth century there was also an Armenian community. The town also suffered frequent fires. In 1772 when the area was annexed to Austria, Zloczow became the capital of a district, which included the large and important community of Brody. Although the city was the capital of a district, the Jewish community was under the jurisdiction of the Brody Jewish community.

Western Galicia (Little Poland)

Krakau (Polish/Ruthenian :Kraków) - recruitment area (Kreis) Crakow city. History.Tradition assigns the foundation of Cracow to the mythical Krak, a Polish prince who is said to have built a stronghold here about A.D. 700. Its early history is, however, entirely obscure. It suffered from Tatar invasions; in 1290 it was captured by Wenceslaus II of Bohemia and was held by the Bohemians until, in 1305, the Polish king Ladislaus Lokietek recovered it from Wenceslaus III Ladislaus made it his capital, and from this time until 1764 it remained the coronation and burial place of the Polish kings, even after the royal residence had been removed by Siegmund III (1587 1632) to Warsaw. On the third partition. of Poland in 1795 Austria took possession of Cracow; but in. 1809

Napoleon wrested it from that power, and incorporated it with the duchy of Warsaw, which was placed under the rule of the king of Saxony.

The former Wojwodschaft (Voivodeship) Krakau in 1775 had 180000 souls.Crakow was a royal large city with more than 4000 houses (around 16000 inhabitants in 1775 and maybe 24000 in 1809 – 8894 inside city walls). [1]

Lublin (Polish/Ruthenian :Lublin) - recruitment area (Kreis) Lublin. The earliest, most significant settlement began in the 6th century, on a hill located in the suburb of Czwartek (in Polish Thursday, most likely in reference to the market day of the settlement). After the Third of the Partitions of Poland in 1795 Lublin was located in the Austrian empire, then since 1809 in the Duchy of Warsaw, and then since 1815 in the Congress Poland under Russian rule. The Wojwodschaft Lublin had, in 1778, around 250000 souls. Lublin town had 2623 souls (1829 houses).

Radom (Polish/Ruthenian :Radom) - recruitment area (Kreis) Radom. The original settlement dates back to 8th–9th century. It was an early mediaeval town in the valley of the Mleczna River (approximately on the location of present-day Old Town). Around the

2nd half of 10th century, it turned into a fortified town called Piotrówka. Radom was founded in 1340, and it belonged to the Sandomierz Voivodeship. Radom capital of the Poviat (district) had, in 1778, 256 houses and 1160 inhabitants.

Sandomir (Polish/Ruthenian :Sandomierz) - recruitment area (Kreis) Kielce-Siedlec. The name of the city comes from Old Polish Sędomir, composed of Sędzi- (from the verb sądzić "to judge") and mir ("peace").After Polish lands were reunified in the 14th century, the former principality became the Sandomierz Voivodeship, incorporating large areas of southeastern Poland. At this time Sandomierz had about 3000 inhabitants and was one of the larger Polish cities. A great fire in 1757 and the First Partition of Poland in 1772, which placed Sandomierz in Austria, further reduced its status. As a result Sandomierz lost its role as an administrative capital. In 1809 the city was damaged during fighting between the forces of Austria and the Duchy of Warsaw during the Napoleonic Wars. The former Wojwodschaft (Voivodeship) Sandomirs had, in 1775, 68825 houses, and around 415000 souls. Sandomir had 2060 inhabitants in 1778 (616 houses) and was the main town of the Powiat (district).

Kielce By 1761 Kielce had more than 4,000 inhabitants. **Note**: Siedlec is not to be confused with the town of Siedlce, capital of Podlachia (see topmost green part of the above map) which was no a western Galician town. The last two circles were Galician, but considered as western Galician district for military purposes.

Myslenice The westernmost of the Galician Circles surrounded by those of Bochnia and Sandec (east), Hungary (south), the Silesia (north) was one of the smallest in Galicia. It comprised 11 towns, 1 fortress, 320. villages, 35311 houses and 248720 inhabitants.

Wadowitz (Polish/Ruthenian :Wadowice) - recruitment area (Kreis) Myslenice. The first permanent settlement in the area of today's Wadowice was founded in late 10th century or early 11th century. According to a local legend, the town was founded by certain 'Wad' or 'Wład', a short form for the Slavic name of Ladislaus (Polish: 'Władysław').

Myslenice (German: Mischlenitz) The name of the city Myślenice goes back to the medieval male name "Myślimir". The first written records are from the years 1253-1258 in the "Code Tynieck". There was a stronghold called "Mislimich". It protected the trade route between Crakow and Węgry (Hungary) which ran on Myślenice. Since the first partition of Poland in 1772 Myślenice was one of Galicia and was part of Austria-Hungary . During this time the town was named Mischlenitz. Myślenice became the siege of a Circle. This happened until 1819, when Wadowice took over this function.

Zamosč (Polish/Ruthenian :Zamość)- recruitment area (Kreis) Zamość. Zamość owes its perfection to two men: Jan Zamoyski and Bernardo Morando. Nobleman Zamoyski wanted to build a private city in the middle of nowhere, and the architect Morando knew how to do it. They worked togheter for 25 years and created a masterpiece which we can still admire today. Little has changed in the general design since Zamoyski founded the city in 1580. Ambitious Zamoyski created a huge "country within the country". His lands within Poland spanned 6 400 km2 with 11 cities and over 200 villages. This was in addition to the royal estates he controlled of over 17 500 km2 with 112 cities and 612 villages.

He founded the private city of Zamość in order to circumvent royal tariffs and taxes as well as the capital for his mini-state and his managment centre. Zamoyski's lands functioned as an almost independent country - with its own army, judicature and university (Academy).

GALICIAN REGIMENTS

Ergänzungsbezirks Kom.		Werb-bezirk	Regular Army	No Landwehr
HQ Recruiting District	Polish - Ruthenian	Recruitment Area (Kreis)	IR	Uhlans Regiment All Circles
Wadowitz	Wadowice	Myslenice	15 - 56	
Salzberg	Bochnia	Bochnia	12 - 57	
Neusandez	Nowy Sącz	Sandec	20 - 1	
Tarnau	Tarnów	Tarnów	12 - 10	
Reichshof	Rzeszów	Rzeszów	29 - 8	
Jassel	Jaslo	Jaslo	40 -20	
Saanig	Sánok	Sanok	22 - 7	
Sambir	Sambor	Sambor	44	
Przemysl	Peremyshl	Przemysl	9	
Stryi	Stryi	Stryi	58	
Lemberg	Lwów	Lemberg	30	
Gródek - Horodok	Gródek Jagielloński	Zolkiew		
Stanislau	Stanisławów	Stanislau	58	
Berezhany	Brzeżany	Brzeżany	24	
Kolomea	Kolomyja	Kolomea	41	
Czortków	Chortkiv	Zalesczyki (Czortków)		
Zolochiv	Złoczów	Zloczów	63	
Ternopil	Tarnopol	Tarnopol	46	
Czernowitz	Chernivtsi	Duchy of Bukowina	No units	former IR 42
Krakau	Kraków	Crakow city	38	
Sandomir	Sandomierz	Kielce-Siedlec		
Zamosč	Zamość	Zamosč	23	West Galicia
Radom	Radom	Radom	50	
Lublin	Lublin	Lublin	55	

Numbers in bold mean a temporary area of recruitment in order to help the main District to reach the stated strength.

K.K. IR 9 – FML prince Adam Czartorisky-Sangusco - 3 battalions [3]

Recruitment: Galicia. 2 Depot companies BrigadeBicking in Lemberg, Division Meerveldt under Hohenlohe-Ingelfingen.

Galicia	Przemysl	09
Depot Kader:	Crakow, then Kaschau	
Commander: oberst	Baron Wenzel Watlet	Baron Carl Mac Elligot

- before Aspern: it was in the BrigadeBrigade GM Johann von Neustädter, Division marquis Hannibal Sommariva, IV Corps, at Dinzlingen and at the defense of Ober-Leuchling (April 21). At Eggmühl it had its 3rd and 4th companies destroyed. The colonel commander was severely wounded and many officer fell prisoners of the enemy. The regiment withdrew towards Bohemia and (April 25) there met its 3rd battalion (major Mesemacre). Later it was assigned to BrigadeNeustädter, Division Dedovich, IV Corps
- at Aspern: with the BrigadeNeustädter, Division Dedovich, IV Corps it marched from Raasdorf till Essling. During the march colonel Watlet was hit and fell onto the ground. Major Mesemacre took the regiment command. The losses at Aspern were: 325 men dead, 395 wounded, 228 missing.
- between Aspern and Wagram: the wounded colonel Watlet was promoted generalmajor and the command of the regiment passed to the former Oberstlieutenant Baron Carl Mac Elligot, now colonel. On June 26 the regiment was assigned to the V Corps Reuss- Plauen watching Schwarze-Laken with the autonomous BrigadeNeustädter then in div. Weissenwolf. There was attached also the 4th battalion Landwehr Seelowitz (Brünn) (major Hoffmann).
- at Wagram: it did not fight at Wagram.
- after Wagram: Brig. Neustädter, autonomous, with Corps.

Some sources [4] referred the engagement of the 3rd battalion in May, first with watching duties in the Avantgarde Brigade GM Armand von Nordmann then in the reserve BrigadeWeissenwolf, Division Kottulinsky, VI Corps at the Ebelsberg battle. It was deployed on the Zieglhuber hill, in reserve, fact not related in the regiment's history. For this source the battalione reached the regiment immediately before Aspern being part of the special task force (Brigade) GM comte Rudolf von Sinzendorff, detached from the Division Dedovich. Probably

IR 31 FML Johann Benjowski   **IR 32 FZM Esterházy**   **IR 33 FML Hyeronimus Colloredo**

IR 34 FZM Davidovich   **IR 35 Erzherzog Johann Nepomuk**   **IR 36 FZM Count Carl Kolowrath**
(from May) FZM Argenteau

▲ Austrian Infantry uniforms regiments nr. 31, 32, 33, 34, 35 & 36

it was there as many other recruits' divisions (two companies) from Moravia, Bohemia and Galicia, which were transferred, hurrying, to reinforce the battered VI Corps, under the reserve Gruppe of general Dedovich. Further research it will be welcome.

K.K. IR 23 – FM Ferdinand Kurfürst (Großherzog) von Würzburg – 3 battalions

2nd Owner: FML Baron Christoph von Lattermann
Recruitment: West Galicia-Poland. - initially 2 Depot companies BrigadeGrosser in Tárnow, Division Meerveldt under Hohenlohe- Ingelfingen. Before Aspern a reserve division remained in Galicia and defended the town of Zamosc.

Poland	West Galicia-Zamosc	23
Depot Kader:	Olmütz	
Commander: oberst	Baron Ferdinand Sterndahl	

- before Aspern: it was in the BrigadeAlois Liechtenstein, Division St Julien, with 2 battalions and took part to all actions in Bavaria together with the Manfredini regiment. However it was employed as reserve and so it did not fight very often. On April 25 the new raised 3rd battalion was the garrison of Braunau on river Inn. The 3rd battalion (only 4 companies) was committed, together with many other reserve divisions and 3rd battalions (garrisons) in the special reserve corps or BrigadeSinzendorf of Division Dedovich later assigned to the VI Corps as reinforcement. At Ebelsberg it was the reserve battalion of the Brigade oberst Anton von Hammer (Division FML Reuss-Plauen, V Corps). On May 6 it returned to the BrigadeSinzendorf of Division Dedovich (VI Corps). At the same time the 1st and 2nd battalions were with Division Baron Philipp Vukassovich (Brigade GM Josef von Pfanzelter) in Bohemia. On May 17 they attacked at the Urfahr battle (Linz) being part of the FML Sommariva column.
The 3rd battalion was assigned to the II Corps (now Hohenzollern) first in the Brigade Mayer and then with GM Wied Runkel, without taking direct part at the Aspern battle.
- at Aspern: the regiment (Battalions 1 and 2) remained with the III Corps in Bohemia.
- at Wagram: the two battalions were with the BrigadeLilienberg, Division St Julien, III Corps and then (after Wagram) with the BrigadeReinhardt, Division St Julien, III Corps.
The regiment was disbanded after the war end.

K.K. IR 24 – GM-FZM Baron Gottfried Strauch – 3 battalions

Recruitment: Galicia. Depot comp: 2 BrigadeBicking in Lemberg, Division Meerveldt under Hohenlohe- Ingelfingen

Galicia	Brzezany	24
Depot Kader:	Neu Sandec - Crakow	
Commander: oberst	Carl Titelsbach von Tigersburg	

- before Aspern: BrigadeTrautenberg, Division Mondet, VII Corps
- between Aspern and Wagram: in campaign in Poland – Silesia. The three battalions marched with the VII Corps (Archduke Ferdinand). The regiment was at the Raszyn battle, where (Brigade GM Baron Trautenberg) it was in reserve duty at Janczewice. They were also at the clashes of Ivanisk, Obroków and Sandomierz. At Sandomierz (June 15) the regiment was with BrigadeGeringer. The struggle was very bloody and forced the Polish garrison to surrender the day after the battle.

K.K. IR 30 – FM Joseph prince De Ligne – 3 battalions

Recruitment: Galicia. Depot comp: 2 BrigadeBicking in Lemberg, Division Meerveldt under Hohenlohe- Ingelfingen. See also IR 41 for the initial organization.

Galicia	Lemberg	30
	Zloczów	
Depot Kader:	Sambor, Lemberg, Bochnia	
Commander: oberst	Earl Alphons Fusco de Matanony	Johann Baptist de Meys

- before Aspern till after Wagram: BrigadeCivalart, Division Mondet, VII Corps in Polish campaign. It was at Raszyn [5] and Warsaw probably only with two battalions. At Raszyn the Civalart brigade had to force the passage towards Iwanowo, to seize the village and to breakthrough till Warsaw. See under IR 41 more details. The regiment took part also at the victorious Jedlinsko battle (June 11-12) led by colonel De Meys. They followed the retreating Poles till Koskie.

K.K. IR 38 – FML Ferdinand duke of Württemberg – 3 Battalions [6]

Recruitment: Galicia. - initially: 2 Depot companies BrigadeGrosser in Tárnow, Division Meerveldt under Hohenlohe-Ingelfingen . The Galician reserve division (2 companies) remained at Home in garrison duties and was at the Zamosc defense (May 19-20) where they were taken prisoners (losing however 17 dead and 31 wounded).

Poland	W.Galicia-Kielce-Siedlec	38	
Galicia	Crakow	38	
Depot Kader:	Lublin, then Brünn, Nikolsburg		
Commander: oberst	Baron Ludwig Piret de Bihain		Emanuel de Lompret

- before Aspern: in was assigned to Brigade GM Josef von Bieber, Division St Julien, III Corps Hohenzollern. At Teugen the regiment occupied the Hausen village. Three companies took part to the attack and lost 239 (out of combat). At Eggmühl it was between the just named village and Laichling with BrigadeBieber, avantgarde Division Vukassovich, III Corps. It fought very hastily around Eggmühl and lost 658 men (dead, wounded and prisoner), while colonel Piret was taken prisoner. Later in the Brigade Josef von Mayer, div.Vukassovich, III Corps participated at the Urfahr battle.

The 3rd battalion on April 25 was committed to garrison the town of Schärding which defended losing 38 men. It was then retreated with the reinforcements of Division Dedovich, BrigadeSinzendorf, VI Corps and was present at Ebelsberg with the Brigade GM chevalier Adrian Joseph Rheinwaldt von Waldegg (V Corps). It was in reserve near the Castle and was engaged in the afternoon counterattacks losing about half of its strength (340 men out of combat). After the retreat to Vienna the 3rd battalion watched the right wing (BrigadeMesko) from Vienna till Leopoldstadt.

- at Aspern: the 3rd battalion (major Wauthier) present (?) in the Brigade GM prince Friedrich von Wied-Runkel or BrigadeMayer, Division FML Franz Weber von Treuenfels, II Corps Hohenzollern. The other two battalions remained at Freystadt with the III Corps. The third, weak, battalion was disbanded and the personnel assigned to the 1st-2nd Battalions reaching a total of 2250 men (two bns.) and a Grenadier division of 280.

- at Wagram: returned to the original BrigadeBieber, Division St Julien, III Corps and took part at the battle losing 353 men (out of combat).

- after Wagram: at Znaim in the same Brigade and without any engagement. During the autumn oberst Piret returned from the prisony and was again at the head of his troops.

K.K. IR 41 – GM-FML Baron Friedrich Kottulinsky – 3 Battalions [7]

Recruitment: Galicia. initially: 2 Depot companies BrigadeBicking in Lemberg, Division Meerveldt under Hohenlohe- Ingelfingen

Galicia	Czortzków	41	
	Kolomea		
Depot Kader:	Tarnów		
Commander: oberst	Martin Becker von Wallensee		oberst Franz Geyger

- before Aspern till after Wagram: according to the "Tabelle" of January 8 the regiment, its Grenadiers and the Staff were at Tarnow. It was enclosed in the Brigade Neustädter (div. Mondet in Tarnow) together with the IR 30 De Ligne one division for each IR 8 Arch. Ludwig, IR 12 Manfredini, Josef Mittrowsky IR 40, IR 29 Lindenau and IR 57 Josef Colloredo. Its third battalion was raised at Stanislau and was attached to IR 44 Bellegarde (Sambor), IR 58 Beaulieu (Lemberg), Palatinal Hussars n. 12 (Zolkiev), 1st Garrison battalion (Czernowitz) to form the Brigade Schauroth (Division Meerveldt) at Lemberg.

On March 1 the regiment had three battalions (the third on 4 companies) and 2 companies were left behind as „Reserve-Division" of the regiment in Lemberg. It went to the Brig Civalart, with the IR 30 , DivisionMondet, VII Corps, then also in Division Schauroth. When Bellegarde took the command of the I field Corps the command in Galicia (interim) went to Prince Hohenlohe-Ingelfingen.

The VII Corps, after the crossing of the river Pilica, gathered at Odrziwol (April 13). Having reached the enemies at Raszyn, GM Civalart was sent (as the main column) across the Ruswa towards Jaworowo, with orders to occupy that village and then to march till Warsaw. However the advance was blocked and the regiment remained almost inactive (nonetheless losing 72 men missing or prisoners). On April 23 the VII Corps entered Warsaw. On May 2 the regiment moved to the Gora's bridges and then reached Sochaczew where it camped. It was then assigned to a new avant-garde unit under its commander, Oberst von Becker, while the third battalion (major Donnhof) remained with the Corps. After the operations against Thorn the Austrians received the news of the

Polish march southwards and of the approach of a Russian army. Archduke Ferdinand ordered to move towards Cracow in order to defend Galicia. The 1st and 2nd battalions (Civalart) remained in Warsaw with Mondet, while the 3rd marched to the south with the Brigade Pflacher.

On June 1 the division abandoned Warsaw and ten days later engaged the enemies at Jedlinsko, seizing the bridges and freeing the town of Radom from the enemy pressure. After a brief pursuit attempt the regiment was recalled at Rawa and Czestochau (Czestokowa) in order to organize the defense of Cracow. On June 21 the regiment took part at the deliverance of Opoczno town. Then it was deployed in the Circle of Crakow defense where it was reached (on July 12) by its 3rd battalion and by the new of the armistice.

Note: the two companies (Reserve division of Lemberg) were gathered by prince Hohenlohe at the time of the Polish advance against Sandomierz and Lemberg too. The force of this territorial defense group was, on May 24, of 3908 men and 386 cavalrymen (the various Reserve companies scattered in Galicia under the three territorial brigades Grasser, Kesslern and Bicking).

K.K. IR 44 – FML Marquis Friedrich Bellegarde – 3 battalions [8]

Recruitment: Galicia. - initially: 2 Depot companies BrigadeBicking in Lemberg, Division Meerveldt under Hohenlohe-Ingelfingen .

Galicia	Sambor	44
Depot Kader:	Olmütz, Lemberg	
Commander: oberst	Louis Dubois de Fiennes	Johann Ogée (O'Schee)

- before Aspern: 2 Battalions with Brigade GM Baron Carl von Riese, Division FML prince Ludwig Hohenlohe-Wartenburg- Bartenstein IV Corps while the third battalion remained with the VII Corps. It fought at Teugen (combat of Dinzling, April 19). The 1st battalion (major Baron Reslitz) seized the village and the 2nd battalion occupied the right wing of the division, till the last houses of the above mentioned location. On April 21 the regiment moved to Laichling through Päring, and deployed in the wood between Unter and Ober Laichling. The local defense caused heavy losses. On April 22 the regiment was again engaged in the woods near Laichling, repulsing the French attacks of Davout's troops. It had heavy losses and many were taken prisoners, reducing its strength by an half battalion. On April 23 it retreated to Ratisbon and then to Bohemia. There it was reached by the third battalion with many recruits from Moravia.

- at Aspern: it was with brig. Riese, div. Hohenlohe. The regiment was in the 5th column (Rosenberg) and marched to Baumersdorf crossin the Russbach. Their 1st and 2nd battalion had to attack the Essling left flank (the 3rd was in reserve). The combats in the woods were very hard and colonel De Fiennes ordered his 1st (major Tacco) and 3rd battalion (hauptmann Schick) to counterattack the French, clearing the woods. During these combats lost his life colonel De Fiennes.On the second day of the battle the regiment renewed the attacks against Essling. The losses of the Bellegarde were around 45 dead and 155 wounded. On May 27 colonel Ogée took the command.

- at Wagram: with the BrigadeRiese, Division Nordmann (Avantgarde left Wing), the regiment marched to Gross Enzersdorf with orders to support the avant-garde. The 1st battalion, again under Reslitz, had orders to defend the village. Gross Enzerdorf was abandoned and the Bellegarde went back on another flanking line on the slopes in front of Markgraf-Neusiedl, from that place till Ober-Siebenbrunn. There was deployed the regiment which repulsed two French attacks. However the enemy artillery enfiladed that oblique line with terrible outcomes.[9] Then the regiment in square formation suffered some cavalry charges and got the order of retreat. Its rests, as those of other units, were assigned to GM Radetzky with the task to rally the troops and to lead them far from the danger.

- after Wagram: IV Corps withdrew towards Nikolsburg without utter combats.

K.K. IR 46 – FML Marquis Johann Gabriel Chasteler de Courcelles – old Tyroler Rgt. - 3 battalions

Recruitment: former Tyrol (1805) then Eastern Galicia. 2 Depot companies BrigadeBicking in Lemberg, Div Meerveldt under Hohenlohe- Ingelfingen. Staff at Pressburg.

Galicia	Tarnopol	46
Depot Kader:	Olmütz, Tarnopol	
Commander: oberst	Carl Steyrer (Steyerer) von Edelberg	Franz Otto von Kirchberg

- before Aspern: it was, with its two battalions [10], BrigadeRiese, Division Hohenlohe Bartenstein, IV

Corps. Note : the regiment was often in the same Brigade of the IR 44 Bellegarde participating at the same actions and battles (see above for details).

At Teugen, however, it had only tasks of support and the two Battalions were divided. One was with the Brigade oberst Carl Steyrer von Edelberg (their commander) together with 1 squadron of Chevaulégers n° 4 Vincent (Division Sommariva) behind the hills of Schneidhart. The 2nd was under the column commanded by von Grill (or maybe Riese, which was the former regiment's commander, actually GM).[11] At Abensberg the 1st battalion returned in the BrigadeRiese, while the 2nd remained with Edelberg. It took part at the Laichling battle (Eggmühl) and lost in the Lüger Wald 65 dead, 243 wounded, 49 prisoners and 79 missing on April 21 ; 28 dead, 96 wounded, 126 prisoners and 68 missing on April 22. Then it withdrew in Bohemia where colonel Steyrer became a major general leaving the command to colonel Franz Otto von Kirchberg. Before Aspern it returned also in the BrigadeRiese.

The third battalion was employed in garrison duties at the bavarian border with the Brigade GM count Rudolf von Sinzendorff, and Division FML Baron Martin von Dedovich.

- at Aspern: was in the BrigadeRiese, Division Hohenlohe Bartenstein, IV Corps only with two battalions. It took part at the attack against Essling. The losses were: 40 dead, 225 wounded, 113 prisoners and 36 missing. On May 25 the regiment officially received its 3rd battalion. [12]

- at Wagram: was in the BrigadeRiese, Division Nordmann (Avantgarde left Wing) with all three Battalions then in the "rescue" BrigadeRadetzky. They fought at Gross Enzersdorf and Neusiedel losing 278 dead, 149 wounded [13], 648 prisoners (practically the whole 3rd battalion).

- after Wagram: IV Corps withdrew towards Nikolsburg without utter combats.

K.K. IR 50 – FML-FZM Earl Leopold Stain – 3 battalions

Recruitment: Upper Austria then West Galicia and Poland. Initially: 2 Depot companies BrigadeEgermann in Sándomierz, Division Meerveldt under Hohenlohe-Ingelfingen. The reserve division remained in Galicia with the VII Corps, fighting at Sandomierz.

Poland	West Galicia-Radom	50
Depot Kader:	Radom, Sándomierz	
Commander: oberst	Baron Franz Mauroy de Merville	Wolfgang von Urban

- before Aspern: the regiment (two battalions) entered Bavaria with the V Corps (archduke Ludwig) in the Brigade GM Josef von Mayer, Division FML Baron Carl von Lindenau. At Teugen (April 19) and Abensberg the Stain and its Brigade were attached to the 1st Reserve (prince Liechtenstein). On April 19 arrived also the 3rd battalion (from Galicia) and took position as garrison along the Inn. The regiment fought at Eggmühl at the right wing of the Reserve corps and was definitively separated from its original V Corps. The 3rd battalion was gathered and added to the Group count Rudolf von Sinzendorff (Division Dedovich) and watched the bavarian border. During the regiment's retreat till Bohemia, the 3rd battalion continued the struggle with the Brigade GM chevalier Adrian Joseph Reinwaldt von Waldegg (V Corps, Reuss-Plauen) and took part at the Ebelsberg battle. The Brigade Reinwaldt was then attached to FML Schustekh defensive system of the Danube (division or "Gruppe" under the III Corps). The 1st and 2nd battalions (BrigadeMayer) were also in Bohemia and on May 18 colonel Mauroy became general major, leaving the command to oberstlieutenant Urban.

- at Aspern: the 3rd battalion was in the Schustekh Group now under the III Corps while the regiment fought with the BrigadeMayer, Avantgarde II Corps Hohenzollern, suffering heavy losses.

- between Aspern and Wagram: the 3rd battalion was first with BrigadeBianchi (detached) later with the. BrigadeWeiss (detached) in the new GM Radetzky division, formed by the IV Corps.

- at Wagram: only the 3rd battalion, which was with the BrigadeWeiss, Division Radetzky, IV Corps

- after Wagram: same formation. On December the regiment was disbanded.

K.K. IR 55 – FZM Heinrich XIII prince Reuss Greitz – 3 battalions

Recruitment: West Galicia and Poland. 1 Depot companies BrigadeGrasser in Tarnow, Division Meerveldt under Hohenlohe- Ingelfingen

Poland	West Galicia-Lublin	55
Depot Kader:	Lublin, Turnau, Tarnów	
Commander: oberst	Franz von Koller	Carl von Gober

- before Aspern: it was with Brigade GM Johann von Neustädter, Division Sommariva, IV Corps Rosenberg. Was in the Haupttruppe column at Teugen, and was deployed in the center of the battlefield at Abensberg. During the battle of Eggmühl it was in the left wing of Rosenberg. After the retreat in Bohemia the regiment and the BrigadeNeustädter were with the Division Dedovich, IV Corps. Its 3rd battalion was assigned to the territorial Corps Kerpen (Styria) .
- at Aspern: always with the BrigadeNeustädter, Division Dedovich, IV Corps.
- between Aspern and Wagram: was reorganized under Division Rohan, IV Corps, whilst the 3rd battalion was still with Corps Kerpen and, later, detached to the Division Jellachich.
- at Wagram: assigned to the V Corps Reuss-Plauen in the BrigadeNeustädter, Division Weissenwolf. It got the 3rd Landwehr battalion Prerau as attachment. During all the described time it was always brigaded with regiment Czartorisky (see above for combats details).
- after Wagram: idem . Having lost its Circle of Recruitment it was disbanded at Turnau.

K.K. IR 58 – FML-FZM Baron Peter Beaulieu – 3 Battalions [14]
Recruitment: Galicia. 2 Depot companies BrigadeBicking in Lemberg, Division Meerveldt under Hohenlohe-Ingelfingen. The Reserve division in Lemberd had 564 men.

Galicia	Stanislau	58
	Stryi	
Depot Kader:	Przemysl, Stanislau then Lemberg	
Commander: oberst	Peter von Fröhauf (Fröhauff)	

- before Aspern: it came with two battalion under BrigadeSchulz, Division FML prince Henri XV Reuss-Plauen then directly under their commander Brigade Oberst Peter von Fröhauff, V Corps archduke Ludwig. The 3rd battalion came from Kalusz nad Stryi and had around 1000 soldiers. The Beaulieu fough at Landshut (21 April) in the rearguard of the Altdorf Hills. It lost few men but all baggages in the retreat. Retreating with the "Hauptkolonne" Baron Bianchi, brig. Fröhauff it was engaged at Neumarkt (April 24). It was the rear guard of the 1st column together with an artillery brigade battery. Prince Reuss-Plauen himself took the head of the regiment attacking a flank of the Bavarians. The regiment lost 16 dead, 57 wounded, and few missing. After the retreat to Linz the regiment was under BrigadeHammer, Division Reuss Plauen, V Corps. At the battle of Ebelsberg the two battalions attacked twice repulsing the French away from the Marketplatz. The battle was also the theatre of the heroic defense led by a young oberlieutenant: Peter von Pirquet. He was surnamed, by the ranks of the regiment, the "last Walloon" and got the Maria Theresia Cross (Ritter) for his energic action. Severely wounded he was found by a French grenadier, who saved his life sending him to the Linz hospital with high regard for his bravery. There the daughter of Baron Beaulieu (he had a castle near Linz) provided to transfer him in a private hospital. [15] The regiment's losse were heavy: 65 men dead, 137 wounded almost all made prisoners. Note that many Austrian wounded were gathered under a wooden arch, waiting a transport, when a French grenade put in fire the building giving them all an horrible death.
The Beaulieu now had all its three battalions (but had a strength of a battalion: 1128 men) and was attached to the BrigadeSinzendorf of the div. Dedovich who marched to Vienna. Being impossible to defend the capital city of Austria, the regiment left the walls to
reach the opposite bank of Danube. The rear guard detachment, around 25 men with all the musicians, went prisoners of the French. The 3rd battalion (hauptmann Wissiak) which was formed only by fresh recruits, was sent to Kremsier with watching tasks.
On May 18 the 1st and 2nd battalions (under brig. Hofmeister) were sent to Pressburg in order to reinforce the garrison (Brigade GM Bianchi). The regiment was not at Aspern.
In June the regiment took position at Engerau and defended the bridges of Pressburg (June 3). There the losses were: 18 dead, 24 wounded, 60 prisoners at the bridge and many other when Engerau fell. And when archduke Johann joined Pressburg (June 23) the weak regiment was assigned to the vanguard unit of FML Nordmann. The Beaulieus took position at Stadtl-Enzersdorf till Flösserhaus, engaging a rifle battle with the French in the two days preceding the Wagram battle. In those days the 3rd battalion reinforced the regiment.
- at Wagram: the 1st, the 3rd Battalions and the companies 7-8 of the 2nd battalion remained with the Brigade GM von Riese, Division Nordmann (Avant-garde of the left Wing) and then reinforced the BrigadePeter Vécsey, (Division Nordmann too). Four companies of the 2nd battalion (320 men) were attached to the 3rd Column of the Inner Austrian army (archduke Johann) in the Brigade GM Baron Bach with the IR 45 Baron de Vaux

IR 37 FML Weidenfeld   IR 38 duke of Württemberg   IR 39 FML baron Duka

IR 40 FZM Joseph Mittrowsky   IR 41 FML Baron Kottulinsky IR 42 FZM Erbach Schönberg

▲ Austrian Infantry uniforms regiments nr. 37, 38, 39, 40, 41 & 42

and sent to garrison Neudorf and Theben. The losses of the 1st and 3rd battalions were: 64 dead, 105 wounded, 113 prisoners.

- after Wagram: the Brigade Bach was followed by Beauharnais and engaged with violence at Stampfen (July 12). Many other men of the Beaulieu there fell prisoners (almost all 320), while few reached Olmütz where the regiment had to reorganize.

K.K. IR 63 – FML-FZM count Ludwig Baillet de Merlemont – 3 battalions [16]

Under the Imperial Act of July 20, 1807, L. 3032, the Emperor Franz stated that the regiment had to cease to be called as Archduke Joseph (since his sudden death) and that it had to get the name of its second Owner, Earl Baillet. By Decree of the army, January 16, 1808 was assigned to the regiment a Circle of recruitment in Galicia. Otherwise many Walloons were stil on duty and the regiment continued to be named as "Walloon". Recruitment: Galicia. 2 Depot companies BrigadeBicking in Lemberg, Division Meerveldt under Hohenlohe- Ingelfingen.

Galicia	Zloczów	63
Depot Kader:	Zloczów	
Commander: oberst	Josef Czerwinka	Caspar von Strauch

- before Aspern: on April 18 it was in reserve and did not fight at Raszyn (BrigadeTrauttenberg, Division Mondet, VII Corps). On April 23 it entered Warsaw. Then it moved north toward Gora in order to build a boats-bridge and to create a bridgehead on river Vistula. Under the command of Oberstlieutenant Strauch all three battalions began the works. Under the continuous harassments of the Poles the bridge was half mounted by May 2 and on the following day it was finished. Oberst Czerwinka took then command with his 1628 men and 3 guns and deployed in the bridgehead on the opposite (Polish) bank of the Vistula. Three Poles battalions attacked at half to 2 hrs. past midnight. The first attack was repulsed but at 2 AM came the second. The Poles arrived till the trenches but were sent back (leaving 100 prisoners). A third assault, which destroyed two guns of the bridgehead, was also repulsed. At 5 AM arrived a fourth attack which finally overrun the defenders. The losses were very heavy (around 499 dead or missing and 600 wounded, 29 officers and 1074 men were made prisoners by the Poles). The rest of the regiment (around 800 men) marched till Nowemiasto where the Poles exchanged and gave back the colonel and large part of the officers as a sign of respect and honour. On May 16 4 companies marched to San-domierz with major De Best. The siege of the town lasted till the capitualtion of June 18. The Baillet lost 11 dead and 16 wounded.

They stood in Sandomierz for a brief time and then returned to Cracow. At the end of June the four companies formed the sole battalion of the regiment together with the remaining 2 companies come back from Nowemiasto. The regiment (battalion) marched to Olmütz and then to Teschen where stood from July 14 till August 14, when it received orders to go to Policzka. There, with new recruits and 400 men released from the prisony (for the armistice), was formed again the second battalion.

▲ Colonel of Hungarian Infantry regiments in 1805. Ottenfeld artwork

▲ Austrian general and grenadier 1809. From Ottenfeld artwork

Notes:

[1]   Geographisch-historische nachrichten von Westgallizen oder den neu erlangten östreichisch-polnischen provinzen, Verlag Johann Otto, 1796.

[2]   These were the Galician companies which completed other regiments (i.e. bohemians or moravians) coming from the military districts called as "help Circles".

[3]   Sypniewski, Alfred Ritter von: Geschichte des k. u. k. Infanterie-Regimentes Feldmarschall Carl Joseph Graf Clerfayt de Croix Nr. 9. Jaroslau: 1894.

[4]   Kerchnawe Hugo, Bei Linz und Ebersberg, anno Neun, Stern, Wien and Leipzig 1910.

[5]   The first Battle of Raszyn was fought on April 19, 1809 between armies of the Austrian Empire and the Duchy of Warsaw. The Austrian army won and the Poles retreated to Warsaw. The Austrian army under the Archduke Ferdinand Karl Joseph of Austria-Este invaded the Duchy of Warsaw in April, 1809. Polish troops under Prince Józef Antoni Poniatowski withstood the Austrian attack on Warsaw defeating them later at Radzymin and reconquered parts of former Poland including Crakow and Lemberg by beating the Austrians at near the villages of Góra and Grochów.

[6]   Spiegefeld, Joseph Freiherr von: Geschichte des kaiserlich und königlichen Infanterie-Regimentes Freiherr von Molinary Nr. 38, seit seiner Errichtung 1725 - 1891.Budapest: 1892.

[7]   Formanek, Jaromir: Geschichte des k. u. k. Infanterie-Regiments Nr. 41. 2nd vol. Czernowitz: 1886/87.

[8]   Branko, Franz Von: Geschichte des k. k. Infanterie-Regimentes Nr. 44 Feldmarschall Erzherzog Albrecht, von seiner Errichtung 1744 bis 1875. Wien: 1875.

[9]   Literarily "hook-like line" or "Hakenstellung". I preferred this translation because it was probably a curved flanking position with a hook-like shape. This was suggested also by the Meyers Großes Konversations-Lexikon 1905: "Hakenstellung, Verteidigungsstellung in Hakenform mit Front nach zwei Seiten". The flank was organized with the six battalions of regiments IR 4 Deutschmeister and IR 49 Kerpen, and with the, now weak, Nordmann's regiments IR 58 Beaulieu, IR 44 Bellegarde and IR 46 Chasteler. The deadly bombardment of the French pieces completely disordered the flank. Large part of the 1st battalion Bellegarde was taken prisoner and so the regiment continued only with two battalions.

[10]   It began with the 1st and 2nd battalion with 6 companies of 160 men and with a raising 3rd battalion with 6 companies of 200 men. Dietrich von Hermannsthal, Friedrich, Geschichte des Tyroler Feld und Land später 46 Linien Infanterie-Regiments errichtet 1745, reduciert 1809, Krakau: des "Czas" 1859.

[11]   This is rather contradictory as many sources refer general von Grill was unfit at the time. His Brigade consisted of IR 22 prince Friedrich Josias Sachsen-Coburg-Saalfeld – 3 bns.; IR 8 archduke Ludwig Joseph – 3 bns. and a Brigade battery.

[12]   All orders of battle stated the regiment with only two battalions at Aspern, but it is possible the 3rd battalion could participate at the battle since its commander, major Neugebauer, was wounded at Essling.

[13]   Strangely the number of wounded soldier is less than that of the dead. This is easily explained, as a general rule, since the main part of the prisoners were also wounded.

[14]   Jacubenz,: Geschichte des k. u. k. Infanterie-Regiments Erzherzog Ludwig Salvator Nr. 58., Verlag des Regiments Vienna: 1904. Sykora Joseph, Geschichte des Kaiserliche-Königliche Linien-Infanterie regiments Nr. 58 von Jahre 1757 bis 6. August 1846, Peter Piller, Lemnerg 1847.

[15]   The legend of Peter Martin stopped after the Ebelsberg wounds. He retired as an awarded Capitän-leutnant but regained the army in 1814 in time to write another page of bravery in Italy. At Cesenatico (near Rimini) on April 23, 1815, in the main place of the town, Piazza Pisacane, Peter Martin Pirquet Von Kriehuber, then major, leading 264 men, attacked by surprise during the night a column of Neapolitans (1800 men of two Murat's battalions). For that action, Pirquet was again awarded in 1818 becoming Baron with the surname "von Cesenatico".

[16]   Nobody could find a "Geschichte des 63. ..." etc. because the regiment was later renamed as K.K. 55 Infanterie-regiment. Its history is written together with the later 55 unit. Beran, Julius: Die Geschichte des k. u. k. Infanterie-Regimentes Freiherr von Merkl Nr. 55. Wien: 1899 and also Nahlik, Johann Edler von: Geschichte des kais. kön. 55. Linien-Infanterie-Regimentes Baron Bianchi, Brünn: 1863.

1705. Aus Muskete umgestaltete Flinte Spunt-Baionett

1722. Ordinäre Flinte

1745. Ordinäre Füsilir-Flinte

1754. Commiss-Flinte

1784. Infanterie-Gewehr

1798. Infanterie-Gewehr

1828. Infanterie-Gewehr

1828. Infanterie (Grenadier)-Gewehr

1842. Infanterie-Gewehr

1854. Infanterie-Gewehr

▲ Austrian weapons: rifles and muskets. From Ottenfeld artwork

Bohemia (Czech: *Čechy*; German: *Böhmen*) is a historical region in central Europe, occupying the western two-thirds of the traditional Czech Lands, currently the Czech Republic. In a broader meaning, it often refers to the entire Czech territory, including Moravia and Czech Silesia, especially in historical contexts, such as the Kingdom of Bohemia.

Czechs are the people of Moravia and Bohemia, but they were above all in this latter region, and they are the 2/3 of the whole population. They could be divided into two large groups: those who dwelled the central part of the region and those who lived near the Saxon-Bavarian borders. True Bohemians were only those living in the central territories (Circles of Rakonitz, Prachin , Czaslau , Béraun and Kaurzim). There practically was utilized only the Bohemian language, while along the borders the largest part of the people spoke German.

In Austria people who spoke only Bohemian (Czech) were called Stokböhmisch while the German speaking people were the Utraquistes. [i]

Circles (Districts) see map-image above (datas from a 1814 gazeteer)

Beraun (Czech: Beroun). Beroun was originally called na Brodě (by the ford), and received the name of Bern, Berun or Verona in the 13th century, when it obtained the privileges of a city from the emperor Charles IV, who was specially attached to the place, calling it "Verona mea." It was on the Beroun river and siege of a battle (1744) between Austrians and Prussians. The whole Circle had around 132.500 inhabitants in 1814.

Budweis (Czech: České Budějovice - German: Budweis or Böhmisch Budweis, also Budjegowitz, often referred to simply as Budweis in English) was the largest city in the South Bohemian Region and main town of the District. Sited on the river Malsch near its confluence into the large Moldaw. Budweis in 1814 had over 600 houses and around 5500 inhabitants. Main towns were:

Krumau (Český Krumlov), south east of Budweis, at the Austrian border, had around 560 houses and 4000 inh. It had an unusually large castle for the town dimensions.

Tabor (Hradiště Hory Tábor or castle of the mount Tabor) was part of the same military Circle; its name means also camp) was a fortress (south east of Časlau), very close to the Moldaw river. In 1814 had 400 houses and around 3000 inhabitants. At the time part of the Budweis District.

Bunzlau (modern Jungbunzlau and current Mladà Boleslav in Czech). The old town (Starà Boleslav) is now part of city Brandýs nad Labem-Stará Boleslav (Brandeis-Altbunzlau). In the 17th and 18th centuries, Mladá Boleslav was an important Jewish center and a Royal castle. In this period, about one half of the town's population was Jewish. Sited on an hill named Hrohka it had 350 houses and 2580 inhabitants. Main towns of the Kreis were:

Reichemberg (Czech: Liberec; at that time also Liberk or Habersdorf) was one of the largest towns in Bohemia with 10.000 inh. and was a border town (Silesia).

Turnau (Czech: Turnov) town on the Jizera river in the northern Bohemia. At the time it was part of the Bunzlau Kreis.Turnau on the Iser river had 300 houses and 2000 inhabitants. It was a town renowned for the gemstones artisans and the Valdštejn Castle, the cradle of the famous Wallenstein family.

Bydzòw or Bidschow (Czech: Bydžov) had 390 houses and 2900 inhabitants. Main towns of this central Kreis were: Arnau (Czech: Hostinné) walled town on the Elbe with 230 houses and 1260 inhabitants.

Starkenbach (Czech: Jilemnice) near the Iser river, 220 houses and 660 inhabitants. Hohenelbe (Czech: Vrchlabí) on the Elbe river, 360 houses and 2300 inh.

Gitschin (Czech: Jičín) In 1710 the town became a property of the House of Trauttmansdorff and in 1814 had around 460 houses and 2400 inhabitants.

Časlau (German: Tschaslau, Csaslau; Czech also Čáslav) south of Königgrätz with only 200 houses and 2000 inhabitants, but site of the grave of Jan Ziska, chief of the Hussite movement. Main towns of the Circle were: Kuttenberg (Czech: Kutna or Kutna Hora) a free town of 716 houses and 4000 souls. Famous for the silver mines.

Chrudim During the reign of Maria Theresa, Chrudim became the centre of the region and, in 1751, the seat of regional offices. The town was not only the natural but also the administrative centre of Chrudim region which had 760 villages and around 248.000 inhabitants. Main towns of the Circle were:

Landskron (Czech: Lanškroun) at the Moravian borde and town of the princes Liechtenstein. Pardubitz (Czech: Pardubiće).

Elbogen (Czech: Loket) a small town surrounded on three sides by the Ohře River, with 241 houses and 2000 souls. The Circle was practically the territory of Egerland, a German speaking land. Main towns of the Circle were: Eger (Czech: Cheb) a large town of 740 houses and around 4000 inhabitants, former leader of the District. Carlsbad (Czech: Karlovy Vary) on the river Töpl, 4400 inhabitants, 1500 houses.

Kaurim or Kaurzim (Czech: Kouřim) was a free Royal town on the Elbe river. It was a little town chief of a Circle of around 145.400 inhabitants. The main cities of the Kreis were: Kolin, site of a famous battle, with 400 houses and 2000 souls. Böhmisch Brod (Czech: Český Brod), Royal walled town, and Brandeis (Czech: Brandýs) then separated from Alt-Bunzlau.

Klattau (Czech: Klatovy) free Royal town at the Bavarian border with around 3000 inhabitants and 450 houses. The Circle had around 140.000 souls, mainly speaking German. Others town of the Circle were:

Taus (Czech: Tauš, current Domažlice) walled town on the road to eastern Bavaria.

Ronsperg (Czech: Ronšperk, current Poběžovice) was a town of Counts Thun und Hohenstein.

Königgrätz (Czech: Hradec Králové). Northern populated Kreis with around 264.000 souls at the Silesian borders, its main town was sited on the Elbe and had around 5000 inhabitants with 700 houses. Was one of the most famous Austrian fortresses. Several churches and convents were pulled down to make way for the fortifications erected under Joseph II, finally dismantled in 1884.

Another large fortress was at Josefstadt (Czech: Josefov, today Jaroměř). Over 1780 to 1787, the Emperor Joseph II built on the left bank of the Elbe and Mettau rivers, the imperial fortress Ples. Later this conurbation took the name of Josefstadt (Joseph town). In 1948 the fortress town was renamed Josefov and incorporated into Jaroměř.

Leitmeritz (Czech: Litoměřice) town of 3000 inhabitants close to the capital Prague on the river Elbe and close to the Saxon border. This Circle had around 300.000 inhabitants and had important border garrisons like Bilin and Tetschen.

Pilsen (Czech: Plzeň) a Royal town of around 5000 souls and 420 houses. The Kreis had around 170.000 inhabitants and the main town were Mies, Plan and Teinitz or Bischofteinitz (Czech: Horšovský Týn) walled town with an old fortress.

Prachin (Czech: Prácheň). It was a large Circle with around 270.000 inhabitants. Officially "Provincia Prachinensi"s or Prachens in German, autonomous region in the southwest of the present Bohemia, created in the late 13th century and abolished by the Austrian Empire's regional reform in 1848. Its boundaries extended through the Bohemian Forest (Gabreta, Böhmerwald or Šumava) in the south, on towards Budweis then to the north, close to the town of Příbram and from here southwest to Markt Eisenstein (Železná Ruda). Ethnic groups of the region included Jews, Roma, Czechs and Germans and by religion were Roman Catholics and Jews. The central geographical feature of the Prachens region is the Otava river or in the local dialect Wotáva. Other principal towns of the former Prachens are Pisek, Strakonitz (Strakonice), Rosenthal (Rožmitál), Winterberg (Vimperk) and Horaschdowitz (Horažďovice) feudal town of the Löwenstein family. These were alss the lands of the Schwarzenberg family.

Prague (Praha, the capital) on the Moldava river, it was the second city of the Empire. In 1814 had around 80.000 inhabitants,

32.000 houses and 8000 garrison soldiers. Since it was the capital of Bohemia, its citizens were commonly engaged in statal/regional jobs, schools and religious affairs. So there was an high number of recruitment exemptions, to which the city supplied with many volunteers and city troopers (Bürger units).

The people from suburbs were commonly enlisted in the nearby Districts like Rakonitz and Beraun.

Rakonitz (Czech: Rakovník) it was a Districts full of hills and woods with, only, 130000 inhabitants. Rakonitz on the Elbe river had around 2700 inhabitants and 347 houses in 1814. Its territory included also the great fortress of Theresienstadt (Czech: Terezín). Its construction started in 1780 and lasted ten years. The total area of the fortress was 3.89 km². The fortification was designed in the tradition of Sébastian le Prestre de Vauban. In peacetime it held 5655 soldiers, and in wartime around 11000 soldiers could be placed here, and neighbouring areas could be inundated.

Saaz (Czech: Žatec) it was another mainly German speaking District with around 116.000 souls. Saaz was a Royal town on the Eger river. Brüx (Czech: Most, bridge) was another walled and fortified (castle) town of this Kreis. Another important town of the area was Chomotau (Czech: Chomutov).

BOHEMIAN DISTRICTS

Region-State	District	1781	1807	1817	Ergänzungs (Werb) bezirks Commando (Heeres)	Kreis (Kraj)
		Year of the recruiting regiment				
Bohemia	Budweis	10	54	54	Budweis	kraj Budejovičko
Bohemia	Tabor				Tabor	kraj Taborski
Bohemia	Kaurim	11	11	11	Beneschau	kraj Kouřimsky Kaurzim (Kourim), Kolin
Bohemia	Caslau	28			Časlau	kraj Časlavsky
Bohemia	Chrudim	15			Hohenmauth	kraj Chrudimsky
Bohemia	Königgrätz	57	28 - 21	21	Königgrätz	kraj Hradečky
Bohemia	Bydzov	21	18	18	Jíčin	kraj Bydzowski Bidschau (Bydzow), Jíčin
Bohemia	Bunzlau	18	17	36	Jungbunzlau (Mladà Boleslav)	kraj Boleslavsky
Bohemia	Leitmeritz	17	56		Theresienstadt	kraj Litomericky
Bohemia	Saaz	36			Komotau	kraj Žatečky Egerland Saaz (Žatec)
Bohemia	Eger –	42	42		Eger (Cheb)	Chebsko- Loketsko
Bohemia	Elbogen			42		
Bohemia	Turnau	--	--	--	Turnau	
Bohemia	Pilsen	35	35	35	Pilsen	kraj Plzensky
Bohemia	Klattau				Pisek	kraj Klatowsky kraj Prachensky
Bohemia	Prachin	25	25	25	(Prachen or Prachin)	
Bohemia	Beraun	54	47		Beraun	kraj Berounski
Bohemia	Rakonitz	47			Prague	kraj Rakovničky Prahsko
Bohemia	Prague			28		
Total	Erbland	14	11	9		

IR 43 FZM Simbschen   **IR 44 FML Marquis Bellegarde**   **IR 45 FML De Vaux**

IR 46 FML Chasteler   **IR 47 FZM Baron Vogelsang**   **IR 48 FML Vukassovich**

▲ Austrian Infantry uniforms regiments nr. 43, 44, 45, 46, 47 & 48

BOHEMIAN REGIMENTS RECRUITMENT 1809

Ergänzungsbezirks Kommando		Werb-bezirk	Regular army	Landwehr
HQ Recr. District	Czech	recruitment area (Kreis)	IR	other
Budweis	České Budějovice	Budweiser	54	4th Fortress Art.
Tabor	Tábor	Taborer		2nd Feldjäger
Kaurzim	Kouřim	Kaurzimer	11	6th Ch.Lég. Rosenberg
Csaslau	Časlau	Tschaslauer		6th Dragoons Riesch
Chrudim	Chrudim	Chrudimer		5th Ch.Lég. Klenau
Königgrätz	Hradec Králové	Königgrätzer	21 - 28	
Stadt Prag	Praha	Prager	**28-11-54**	1st Fortress Art.
Bidschow	Bydzow	Bidschower	18	
Jung-Bunzlau	Mladá Boleslav	Bunzlauer	17	
Leitmeritz	Litomeřice	Leitmeritzer	36	1st Feldjäger 3rd Feldjäger
Saaz	Žatec	Saazer	42	
Eger	Cheb	Elbogener		5th Feldjäger
Pilsen	Plzeň	Pilsener	35	
Klattau	Klatovy	Klattauer		
Pisek	Pisek	Prachiner	25	4th Feldjäger
Beraun	Beroun	Berauner	47	
Rakonitz	Rakovník	Rakonitzer		

Numbers in BOLD mean a temporary area of recruitment in order to help the main District to reach the stated strength.

K.K. IR 11 - FZM Erzherzog Rainer Joseph – 3 Bns (Archduke Rainer) [iv]

2nd Owner (Inhaber): from 1801 FML Count Vincenz Kolowrath-Liebsteinsky
Recruitment: 2 Depot companies Brig. and Div. Karl Kinsky in Prague under Riesch and Loudon. Bohemia

Bohemia	Kaurzim District	11
Depot Kader: Prague	between Aspern and Wagram led by Oberst	
Commander: oberst	Franz von Dolle, dead at Aspern	Hermann von Faber (Fabre)

- before Aspern: Brigade GM Baron Theodor Wacquant-Geocelles, Division FML Josef von Ulm, I Corps Bellegarde.
- at Aspern: Hauptmann Murmann of the 2nd Bn distinguished during the assault at the Churchyard of Aspern. In the 2nd day of the battle, two comp. under Hauptmann Vernholz were at the Aspern defense. Both MTO.
- at Wagram: Brig. Wacquant, Div. Dedovich, I Corps. Clash at Aderklaa. During the retreat the commander of the 1st battalion (Hauptmann Fabary) was mentioned for bravery. The regiment lost 95 men dead and 520 wounded.
- after Wagram: it fought at Znaim, on the hills of Oblas, Pumlitz and Tesswitz, losing other 6 dead and 120 wounded. Then retreated under their colonel command in the Brig. Fabre, Div. Henneberg, I Corps.
Note: it will change its pink facing/white buttons in dark blue/gold buttons from 1810.

K.K. IR 54 – FML Baron Joseph Froon von Kirchrath – 3 Bns [v]

Bohemia	Budweiss	54
Bohemia	Tabor	
Commander: oberst	Baron David Andrássy [vi]	

Recruitment: Bohemia - Moravia. 2 Depotcompanies Brig. and Div. Richter under Riesch and Loudon

The regiment recruited till 1806 in Franconia. After it was assigned to Beraun in Bohemia with a supporting District in Galicia (Sambor and Sanok). From 1807 Budweis-Tabor.
- before Aspern: Brigade GM Carl von Fölseis, Div. Brady, II Corps and Brig. Fölseis, then Division FML Franz Weber von Treuenfels, II Corps. During the attack against Stadt-am-Hof (Ratisbon) distinguished itself the 3rd Bn under Oberstleutnant Taizon. Lost 31 dead, 141 wounded and 71 prisoners of the French. During the retreat GM Fölseis kept the 1st battalion inside Ratisbon in order to cover the cavalry retreat. The third battalion (Taizon) remained in reserve at Eisenstein and reached the regiment on June 30 before Wagram. The regi-

ment was sent towards Hiller's V Corps in order to try the link with the main army. At the time of the battle of Urfahr-Linz the 1st and 2nd battalions were under Brigade GM Andreas von Schneller, Division Franz Saint Julien-Waldsee, but in reserve.

- at Aspern: 2 Bns with Brigade GM Baron David Andrássy (in place of GM Koller), Division FML Baron Thomas von Brady, 3rd column FML prince Franz Xavier von Hohenzollern-Hechingen (II Corps). The regiment, deployed in square, fronted the French Cuirassiers charge. In the second day they were at the Esslingen [vii] clash. The Oberstleutnant Peter Gerditsch died at Aspern and the regiment lost 30 men dead, 154 wounded.

- at Wagram: Brig. Paar, Div. Brady, II Corps again 3 Bns. Attached to the Hardegg avant-garde the regiment deployed at Baumersdorf (Parmarsdorf), which was defended by Major Rothmund battalion. Regiment lost 76 men dead, 474 wounded, 292 were never found (dead or prisoners) and 28 were taken prisoners.

- after Wagram: at Znaim on the right bank of the Thaya river on the Oblas and Pumlitz hills, and town Tessnitz. with Brig. Quallenberg, Div. Buresch, II Corps. Then retreated in Hungary through Neutra till Pressburg.

-

K.K. IR 21 – FML Viktor Ludwig Prinz Rohan – 3 Bns

Recruitment: Bohemia. 2 Depotcompanies Brig Szénassy in Jaromirz, fortress Josefstadt under Riesch and Loudon . In February the battalion was at Gitschin then to Prague.

Bohemia	Königgrätz (part of Chrudim)	21
Depot Kader:	Josephstadt	
Commander: oberst	Chevalier Johann Altstern Oberstleutnant Ludwig von Krause after Aspern	

- before Aspern: detached Brigade, called "Light Corps", [viii] Peter Vécsey, IV Corps Rosenberg then the first battalion sent under Brig. Peter Vécsey, I Res. Corps in reconnaissance toward Ratisbon, while 2nd and 3rd Bns under Oberstleutnant von Krause had the task to watch the Danube pontoon-bridges laid south east of Ratisbon. The provisional bridgehead was attacked by the French and the Austrians forced to return on the left Danube bank. The two battalions under bombardment lost 35 dead, 84 wounded and 111 missing. The first battalion left the watch at the Ratisbon stone-bridge without fights retreating till Cham and then to Budweis in Bohemia where the regiment was gathered under Brig. Wied Runkel, Div. Weber, II Corps.

- at Aspern: Brig. Altstern, Div. Ulm, II Corps and Brig. Wied Runkel, Div. FML Franz Weber von Treuenfels, II Corps Hohenzollern. The 3rd battalion (Krause) was committed for the attack towards Esslingen: losses of the regiment were 38 men dead, 169 wounded. During the night the regiment withdrew to Baumersdorf camp and there received some replacements. Commander Altstern commanded now a brigade.

- at Wagram: Brig. Altstern, Div. Ulm, II Corps the regiment, led by von Krause, with 1st battalion (Oberstleutnant Pfleger von Lindenfeld), 2nd Bn (Major de Chaudelot) and 3rd Bn (Oberstleutnant Müller von Hohenthal), deployed at Baumersdorf. The defense was stubborn with bayonet's countercharges and led to many deads and around 200 wounded. On the second battle day the regiment was taken by crossing bombardments and had to retreat with the II Corps suffering a violent charge by the French cavalry. At Wagram it lost 5 officers dead, 14 wounded, 3 wounded and prisoners; 429 troopers dead, 696 wounded, 184 missing and 388 prisoners of the French.[ix] Brigadier Altstern (Div. Siegenthal then Ulm, II Corps) led the retreating regiment till the Thaya river.

- after Wagram: it did not take part at the Znaim battle. Retreated in Moravia and finally to the depot at Königgrätz).

K.K. IR 28 – FML Baron Michael Frelich (Frehlich, Fröhlich) – 3 Bns [x]

Recruitment: Bohemia. 2 Depotcompanies Brig. de Baut in Chrudim, fortress Königgrätz under Riesch and Loudon. Before 1806 it had recruited also in Upper Rhine territories.

Bohemia	Caslau and Chrudim	28
Depot Kader: Prague	Kuttenberg (Bohemia)	
Commander: oberst	Baron Carl Mécsery	

- before Aspern: Brigade GM Carl von Fölseis, Div. FML Franz Weber von Treuenfels, II Corps Kolowrath. It had 66 officers and 3552 men. Then assigned to Brig. GM prince Friedrich von Wied-Runkel, Div. Brady, II Corps. Did not fight in Bavaria.

- at Aspern: Brig. Wied Runkel, Div. Weber, II Corps or 3rd column. The regiment reached Hirschstetten and deployed itself in three "battalions-massen" repulsing with fire a bloody charge by D'Espagne cuirassiers. The

same scene repeated the day after. The regiment lost 32 dead, 233 wounded (of which 31 were made prisoners). At the end of June (Brig. Wied Runkel, Div. Brady, II Corps) replacements brought the strength up to 4202 men.
- at Wagram: Defense of Baumersdorf: 3rd battalion was with Brig Wied Runkel, Div. Ulm, II Corps but the 1st and 2nd battalions were with avant-guard Hardegg inside the village. In the two days of the battle the regiment lost: 16 officers wounded (of which 4 died), 62 dead, 275 wounded, 190 missing and 276 taken prisoners.
- after Wagram: Battle of Znaim. Brig. Hardegg, Div. Ulm, II Corps. The regiment took position at Tief-Maispitz and Brenditz with the task of supporting and covering the retreat of the army reserve artillery. Other part of the unit retreated with IV Corps Rosemberg with Baron Carl Mécsery.

K.K. IR 17 – FML-FM Heinrich XV Prince Reuss Plauen – 3 Bns
Recruitment: Jungbunzlau District 2 Depotcompanies Brig. and Div. Schönthal in Pilsen under Riesch and Loudon.

Bohemia	Leitmeritz		17
Bohemia	Bunzlau		
Depot Kader:	Leitmeritz-Jungbunzlau		
Commander: oberst	Baron Ernst Oberndorf		

- before Aspern: Brig. Am Ende, Div. Vogelsang, I Corps Bellegarde gathered at Plan and advanced (April 10) inside Bavaria. Also parte of the strong avant-garde of Baron Crenneville. On April 14 fought at Ursensollen. On April 20 approached Ratisbon seizing the city and forcing the French to surrender. Then retreated till Cham in the Brig. Henneberg, Div. Vogelsang, I Corps.
- at Aspern: Brig. Henneberg, Div. Vogelsang, I Corps or 2nd column, in which was the 3rd battalion. The other two battalions were with the Brig. Wacquant with IR 11 and IR 47 (Div. Ulm) and took part to the seizing of Aspern. It took part also at the 2nd day of the battle. Mentioned Obertsleutnant Count Bentheim and Major Seidenhofer. [xi]
- at Wagram: Brig. Henneberg, Div. Dedovich (under Wacquant's provisional command), I Corps. Colonel Oberndorf defended the village of Deutsch-Wagram and was also wounded. Involved in the clash of Aderklaa. Mentioned the colonel, the two Majors Karg and Schlosser.
- after Wagram: Brig. and Div. Henneberg (maybe with Brig. Fabre), I Corps at Znaim fighting for the defense of the Teschwitz bridge.

K. IR 18 – FML Count Patrick Stuart [xii] (then) FML Baron Constantin D'Aspre – 3 Bns [xiii]
Recruitment: 2 Depotcompanies Brig. Szénassy in Jaromirz, fortress Josefstadt under Riesch and Loudon

Bohemia	Bidzow		18
Depot Kader:	Neu Bidzow		
Commander: Oberstleutnant	Anton Grimmer von Riesenburg	1st Bn – Major Kirchlebsky	

- before Aspern: 5527 men, 2nd Bn (Major Baron Carl Boeck), 3rd Bn (Oberstleutnant Wilhelm von Feuchtersleben) and 1st Bn were with Brigade GM prince Friedrich von Wied-Runkel, Div. Weber then Division FML Baron Thomas von Brady, II Corps Kolowrath. Two battalions with Wied-Runkel took part at the Kolowrath advance at Eckmühl. A division of the regiment undet Hauptmann Baron Imhoff defended the Jakobs-Tor at Ratisbon losing 5 men dead, 55 wounded and 220 prisoners.
The third battalion was detached to the IV Corps (April 6) and sent to reach the connection with the retreating V and VI Corps, with the Landwehr Brigade GM Richter and then with the Brigade GM Rudolf von Sinzendorff, both under FML Dedovich. The battalion was ordered to defend the powerful bridgehead of Oberhaus being part of the Oberst Grätze detachment (a colonel of a Border Regiment or Grenzer). But the French advance forced to send away guns and ammunitions of Oberhaus, sending them to Linz by boats. One division of the battalion remained at Oberhaus, another at Passau.
The Div. Dedovich was attached to the V Corps Hiller and was in reserve in the woods behind Ebelsberg, on the right Danube bank. The 3rd battalion was sent to support the Vienna Volunteers inside the town and it lost 16 men dead, 22 wounded, 10 prisoners and 208 missing. Then retreated to Vienna and joined the main army on the left Danube bank. The other two battalions remained with the Brig. Wied Runkel, Div. Weber, II Corps in Bohemia. The three battalions assembled together before Aspern. On May 1st Major Kirchlebsky left for a different command. The 1st Bn was now under Boeck and the 3rd under Major Lorenz Volk.

- at Aspern: Brig. Wied Runkel, Div. Weber, II Corps and during the battle to Brig. Altstern, Div. Ulm, II Corps, after the death of FML Franz Weber von Treuenfels. The regiment took part to all clashes of the Wied Runkel Brigade (expecially Esslingen assault). The losses were: 72 dead, 689 wounded, 157 prisoners.
- between Aspern and Wagram: its Owner became D' Aspre. [xiv] Brig. Wied Runkel, Div. Ulm, II Corps.
- at Wagram: Brig Wied Runkel, Div. Ulm, II Corps then Brig. Wied Runkel, Div. Siegenthal, [xv] II Corps and again Brig. Wied Runkel, Div Ulm, II Corps. During the battle the regiment was in the second line (with IR 28) protecting the road of Baumersdorf. For some time it was led directly by Hardegg, who was in the town.
- after Wagram: Brig Wied Runkel, Div. Ulm, II Corps. The regiment was at Znaim behind the cavalry Reserve between Blenditz and Maispitz. Then retreated in Bohemia reaching in autumn the new Depot location of Gitschin.

K.K. IR 36 – FZM Count Carl Kolowrath-Krakowsky – 3 Bns [xvi]

Recruitment: 2 Depotcompanies Brig. and Div. Schönthal in Pilsen, under Riesch and Loudon.

Bohemia	Brüx then Leitmeritz	36
Depot Kader:	Leitmeritz - Theresienstadt	
Commander: Oberstleutnant	Count Wenzel von Klenau then Joseph Fischer von See -Oberstleutnant Wappel	

- before Aspern: Brig. Am Ende, Div. FML Ludwig Vogelsang, I Corps Bellegarde then Brig. GM Baron Josef Henneberg, Div. Vogelsang, I Corps. Did not fight any battle.
- at Aspern: Brig. Henneberg, Div. Vogelsang, I Corps . The regiment deployed in fron of Hirschstetten. The commander of the 3rd Bn Hauptmann Baron Bienefeld distinguished himself during the attack against Aspern's Churchyard. The regiment lost 7 officers and 127 men dead, 21 officers and 595 men wounded; 204 men missing (a total of 28 officers and 928 men, the largest losses of the I Corps). On May 27 FML Vogelsand retired himself and gave the command to FML Nostitz. Colonel Klenau was promoted Generalmajor and left the command to the (fresh) colonel Fischer, while the former Major Senitzer became Oberstlieutnant.
On June 22 the regiment received 800 replacement troopers and FML Nostitz left for another command. The division was provisionaly led by GM Wacquant. Colonel Fischer, ill, left the command to Oberstleutnant Wappel, while the 1st battalion was now under Hauptmann Haberein.
- at Wagram: Brig. Henneberg, Div. (column) Dedovich, under provisional command of Wacquant, I Corps. The regiment deployed behind the Russbach creek. The 3rd battalion (Haberein) sent, autonomous, went behind the village of Wagram, was attached to the Stutterheim vanguard. During the night Brig. Henneberg, Div. Fresnel, I Corps (1st and 2nd battalions). The 3rd battalion then took part at the defense of Aderklaa with the other two battalions. The I Corps then retreated to Gerarsdorf. The regiment lost 67 men dead, 324 wounded (was also wounded the interim commander Wappel who left the command to Major Rasquin), 6 prisoners and 390 missing. Captain Haberein was awarded with the MTO Cross.
- after Wagram: Brig. Henneberg, Div. Henneberg (interim), I Corps . The provisional brigade camped on the Weingebirge in front of Znaim. Colonel Fischer take again command. After the hard battle the regiment lost its former commader Wappel and other 91 men dead, 496 wounded, 14 prisoners and 275 missing.
Note: facings of the regiment got the ancient name of colour "gris de lin". From 1807 it was also called as Leinblüthenfarbe; from 1860 also Blaßrot.

K.K. IR 42 – FML-FZM Carl Eugen Erbach Schönberg – 3 Bns [vii]

Recruitment: Bohemia. 1 Depotcompanies Brig. Ullrich in Elbogen, Div. Karl Kinsky under Riesch and Loudon. Depotdivision at Theresienstadt.

Bohemia	Eger	42
Depot Kader:	Elbogen - Eger	
Commander: Oberst	Chevalier Franz Rousseau	Wilhelm von Brixen

- before Aspern: Brigade GM Count Johann Nostitz, Division FML Ludwig Vogelsang, I Corps Bellegarde (2 Bns), and 3rd Bn with the II Reserve Corps then to Brigade autonome GM Baron Carl von Am-Ende in Bohemia to watch the Saxon borders at Pascopol. Regiment with Brigade Nostitz, Division FML Count Johann Fresnel von Hennequin, I Corps.
- at Aspern: Brigade Nostitz, Division Fresnel von Hennequin, I Corps. Deployed on the hills behind Gerasdorf. It took part to the assault at Aspern. Later with the Brig. Clary, Div. Fresnel, I Corps then Brig. Schaeffer, Div. Nostitz, I Corps then Brig. Nostitz, Div. Fresnel, I Corps. Colonel Rousseau left after a severe wound and the command went to colonel von Brixen.

- between Aspern and Wagram: 3rd Bn always with the independent Brig. Am Ende under Kienmayer Corps.
- at Wagram: Brig. Clary, Div. Fresnel, I Corps. The regiment was between Baumersdorf and Wagram. During an attack died its commander and was substituted by Major Fromm. On the second day of the battle the regiment was between Aderklaa and Wagram. Also the new regiment commander died during an attack. The regiment was now under Major Schober. The 2nd battalion (Hauptmann Höckner) seized Aderklaa. As award for having fought in a so brave way the regiment got the honour to be allowed to play the "Grenadiersmarsch in every occurrence desired …". Archduke Charles himself mentioned the bravery of the Erbach's Leibbattalion (the 1st).
- after Wagram: Brig. Clary, Div. Fresnel, I Corps and return to Bohemia. The total losses of the two Erbach battalions during the summer were: 18 officers and 900 men, of which 3 officers and 49 men dead.
Note: this famous regiment had often nicknames like "42er" (Zweiundvierziger) or the Erbacher"

K.K. IR 35 – Erzherzog Johann Nepomuk (from May) FZM Count Eugen Argenteau – 3 Bns [xviii]
Recruitment: Bohemia. 2 Depotcompanies Brig. and Div. Karl Kinsky in Pilsen under Riesch and Loudon.

Bohemia	Klattau -Pilsen	35
Depot Kader:	Pilsen	
Commander: Oberst	Joseph Schäffer von der Mulda	

before Aspern: mobilized as Rgt. Archduke Johann Nepomuk in Brigade GM Baron Ferdinand Wintzingerode-Ohmfeld, Division FML Count Johann Fresnel von Hennequin, I Corps Bellegarde. Successively in Brig. Henneberg, Div. Vogelsang, I Corps and then also Brig. Wartensleben, Div. Fresnel, I Corps. In April it was on the Kieselberg hills near Ursensollen, where Hauptmann Baron Hromada (then promoted to major) attacked the French in the wood, repulsing them with two companies of the regiment. On May 1st the regiment was given to FZM Count Argenteau.
- at Aspern: Brigade GM Count Johann Nostitz (Brig. Lützel ?), Div. Fresnel, I Corps and Brig. Schäffer, Div. Nostitz, I Corps or 2nd Column during the battle. At 3 PM it attacked Aspern village with the 1st battalion and part of the 2nd. The 3rd battalion was in reserve. The regiment lost: 3 officer and 85 men dead, 10 officers and 544 men wounded, 116 men prisoners or missing. Later it was again in the Brig. Wartensleben, Div. Fresnel, I Corps.
- between Aspern and Wagram: for a short period it trained with the Div. Nordmann, Avantgarde left Wing .
- at Wagram: Brig. Motzen, Div. Fresnel, I Corps (interim led by colonel Schäffer). The regiment took position at Baumersdorf. The Oberstleutnant Matthias Dittmayer, with his 16th company, assaulted and conquered one enemy gun, one Eagle of the 116e infantry and around 200 prisoners, receiving the MTO Cross award. During the 2nd battle-day the regiment was between Wagram and Baumersdorf.
- after Wagram: Brig. Schäffer, Div. Fresnel, I Corps . At Znaim the regiment deployed on Esseklee hills. It received order to stop the

K.K. IR 25 – FML Count Franz Julius Zedtwitz (but formally Vacant) – 3 Bns [xix]

Till 1806 it was the "Bavarian" regiment having Reichswerbung at Salzburg, Passau and Ratisbon and it was supported by the Galician Kreis Stanislau. After 1807 it became a Bohemian unit recruiting in Pisek and partially at Klattau. That was the so called Prachiner area. Recruitment: 2 Depotcompanies Brig. and Div. Richter in Pisek under Riesch and Loudon.

Bohemia	Prachin	25
Depot Kader:	Pisek	
Commander: Oberst	Kurz von Traubenstein then Oberst Carl von Quallenberg	

- Before Aspern: Brig. GM Carl von Fölseis, Div. Brady, II Corps Kollowrath then Avantgarde FML Count Johann Klenau, II Corps. On April 17 it fought a clash at Weichs with its 7th division (Hauptmann Theiss), then came to Ratisbon to garrison the city and was engaged first in the attack of Stadt-am-Hof, then in the town defense where, for the main part, it was taken prisoner after an hard struggle, losing, as prisoners, 2 Staff's and 23 officers with the colonel commander Kurz, and up to 1522 troopers (65 dead and 100 wounded). General Fölseis led the garrison
The regiments was completely reorganized (May 10 at Zwettel) after the Ratisbon affair. Later was with the Brig. Oberst Baron Franz Koller [xx] (GM after May 18), Div. FML Baron Thomas von Brady, II Corps, now, Hohenzollern. The new Staff was Oberst Quallenberg, commander, Major von Annaker (1st Bn), Major Eckhardt (2nd Bn) and Oberstleutnant Kirchlepsky (3rd Bn).

- at Aspern: before the battle beginning it was (reorganizing) Brig. Paar, Div. GM Wenzel Buresch von Greifenbach, II Corps Hohenzollern became Brig. Koller, Div. Brady, II Corps and finally to the Brig. David Andrássy, Div. Brady, II Corps Hohenzollern (3rd column). It deployed in line near Wagram and was ordered to attack Aspern village. During the first battle-day, colonel Quallenberg was wounded and the command was taken by Kirchlepsky. At Aspern the regiment lost 156 men dead, 592 wounded and 51 missing.

- at Wagram: Brig. Count Paar, Div. Brady (then von Buresch – interim), II Corps. The regiment deployed at Baumersdorf where it sufered an heavy bombardment. The orders for the following day were to sustain the line behind the Russbach creek. Tactical orders were to spread out some skirmishers (Plänklers) screens and to deploy in battalion Masses (eventually forming Squares). After having suffered utter heavy bombing, after having partially seized again Baumersdorf the regiment was charged by the French cavalry. The Square were not enough to avoid the retreat and the units reached Enzelsfeld. Losses were heavy: 53 dead, 536 wounded, 11 prisoners and 99 missing men.

- after Wagram: the 1st battalion (now Major Eckhardt) retreated with the IV Corps Rosenberg, attached to the rearguard of Radetzky till Laa. Then it was formed a new rearguard brigade, with all the remnants of II Corps units, under the command of Baron Carl Mécsery (IR 28). The regiment was in the Brig. Oberst Carl von Quallenberg, Div. von Buresch, II Corps. It withdrew till Klein- Tesswitz where it was deployed, reaching after Znaim and Winau where it was during the battle, without fighting. By January 1st, 1810 the regiment will be property of FML Thierry de Vaux.

K.K. IR 47 – FML-FZM Baron Ludwig Vogelsang – 3 Bns lxxi|
Recruitment: Bohemia 2 Depotkomp Brig and Div. Karl Kinsky in Prague under Riesch and Loudon

Bohemia	Beraun	47
Depot Kader:	Prague	
Commander: Oberst	Joseph Weiss von Finkenau after Wagram oberst Friedrich Count Bentheim- Steinfurt	

- before Aspern: in March had, commander Oberst Joseph Weiss von Finkenau, Oberstleutnant Heinrich Van der Gracht, 1st major Ludwig Grötz, 2nd major Johann Frisch. Commander of the Prague depot division Oberstleutnant Michael Aichinger; marched with the Brigade GM Baron Theodor Wacquant-Geocelles, Division FML Josef von Ulm, I Corps Bellegarde.

- at Aspern: Brig. Wacquant, Div. Dedovich, I Corps then Brig. Wacquant, Div. Ulm, I Corps. The regiment attacked the village of Aspern, aflame. The losses were: 42 men dead, 413 wounded, 111 prisoners, 90 missing.

- between Aspern and Wagram: Weiss was promoted and left the command to Oberst Bentheim- Steinfurt, while the regiment received 800 new recruits.

- at Wagram: Brig. Wacquant, Div. Dedovich (under Wacquant provisional command), I Corps. The regiment occupied the left wing of the Austrian first line behind the Russbach creek. After a French attack and the counterattack general Wacquant was wounded and left command to GM Henneberg. On the second day battle the regiment was sent, in reserve, behind Wagram (now Brig. Clary, Div. Dedovich, I Corps). The French breakthrough at Baumersdorf threatened a surrounding maneuver against Wagram. So the regiment deployed and countercharged the French two times. The regiment lost: 75 men dead, 563 wounded, 359 prisoners and 151 missing.

- after Wagram: Brigade Oberst von Faber (Fabre), Div. Henneberg, I Corps. At Znaim it had a marginal part, being present to some skirmishing actions on the Weinbergen hills. There it lost 1 dead, 52 prisoners and 53 missing men. On July 27 the regiment came in the Div. Fresnel.

Archduke Charles: "Der Schutz des Vaterlandes ruft uns zu neuer Thaten"
(The Fatherland's Shield calls us to new Events) or

THE HUNGARIAN ROYAL ARMY

HUNGARIAN INFANTRY REGIMENTS 1805-1809

I n the Austrian Empire some lands (Tirol, Northern Italy, Netherlands) relied on free recruiting, while Hungary, as for the Insurrectio troops, filled the ranks by local officials according to quotas imposed by the Hungarian Diet and on volunteers. Hungary was ruled by its own "Diet" (parliament), which enjoyed a degree of independence.

Against 5.600.000 Germans, 3.770.000 Poles and Ukrainians and 4.730.000 Czechs and Moravians, Hungary opposed 4.500.000 Hungarians, 1.300.000 Slovaks, 1.700.000 Romanians, 600.000 Croats and Serbs . 4.750.000 of others (Italians, Tyroleans and other nationalities) had abandoned the Austrian recruitment. The Hungarians enjoyed great reputation as horsemen and fighters. The Romanians were imagined as short, robust, rancorous and brutal, while the Serbs and Croats were considered as blunt men, "indomitable fighters" and serious drinkers. Before 1805 the term of service was reduced to 10 years in the infantry, 12 in the cavalry and 14 years in the artillery and engineers. The hussar regiments had no problems with keeping their strength, as there were many volunteers in Hungary, who happily joined their favorite and traditional branch. The 'Hungarian' regiments were the largest of all.

Austrian infantry was divided into two groups; 'German' and 'Hungarian' regiments.

The 'Hungarian' regiments were renowned for their fierce fighting spirit, and their grenadiers were best of them. " ... *The Hungarian infantrymen were at their best when they were in the immediate presence of the enemy, which encouraged Armfeldt to describe them as among the best of Maria Theresa's foot soldiers. The difficulty was not to get them to fight, but to enlist in the first place... they were convinced that they were unsuitable for dismounted service.*" (Duffy - "Instrument of War" Vol I, p 237)

MILITARY REFORMS

After 1800 and the first army reorganization the K.K. Österreichisches Heer improved its organization with a new recruiting system and the widening of the duty services, created new units and enlarged the hungarian troops (probably either for having lost a large amount of crown lands, either under the direct French threats). The great test for this new army was completely failed in 1809, but this, really, could have been considered as the first trial to organize the future "vielen Völkern K.u.K. Armée".

The "Stand" of the Royal hungarian regular army was, initially, of 12 infantry regiments and 10 light cavalry regiments (Hussars); we must assume the Siebenbürgen or Transylvanian Hussars as part of another territory, the military Border.

From 1802 the peacetime strength of the hungarian infantry regiment was of 3857 men (without officers and the 63 Musikanten) and comprised 2 grenadiers companies, 18 fusiliers companies, a total of 46.284 "Magyars" in the 12 regiments. The Hussar regiments had 1698 hussars (without officers); therefore in 10 regiments the hungarian cavalry had 16.980 hussars in field.

Rapid reforms were made from 1805, too fastly for the Austrian pace. So when the army began a new campaign, the new rules caused only confusion (Archduke Charles had realised the danger in the field, and apparently never applied the new regulations for his own forces).

The main change would have been each infantry regiment to be arranged in one grenadier and four fusilier battalions, each battalion being of four companies of a nominal 160 men each. The 1807 regulations, supervised by the Archduke Charles, returned to the previous organisation (three battalions and two grenadier companies per regiment, field battalions of six companies and garrison battalions of four), wartime establishments now being the same as peacetime save for the increase of the third battalion to six companies and the detachment of the grenadiers to composite battalions.

Infantry regiment had three field and one depot battalion. Austrian battalion was probably the biggest battalion in Europe. It consisted of approximatively 1.200 men, while the French battalion was only 840 men strong.

All Austrian regular troops were well supplied and equipped. Every soldier carried a fur-covered leather backpack called Tornister. There was 1 tent for every 5 men, 1 wagon for each company, 4-6 carts and wagons and 30 pack-horses with ammunition (on average 36 rounds for every soldier) for every battalion of 6 companies. Officers were also allowed individual packhorses.

The senior officers and generals however brought excessive baggage, numerous carts and horses. It slowed down movements of the army. In 1809 regiment of infantry had 26 packhorses, while Grenzer regiment only 7. The supplies for infantry regiment were carried on 13 wagons (4 horses each) and 26 pack animals.

In March 1809 Austria had 46 'German' and 15 'Hungarian' infantry regiments. The grenadiers were detached and formed in 21 grenadier battalions. The hungarian regiment had their Staffs and Depot (Kader) in Hungary (many Hussars regiments had their depots in nearby Galicia). Austria also had one infantry regiment (of 10 independent coys) for the guard and escort of staffs. These troops were called Staff Infantry. The 5th and 6th Regiment were disbanded in 1807 and served as garrisons in numbered battalions.

In 1809 (*Europäischen Annalen 1810*, St.5, pages 183-184) one hungarian regiment in companies had 3584 men, or 2 battalions of 6 companies and one (the third) of 4 companies, plus two grenadier comp. and 1 or 2 depot companies. Every company was about 180 men strong. The hungarian Hussars regiments had 8 squadrons and 1168 horses. In December 1809 when the army took its quarters, in Hungary came back 19 brigades or 33 regiments counting also the Grenzers.

After the 1809 defeats the 3rd battalions were disbanded, all companies were reduced to 60 privates in 'German' and 100 in 'Hungarian' infantry. Austria also had lost many former recruiting areas and 6 Wallons regiments, recruited in Belgium till the end of the century, were definitively moved to Bohemia. When in 1814 Austria recovered some of its former territories (parts of Northern Italy) they formed new regiments (1st, 2nd, 3rd and 4th Provisional Infantry Regiment and four battalions of light infantry). The provisional regiments became regular units and were numbered: 13th, 23rd, 38th and 43rd. The four battalions of light infantry formed a new 45th Infantry Regiment.

The 1810 Reforme (imperial Handbillet 9 August 1810 sent to FM Bellegarde) stated the infantry companies had to pass from 120 to 100 men (Gemeine) and the hungarian company had to be reduced from 180 to 120 men. The Hussars squadrons were of 130 men, but they had increments of 20 Ersatz men per year, so, i.e. in 1814, the Hussars squadron had 210 horses.

ORGANIZATION

Regimental Staff		
3 Senior Officers: Inhaber, Oberst (colonel) and Oberstleutnant		
2 Majors	1 Regimental adjutant	6 'Kaiserliche Kadetten' (Officers' sons selected by Hofkriegsrat. The more competent were appointed as NCOs in companies.)
9 Fouriers	1 Drum-major	others: provost, chaplain, auditor, accountant, surgeons, musicians

Battalions		
1st or Leib Battalion (Fusilier Comp.x 6)	2nd or Oberst Batt. (Fusilier Comp. x6)	3rd Oberstleutnant or Depot Battalion (Fusilier Companies x 6) 4 in peace

(Until 1809 the Depot Btn. had only 2 companies. In wartime the battalion increased to 6 companies and often served in the field as 3rd Field Battalion.)

Companies in wartime - 'German' fusilier company had 180 men while 'Hungarian' company 200		
3 Officers: Hauptmann, Oberleutnant, Unterleutnant		
1 Ensign {Fahnrich}	2 Senior NCOs {'Prima Plana'}: sergeant-major {Feldwebel} and fourier {Fourierschutzen}	6 (4 in peacetime) Sergeants {Korporalen
	12 (8 in peacetime) Corporals (Gefreiter)	7 Vize-Korporals (in wartime they took up the rank of 'Korporalen')
1 Sapper {Zimmermann}	2 Drummers	150-200 privates.

The hungarian and the Siebenbürgisches Line Infantry regiments of the Austrian army had: 2 Grenadiers coys and 16 Fusiliers coys. Hungarian companies could have around 180 men.

Staff	Hungarian Regiment infanterie		
1	Superior and Regiments Inhaber	1	Superior and Regiments Commander
1	Oberstlieutenant	2	Major
1	Regiments Kaplan (priest)	1	Regiments Auditor
1	Regiments Feldarzt	1	Regiments Rechnungsführer
1	Regiments Adjutanten	6	K.k. ordin. Cadetten
3	Ober-Ärzte	9	Unter-Arzten
9	Fourieren	1	Regiments Tambour
4	Fourierschützen	8	Hautboisten (Hoboisten)
1	Profosen	5	Privatdiener
	total	56	

Staff	Hungarian Regiment Grenadier Company		
1	Hauptmann	1	Oberlieutenant
1	Unterlieutenant	1	Feldwebel
6	Corporalen	1	Fourierschützen
2	Tambouren	1	Zimmermann (carpenter)
2	Privatdiener	--	Gemeine (in the stated number)

Staff	Hungarian Regiment Fusilier Company		
1	Hauptmann or Capitan-Lieutenant	1	Oberlieutenant
1	Unterlieutenant	1	Fähnrich or Führer
1	Feldwebel	8	Gefreiten
6	Corporalen	1	Fourierschützen
2	Tambouren	1	Zimmermann
2	Privatdiener	?	Gemeine (in the stated number)

The austrian new recruitment system was ruled by the Kaiserliche Conscriptions-und-Werbbezirke System of October 25, 1804. It was not allowed to the hungarian regiments and military districts to enroll a german or hereditary land citizen (Allerhöchsten Befehl 28 June 1808). As per art. 1, in 1807 Hungary had 12000 recruits and, from 1808 they began to enroll also Jews (Juden). I.e. in a contingent ripartition of 392 men, city of Pest counted 38 christian recruits and 4 jews.

Therefore the hungarians could, for the first time, raise their artillery, engineers and train units. Hungarian nobles, students or other men, who were free from duty, could enroll also in german units as volunteers (in the same way a hungarian citizen, who had been resident in the hereditary lands for an uninterrupted period of 10 years, was considered as being a german recruit).

MILITARY RANKS COMPARISON TABLE (Vladimir Brnardić – Enrico Acerbi)

Austrians	Grenzregiments (historical Croatian)	Magyar	French
Generalissimus			
Feldmarschall General der Infanterie	Maršal	Gyalogsági tábornok	Marechal
	General pukovnik		Colonel génèral
Feldzeugmeister General der Kavallerie	General armije	Táborszernagy Lovassági tábornok	Général en chef
Feldmarschal Lieutenant	General divizije Podmaršal	Altábornagy	Général de division
Generalmajor	Brigadni general	Vezérőrnagy	Général-de-brigade
	Brigadir		adjudant commandant
Obrist / Oberst	Pukovnik	Ezredes	Colonel Chef-de-brigade
Oberstlieutenant	Potpukovnik	Alezredes	Colonel major
			Colonel en second
			Lieutenant Colonel
Obertswachtmeister Major	major, četnik	Őrnagy	Major / Chef-de-bataillon

Austrians	Grenzregiments (historical Croatian)	Magyar	French
Hauptmann Rittmeister	kapetan, stotnik, satnik	Százados	Capitaine
Capitain-Lieutenant			------
Oberlieutenant	Natporučnik	Főhadnagy	Lieutenant
(unter) lieutenant	Potporučnik	Hadnagy	Sous Lieutenant
Fähnrich	Zastavnik	Zászlós	------
	časnički namjesnik		Adjudant major
Cadet		Hadapród	
Feldwebel Oberjäger Wachtmeister	Feldbaba Stražmeštar	Örmester	Sergent Major
Corporal Unterjäger	Kaplar	Tizedes Kápral	Sergent
Fourier	opskrbnik, končar		Caporal Fourrier
Gefreyte (gefreiter)	Kaplar	Örvezetö	Caporal
Gemeine Soldat	Vojnik ?Pozornik ?	Katona (Huszár)	Soldat
Tambur	Dobošar ?	Század-dobos	Tambour
Pfeiffer	Svirač ?		
Zimmermann	Pionir ?	Utász	Pionier

NORTHERN-EASTERN HUNGARY

Ergänzungsbezirks Kom.		Werb-bezirk	Reg army	other
HQ Recr. District	hungarian name	recruitment area (Kreis)	K.K. IR	
Pressburg	Poszony	Pozsony - Nyitra		Pressburg is Bratislava (Slovak.) both Insurrectio 1st. and Pressburg cavalry. Neutra Insurr. 3rd Neutra Hussars
Trentschin	Trencsén	Trencsén	2	

IR 49 FZM Kerpen   IR 50 FZM Stain   IR 51 FML Splényi

IR 52 Erzherzog Franz Carl   IR 53 Johann Jellachich   IR 54 FML Baron Froon

▲ Austrian Infantry uniforms regiments nr. 49, 50, 51, 52, 53 & 54

Raab	Györ	Györ		Insurr. 6th and 7th batt.
		Veszprém	19	Insurr. 9th batt. Veszprém cavalry
Komorn	Komarom	Komarom		Insurr. 7th batt.
Gran	Esztergom	Esztergom		Insurr. 4th batt. Primartial Hussars
		Hont and Bars counties	33	Insurr. 4th batt. Bars cavalry Nógrad cavalry.
		Zólyom		
		Árva - Liptó		
Lizenz	Losoncz	Nógrad	32	
		Gömör	60	Insurr. 17th batt. Heves cavalry
Kaschau	Kassa	Abaúj-Torna		Heves cavalry
		Borsod	34	Insurr. 16th batt. Heves cavalry
Erlau	Eger	Heves	32	Insurr. 15th batt. Heves cavalry
Munkatsch	Munkács	Bereg	34	Insurr. 11th and 12th batt. Szátmar cavalry Szabolcs cavalry
	Szatmárnémeti	Szátmar and Szabolcs	39	
Ungwar	Ungvár	Ung and Zemplén	34	Insurr. 18th batt.
Preschau	Eperjes	Sáros and Szepes (Zips)	60	with Abaujvár county Insurr. 19th batt. Zemplén cavalry

Large Numbers in bold mean a temporary area of recruitment in order to help the main District to reach the stated strength. These areas were named Aushilfe kreise (Antheil Ergänzung) (Helping Circles).

1809 REGULAR INFANTRY K.K. (Kaiserliche königliche) Ungarischen Infanterie Regimenter
Pressburg and the Slovak Regiments

or Preßburg, Hungarian: Pozsony, former Slovak name, Prešporok, was named as Bratislava, only on March 6, 1919. Pressburg flourished during the 18th century reign of Queen Maria Theresa, becoming the largest and most important town in Hungary. The population tripled; many new palaces, monasteries, mansions, and streets were built, and the city was the centre of social and cultural life of the region. However, the city started to lose its importance under the reign of Maria Theresa's son Joseph II, especially when the crown jewels were taken to Vienna in 1783 in an attempt to strengthen the union between Austria and Hungary. Many central offices subsequently moved to Buda, followed by a large segment of the nobility. The first newspapers in Hungarian and Slovak were published here, "Magyar hírmondó" in 1780, and "Presspurske Nowiny" in 1783. In the course of the 18th century, the city became a centre for the Slovak national movement.

19th century history was closely tied to the major events in Europe. The Peace of Pressburg between Austria and France was signed here in 1805. Theben Castle was ruined by Napoleon's French troops in 1809.

Pressburg fortress was destroyed by the French at the end of the 1809 campaign, because of its strong symbology. The fortress or Devín Castle (Slovak: Devínsky hrad, Hungarian: dévényi vár, German: Burg Theben) was a castle in Devín, which was a suburb of Pressburg. Owing to its strategic position, the cliff (altitude of 212 meters) at the confluence of the Danube and Morava rivers was an ideal place for a fort. The Hungarians regarded it as the western gateway of the Kingdom of Hungary. The last owners of the Devin Castle were the Counts of the Pálffy family. In 1809, after the Siege of Pressburg, was the castle (still considered a threat) destroyed by the forces of Napoleon

K.K. IR 2 – FML-FZM baron Johann Hiller – 3 battalions

Recruitment: 2 Depot Companies Brig. Kerekes in Pressburg under Alvinczy. It began the campaign at Vienna in January in the brig. Ignaz Buol von Berenburg with 2 batt. (6 comp.) and the third batt. (4 comp.). An hungarian brigade under german command.

Nyitra	Neutra	
Türocz	Turócszentmárton	
Trencsén	Trencsén	2
Pozsony	Pressburg	
Depot Kader	Pressburg	
Commander: oberst	Prince Philipp Hessen Homburg	Franz von Torri (officially after Wagram)
Oberstleutnant	Franz von Torri	István Papp (wounded)
Majors	István Papp	Wilhelm Hahn

before Aspern: in the V Corps archduke Louis, Div. Lindenau, Brig. von Buol, later Brig. prince Hessen Homburg (the colonel). On April 10 they invaded Bavaria. During the first combat at Landshut the regiment crossed the bridges, supporting the avant-garde along the Altdorf road. The division then entered the ranks of the 1st Reserve Corps; so at Teugen it was with the 3rd Column Liechtenstein, and it continbued with the 1st Reserve Corps at Abensberg and Eggmühl. On April 20 they were at Ratisbon when the city surrendered, marching behind the Vécsey vanguard group.

After the retreat in Bohemia it was attached to the IV Corps, Div. Hohenlohe Bartenstein, Brig. Reinhardt.

at Aspern: in the 4th-5th Column (Rosenberg) under command of the FML baron Martin von Dedovich, again Brig. Hessen Homburg. The regiment was attached to the 5th Column on the left bank of the Russbach between Deutsch-Wagram and Baumersdorf. It had the task to attack Essling and did it for the two battledays. At Aspern it lost 68 men dead, 385 wounded and 19 missing, with no prisoners fallen in French hands.

at Wagram: in the 4th Corps (Rosenberg) with the division Hohenlohe Bartenstein, Brig. Hessen Homburg. At 4 AM of July 6, after a day of defensive combats, the 4th Corps formed three columns. Two had orders to attack and seize the area between Grosshofen and Glinzendorf, the third (cavalry) to support the left flank and to link with archduke John's Corps. The first column under prince Hohenlohe was practcally the prince Hessen-Homburg brigade. They had to seize Grosshofen and they did it. The French cavalry counterattack sent the regiment backwards. Having a new line along the Russbach, partially defended in skirmish order, the regiment was attacked by the French division Morand (the 3rd battalion in square, was attacked by the French Guard cavalry). The regiment lost 44 men dead, 277 wounded, 216 missing.

The Rosemberg's troops were not at the battle of Znaim, crossing the Thaya river at Laa.

Upper Hungary

Upper Hungary was an historical area of current Slovakia. Historically there were different meanings:

1. The older Hungarian term Felső-Magyarország (literally: "Upper Hungary"; Slovak: Horné Uhorsko; German: Oberungarn) formally referred to what is today Slovakia in the 16th-18th centuries and informally to all the northern parts of the Kingdom of Hungary in the 19th century.

2. The Hungarian Felvidék (literally: "Upper Country", "Upland", "Highland"; Slovak: Horná zem; German: Oberland) has had several informal meanings:

In the 19th century and part of the 18th, it was usually used:

a- to denote the mountainous northern part of the Kingdom of Hungary as opposed to the southern lowlands

b- more generally, to denote regions or territories situated at a higher altitude than the settlement of the speaker

c- as a synonym for the then-meaning of Felső-Magyarország

After Transylvania, Upper Hungary (the territory of present day Slovakia), was the most advanced part of the Kingdom of Hungary for centuries (the most urbanized part, intense mining of gold and silver), but in the 19th century, when Buda/Pest became the new capital of the kingdom, the importance of the territory, as well as other parts within the Kingdom fell, and many Slovaks were impoverished.

K.K. IR 34 – FML-FZM baron Paul Davidovich - 3 battalions

Recruitment: 2 Depot Companies at Kaschau with Brig. Elsnitz under Alvinczy. Staff at Sandomir (Galicia) and Cracow. It began the war in the Brig. GM Graf Karl Civalart (Div. Hohenzollern) then in campaign with Brig. Trautenberg, Div. Mondet, VII Corps, archduke Ferdinand.

Abaúj-Torna	Kaschau (Kassa)	
Bereg	Munkács	
Borsod	Miskolcz	**34**
Ung	Ungvár	
Ugocsa	Nagyszőlős	
Zemplén	Sátoraljaújhely	
Depot Kader	Kaschau	Tarnow (Galicia)
Commander: oberst	Johann Schmelzern von Widmannsegg	baron Ludwig Gabelkoven in 1810
Oberstleutnant	Franz Geiger	Sigmund Szinkovits
Majors	major Peremanns Johann A. Enyetter	Johann Kirchenbetter von Ritterskirchen

before Aspern: on April 4, the regiment left the works in Sandomierz to reach the Brig. Pflacher at Opatow. The brigade (3 batt. Davidovich, 3 batt. Weidenfeld IR 37 plus one six pdr. battery) marched to Odrzywól to reach the division Mondet. At Raszyn the regiment took position on the road to Jaworów, in front of the height of Wygoda Karczina, part of the GM Mohr vanguard (together with 2 walachian battalions and six sqns.) The regiment attacked the village of Falenty and advanced till Raszyn. It had very few losses: 1 man wounded and 4 prisoners. On April 23 they entered Warsaw. In May the 2nd batt. was with colonel Mercy on garrison duties.

at Aspern: on May 22, the Corps left Poland in order to defend Galicia gainst the russian advance. Div. Schauroth with 5 batt. and 13 sqns. marched to Opatow (with the 1st battalion under obertslieutenant Geiger).

between Aspern and Wagram: on June 3, the Corps vanguard Brig. Geringer (with 2nd and 3rd batt.) were at Opatow with orders to reach Sandomierz. Two companies attacked in that place, but with poor luck: they lost 9 men dead, 12 wounded and 160 prisoners. On June 6 the archduke ordered a probe attack against Sandomierz. The 2nd battalion was in first line and lost 2 dead, 41 wounded and 12 prisoners.

During the night on June 16 the Austrian attacked again Sandomierz. GM Geringer divided the attacker in four columns:

1st Column Oberstlieutenant Geiger: 1st batt. IR 34; IR 24 Strauch 3 comp; 1 Sqn. towards Andruszkowice;

2nd Column under Major Peremanns: 2nd batt. IR 34; IR 24 Strauch 2 comp at Koberniki;

3rd Column under colonel Schmelzern: 3rd batt. IR 34; IR 24 Strauch 2 comp; 2 Sqns. at the Marien-Kapelle on the Opatow road.

4th Column under major Szinkovics: one batt. IR 37 Weidenfeld; IR 24 Strauch 3 comp; at Kruków.

20 guns prepared the attack shooting from 11 PM till 1 AM in the night. However the town resisted and the Austrian went back losing (the 34th regiment) 24 officers and 700 men (107 dead, 331 wounded, 163 prisoners, 123 missing, 32 of whom later rejoined the unit). Polish general Sokolnicki surrendered on June 18, making that sacrifice totally unuseful. In the meanwhile FML Schauroth division (Brig. Geringer, Pflacher and Speth) concentrade its troops near Opatow waiting for the joint Russo-Polish push. The regiment (now with only 2287 men) took position at Ostrowiec (3rd batt.), Iwaniska (2nd batt.) and Radom (1st batt.).

at Wagram: the VII Corps retreated till Wadowice district, having lost Cracow (Russians) and there had the new of the Znaim armistice.

Zips Territory

Spiš (Slovak; Latin: Scepusium, German: Zips, Hungarian: Szepesség, Polish: Spisz) is a region in the current north-eastern Slovakia, with a very small area in south-eastern Poland and a former county of Hungary (Szepes). The subsidiary of the Hungarian Chamber (the supreme Habsburg financial and economy institution in the Kingdom of Hungary) responsible for eastern Slovakia and adjacent territories (i.e. not only for Szepes) was called the Szepes Chamber (Zipser Kammer in German), and it existed from 1563 to 1848. Its seat was the town of Kassa, today Košice, sometimes Eperjes, (today's Prešov).

During the medieval time the Zips town had many privileges. After the Polish conquest the privileged status became to fade away (they however maintained some autonomy, in respect of the Polish kings, who did not change the privileges) and it was created the "Province/Union of 13 Szepesi towns" in 1412. The remaining 11 towns of the former 24 towns, which created the "Province/Union of 11 Szepesi towns", were not able to maintain their privileges and as early as in 1465 they were fully incorporated into the Szepes county, i. e. they became subjects of the lords of the Spiš Castle. Most of them gradually turned into simple villages and largely lost their German character. Maria Theresa of Austria decided to recover them by force: she took advantage of the Polish noble insurrections in the second half of the 18th century and occupied the towns in 1769 (with the apparent consent of the then Polish king Stanislaus II of Poland) without debt repayment. This act was confirmed by the First Partition of Poland in 1772. In 1773 when the pawn was cancelled. In 1778 the 13 towns regained their privileges of 1271, the privileges were extended to the other 3 previously pawned towns, and this newly formed entity was named "Province of 16 Szepes towns". The capital of the province was Spišská Nová Ves. However, the privileges were gradually reduced and some 100 years later only religious and cultural rights remained. Finally, the province was dissolved altogether and incorporated into Szepes county in 1876.

The German people widely dwelling the area during the napoleonic wars, progressively decreased. According to censuses carried out in the Kingdom of Hungary in 1869 the population of Spiš county comprised the following nationalities: Slovaks 50.4%, Germans 35%, Ruthenians (Rusyns) 13.8% and 0.7% Magyars (Hungarians). Hardly any Hungarians lived in the territory during the existence of the Kingdom of Hungary.

K.K. IR 60 – FZM Graf Ignaz Gyulai von Máros-Nemeth und Nadaska - 3 battalions

Recruitment: 2 Depot Companies at Eperjes Brig. Elsnitz under Alvinczy. Staff at Tarnow (Galicia) moved to Retz (Austria) under brig. GM Federico Bianchi, V Corps.

Gömör	Rozsnyó	
Sáros	Eperjes	60
Szepes (Zips)	Lőcse	
Depot Kader	Eperjes	1810 Lemberg (Galicia)
Commander: oberst	Andreas Máriássy de Markus et Batis-Falva	count Anton Weissenwolf and finally baron Joseph von der Trenck
Oberstleutnant	baron Joseph von der Trenck	
Majors	Johann Nepomuk Ürményi major von Czárnotzay	Major Fligely (recruits)

before Aspern: entered Bavaria with the V Corps archduke Louis, Division FML prince Henry XV Reuss-Plauen, Brig. GM baron Federico Bianchi. At Abensberg the brigade was sent ahead to support the battered brig. Thierry, without success. During the retreat, on April 21, the 3rd battalion was sent to Seelingthal and Landshut, in the center of the incoming battle, in order to support the rearguard of GM Radetzky. Led by the Oberstleutnant baron Joseph von der Trenck, the battalion was part of the Detachment colonel baron Emerich de Bakonyi, former regiment's oberstlieutenant and actually colonel commander of IR 39 Duka. Defending Seelingthal town and the half destroyed bridges the regiment lost 15 men dead, many wounded and around 136 prisoners (with 9 supply wagons, the blacksmith workshop and 22 train horses). On April 22 it came under the united Corps of FML Hiller. It fought at Neumarkt (110 dead, 116 wounded), Efferding (lost 235 prisoners) and Ebelsberg (Brig. Bianchi; it lost 4 dead, many wounded and 96 prisoners) being now definitively part of the VI Corps baron Hiller, Div. FML Friedrich von Kottulinsky, from May 17. The 3rd batt. was disbanded in order to replace the 1st and 2nd batt. Then 994 men arrived from Eperjes as replacements.

at Aspern: it was in the 1st Column (VI Corps Hiller) with two battalions, 1717 men in the Brig. Bianchi (Div. von Kottulinsky under command of GM Hohenfeld), supporting also the Avant-garde Brig. Nordmann and being part of it during the attack against Aspern (extreme right wing of the 1st column, area of Au). It lost at Aspern 55 men dead, 81 prisoners and 367 wounded. On May 25, FML Klenau took command of the VI Corps.

between Aspern and Wagram: on May 28 the Brig. Bianchi was detached to the Pressburg defence. On June 23 archduke John took command at Pressburg and Bianchi returned to the VI Corps. On July 2 the regiment received the 3rd battalion (major Fligely).

at Wagram: was with the VI Corps, Div. Hohenfeld, Brig. Bianchi and retreated after two days of battle.

after Wagram: the 3rd battalion retreated with FML Wallmoden Corps till Korneuburg where it fought with Masséna. FML Klenau with the main group was, on July 9, at Ober Hollabrunn (combat of Schöngraben), with the regiment under its former commander GM Máriássy. At Wagram and during the retreat the regiment lost: 29 men dead, 186 wounded, 89 prisoners and 92 missing (a total of 396). It did not fight at Znaim.

THE SIEGE OF PRESSBURG

Austrian imperial units built a fortified bridgehead on the right bank of the Danube on the site of today's Sad Janko Kral near Petrzalke (Engerau). The defenders were 5672 men with 22 guns, commanded by general Bianchi, with two battalions of the K.K. IR 60, Slovak soldiers from northern Hungary. The French failed to capture the bridgehead cattle even after some bloody attacks and an heavy bombing of the city, both unable to break resistance. Fortress Pressburg resisted opening its gates only on July 14, on the basis of the ceasefire after the lost battles, for the Austrians, at Wagram and Znaim. Being Pressburg hard to hit, however the town suffered several fires, which put in ashes 143 houses and killed hundreds of people. French artillery attacks are today witnessed by the cannonballs in the walls of few houses.

The troops in Pressburg were:

May 16

Brigade GM Josef Hoffmeister von Hoffenegg (2 sqns. O'Reilly Chevaulegers then 7 sqns. 870 c., IR 58 Johann Peter baron von Beaulieu-Marconnay – 2 batt. 1420 men.

16 6pdr guns, 4 12 pdr guns and 2 7 inch. howitzers.

May 28

Brig. GM Federico Bianchi; IR 60 FZM Graf Ignaz Gyulai – 2 batt. (1265); IR 39 Duka 2 batt. (914 men).

May 28 – Landwehr Brigade GM count Rudolf von Sinzendorff - Niederösterreichische Landwehr battalions Schönborn (640 m.) – Gilais (538) – Praschma (460) and Beisselt (435).

K.K. IR 33 – former **FZM Graf Anton Sztáray - 3 battalions** – 1809 first vacant then
K.K. IR 33 – **FZM-FML Graf Hyeronimus Colloredo-Mansfeld**

Recruitment: 2 Depot Companies Brig. Kerekes in Pressburg under Alvinczy. Staff at Vienna. It began the campaign with V Corps archduke Louis, Div. Lindenau, Brig. Buol. Later in Brig. prince Hessen Homburg.

Bars	Aranyosmarót	
Hont	Ipolyság	33
Zolyóm	Besztercebánya	
Depot Kader	Gathering Place: Altsohl (Zolyóm)	
Commander: oberst	baron Ludwig Anton König von Cronburg	
Oberstleutnant	count Anton Weissenwolf	Ferencz Födor
Majors	David von Porubzky	Johann Zsigray

before Aspern: At Teugen with the 3rd Column Liechtenstein, the 1st Reserve Corps at Abensberg and Eggmühl. After the retreat in Bohemia it was attached to the IV Corps, Div. Hohenlohe Bartenstein, Brig. Reinhardt. It was always in the same brigade of the 2nd K.K. regiment (see above). at Aspern: in the 4th Column (Rosenberg) under command of the FML baron Martin von Dedovich, again Brig. Hessen Homburg. The 2nd battalion under major Porubzky firmly stood under a French cavalry charge gaining many awards.

at Wagram: in the 4th Corps (Rosenberg) with the division Hohenlohe Bartenstein, Brig. Hessen Homburg. The Rosemberg's troops were not at the battle of Znaim.

after Wagram: Garnison in Vienna.

Notes

1   Number of slav civilians (Militär-Grenze people not included).

2   According to Dienst Reglement (fur die kaiserliche königliche Infanterie, Wien 1807) there were 12 corporals (6 in peacetime) per fusilier and Grenzer company, 13 (6) per grenadier company, 12 (8) unter-jagers per jager company.

3   Kirchthaler, Ludwig: Geschichte des k.u.k. Infanterie-Regiments Nr. 2 für immerwährende Zeiten Alexander I. Kaiser von Rußland. Wien: 1895.

4   At Lambach von Buol was called back to Klagenfurt and the brigade command was taken by prince Hessen. The oberstlieutnant von Torri took the regiment's command.

5   After the famous archduke Charles speech "Der Schutz des Vaterlandes ruft uns zu neuen Thaten .. and so on" the troops received, along with the order to advance, an extra supply of ¼ mug of cooked-wine (vin brulé) and 1 more pound of meat.

6   Kreipner, Julius: Geschichte des k. und k. Infanterie-Regimentes Nr. 34 für immer-währende Zeiten Wilhelm I. Deutscher Kaiser und König von Preußen: 1733 - 1900. Kaschau: 1900.

7   Dead at Sandomierz on June 16.

8   Rupprecht von Virtsolog, Coloman: Geschichte des k. k. 60. Linien-Infanterie-Regimentes gegenwärtig Gustav Prinz von Wasa. Wien: 1871.

9   Transferred after Wagram to IR 60 as colonel commander.

▲ Austro-Hungarian infantry 1809. From Ottenfeld artwork

CENTRAL HUNGARY

Ergänzungsbezirks Kommando	hungarian	Werb-bekirk recruitment area (Kreis)	Regular army IR	other
HQ Recr. District				
	Máramarossziget	Máramaros	None	Grenzer 2nd Walachen Insurr. 13th batt. Szatmar cavalry
Debreczin	Debrecen	North Bihar- Hajdú	39	Insurr. 14th batt.
Grosswardein	Nagyvárad	South Bihar	37	Bihar cavalry
		Hajdú (Haiducken Städte)	**39**	Szabolcs cavalry
Szegedin	Szeged	Csanad - Csongrad		Szátmar cavalry
Tschabe	Békéscsaba	Békés	**37**	Bihar cavalry
Arad	Arad	Arad-Zárand	61	together with the Banat
Pest-Ofen	Pest	Town and Ofen district		military administrative
Pest-Ofen	Pest	Pest-Pilis		Insurrectio 2nd batt.
		Pest-Solt	32	(with Bács and Hont) Pest cavalry
	Kecskemét	Jazygier (Jász)		Nógrad cavalry
		Kumanien (Nagy Kun)		also Bács-Kis Kun areas Nógrad cavalry
Sollnock	Szolnok	Szolnok		
Stuhlweissenburg	Székesfehérvár	Fejér	19	Insurr. 10th batt. Veszprém cavalry

Large Numbers in bold mean a temporary area of recruitment in order to help the main District to reach the stated strength. These areas were named Aushilfe kreise (Antheil Ergänzung) (Helping Circles).

1809 REGULAR INFANTRY
K.K. (Kaiserliche königliche) Ungarischen Infanterie Regimenter Stuhlweissenburg (Székesfehérvár)
The name Székesfehérvár means „white castle with the chair/seat" and the city is known by translations of this in other languages (Latin: Alba Regia, German: Stuhlweißenburg, Slovak: Stoličný Belehrad, Croatian: Stolni Biograd). The word szék (meaning „seat" as „throne") is related to its important role in the first centuries of the Kingdom of Hungary: székhely means a (royal) residence, center. In accordance of the obligation from the Doctrine of the Holy Crown, the first kings of Hungary were crowned and buried here. Székesfehérvár or ALBA REGIA, using its medieval name, was the cathedral seat of Saint Stephan I (Saint Stephan) and also a coronation and burial place of the Hungarian kings during the centuries of the Middle Ages.

K.K. IR 19 – FM Jozséf Alvinczy de Berberek – 3 battalions
Recruitment: Staff with the Brig. baron Franz Weidenfeld in Ofen. The 2 Depot comp. were at Stuhlweissenburg (Székesfehérvár), then in Ofen. The HQ was transferred with its 2 batt. (6 comp.) and the 3rd (4 comp.) at Agram (Brig. GM Franz von Marziani).

Esztergom (Gran)	Gran	
Moson	Magyaróvár	
Veszprém	Veszprém	
Komarom	Komorn	19
Györ	Raab	
Szolnók-Nagy Kun	Törökszentmiklós	
Fejér	Stuhlweissenburg	
Depot Kader	Stuhlweissenburg	
Commander oberst	Johann von Seethal (till Piave Battle, wounded)	chevalier Arnold Albeck
Oberstlieutenant	Franz Schmauser von Leidenfeld	chevalier Arnold Albeck
Majors	Friedrich Mumthe von Heldenfeld	Carl von Szent-Iványi Ignaz Trachberger Carl Rom baron Ignaz Splényi

before Aspern: entered the campaign with the IX Corps Gyulai, Div. Gorupp and Brig. Marziani, in the Inner Austria army of archduke John. It was in the first line at Sacile. On May 2, at Montebello and Olmo (near Vicenza) it lost 40 men dead, a very high number of wounded (no available datas), 60 missing and 180 prisoners, while covering the Austrian withdrawal from Venetian land. At that time the regiment was attached to FML

IR 55 prince Reuss Greitz   **IR 56 FM Wenzel Colloredo**   **IR 57 Joseph Colloredo**

IR 58 FZM Beaulieu   **IR 59 FML von Jordis**   **IR 60 FZM Graf Ignaz Gyulai**

▲ Austrian Infantry uniforms regiments nr. 55, 56, 57, 58, 59 & 60

Frimont rearguard, Brig. Marziani, deployed in line near the Alpone stream.

During the retreat, in May, it had several combats at the Piave and Tagliamento battles. The regiment opened the column in the difficult crossing of river Tagliamento river. On May 14 a bunch of 150 recruits of IR 19 defended Raibl pass in the Alps. In Carniola the regiment was attached to Div. Albert Gyulai, brig. GM count Colloredo, 1868 men in total, 500 of which were sick. The regiment (now 1st and 2nd batt.) were attached to brig. Longueville, Div. Frimont at Villach.

between Aspern and Wagram: it was with the Div. FML Jellačić, Brigade GM Kleinmayer acting as a reserve corps but being partially involved in the battles of Papa (3rd battalion under hauptmann Bartholémy, which had reached the regiment) and Raab (all three battalions and the Grenadiers in the center, Szabadhegy hills, with Jellačić). The losses were: at Papa 2 dead, many wounded and 44 prisoners; at Raab, 79 dead, 228 wounded, 171 prisoners and 216 missing. At Raab Albeck had officially the rank of colonel commander.

After Raab the regiment was reorganized in the fortress of Komorn (div. Colloredo brig. De Vaux).

at Wagram: the regiment reached the Pressburg Bridgehead in the former Defence-Corps Bianchi, Brig. De Vaux. It successively participated to the attempt to reinforce the Emperor at Wagram with the archduke's John Corps, bur, on July 11, it withdrew to Komorn, after the imperial order to abandon Pressburg.

The Hajducken Towns and Debrecen

In 1604-1606, István Bocskay, Lord of Bihar, led an insurrection against the Habsburg Emperor, whose army had recently occupied Transylvania and begun a reign of terror. The bulk of Bocskay's army was composed of serfs who had either fled from the war and the Habsburg drive toward Catholic conversion, or been discharged from the Imperial Army. These peasants were known as the "hajduk", a term associated in the Hungarian language with the cattle drovers of the Great Plains. As a reward for their service, Bocskay emancipated the hajduk from the jurisdiction of their lords, granted them land, and guaranteed them rights to own property and to personal freedom. The emancipated hajduk constituted a new "warrior estate" within Hungarian feudal society. Many of the settlements created at this time still bear the prefix Hajdú such as Hajdúbagos, Hajdúböszörmény, Hajdú-dorog, Hajdúhadház, Hajdúnánás, Hajdúsámson, Hajdúszoboszló, Hajdúszovát, Hajdúvid etc., and the whole area is called Hajdúság (Land of the Hajduk).

Debrecen

Is now the second largest city in Hungary after Budapest. The " biggest village in Europe ", as the town was still described by an English traveller at the end of the 18th century, started to assume a more urban appearance in her outlook, too. After the largest fire of her history in 1802 Debrecen rose again from its ashes with the vitality of the phoenix, the symbol bird of the town. Near Debrecen there is the famous hungarian Puszta.

Puszta or Hortobágy ranges from the edge of the Hajdúság to the Tisza River; it is a saliferous, grassy desert of 115 km² home of the hungarians horses farms. Hortobágy is more renowned for its herdsmen than for its natural beauty. The herdsmen are the symbol of the 'puszta', freedom and the natural way of life.

K.K. IR 39 –FML baron Peter Duka – 3 battalions

Recruitment: 2 Depot comp. at Debrecen in the Brig. Elsnitz (Kaschau) under Alvinczy. Staff was at Sandec (Galicia), and then at Ofen (Budapest). The regiment moved to Mistelbach (Austria) under brig, GM Federico Bianchi.

Hajducken Städte	Debrecen	
Bihar North	Nagyvárad	39
Szatmár	Szatmárnémeti	
Szabolcs	Nyíregyháza	
	Debrecen	
Commander oberst	baron Emerich Bakonyi	baron Carl Rosenfeld at Aspern. Johann Windrich (interim) Maj. Michael Schuller after Wagram
Oberstlieutenant	baron Carl Rosenfeld	Johann Windrich
Majors	Johann Windrich	Michael Schuller
	Johann Habinay	Gabor Szilásyi

before Aspern: entered Bavaria with the V Corps archduke Louis, Division FML prince Henry XV Reuss-Plauen, Brig. GM baron Federico Bianchi. At Abensberg the brigade was sent ahead to support the battered brig. Thierry, without success. During the retreat, on April 21, the regiment acted as rearguard at Seelingthal (Landshut bridges); its 3rd batt. was in the Detachment colonel baron Emerich de Bakonyi, regiment's colonel commander. On April 22 it came under the united Corps of FML Hiller. It fought at Neumarkt (made a sturdy defence together with the IR 14 Klebek), Efferding (12 dead and 20 men missing) and Ebelsberg (Brig. Bianchi) being now definitively part of the VI Corps baron Hiller, Div. FML Friedrich von Kottulinsky. During the first part of the campaign the regiment lost: 157 men dead, 244 wounded and 536 missing, mainly prisoners. Also the 3rd battalion of the Dukas gave their men to replemish the other two battered battalions (like the twin IR 60).

at Aspern: during the days preceding the battle, the regiment had a combat at Stammersdorf and lost its colonel, severely wounded in a knee.

In the battle it was in the 1st Column (VI Corps Hiller) in the Brig. Bianchi (Div. von Kottulinsky under command of GM Hohenfeld), supporting also the Avant-garde Brig. Nordmann and being part of it during the attack against Aspern (extreme right wing of the 1st column). Its two battalion lost: 48 men dead, 181 wounded, 65 missing. The regiment two battalions together now counted around 773 men only.

On May 25, FML Klenau took command of the VI Corps and Oberstlieutenant Windrich became the interim commander.

between Aspern and Wagram: on May 28 the Brig. Bianchi was detached to the Pressburg defence. On June 23 archduke John took command at Pressburg and Bianchi returned to the VI Corps. On July 4 the regiment received the 3rd battalion from Prossnitz (hauptmann Grubits). Now the regiment had 1353 men with the 1st battalion led by major Habinay and the 2nd by hauptmann Del Rio.

at Wagram: was with the VI Corps, Div. Hohenfeld, Brig. Bianchi and retreated after two days of battle. It lost 156 men dead, 263 wounded many of which deceased or were taken prisoners, 45 missing.

after Wagram: the regiment retreated through Korneuburg where it had a combat (1 dead and 33 wounded), and joined the brigade at Hollabrunn (combat of Schöngraben with 1 man dead and 12 wounded). It did not fight at Znaim and remained with only 758 men.

K.K. IR 37– FML baron Carl Philipp Weidenfeld – 3 battalions

Recruitment: 2 Depot comp. Brig. baron Lippe in Temesvár under Alvinczy (Nagyvárad).

Csongrád	Szeged	
Békés	Békéscsaba	
Csanád	Makó	37
Bihar South	Bélenyes	
Depot Kader	Grosswardein - Nagyvárad	
Commander oberst	Benedikt Reichlin von Meldegg	
Oberstlieutenant	Maximilian Pulszky von Cséfalva	
Majors	Sigismund Szinkovics	
	Johann Limberger	

before Aspern: at Cracow with Brig. Pflacher, Div. Dinnersberg then again in Brig. Pflacher, Div. Mondet, VII Korps archduke Ferdinand in Poland with 2072 men. During the battle of Raszyn it acted as support unit losing 9 men prisoners and 3 missing, while its 1st battalion had 22 wounded and 4 dead. On April 23 it entered Warsaw with the Corps. GM Trautenberg had the place command.

- between Aspern and Wagram: one battalion was with the colonel Schmelzern detachment (June 5) in the probe attack at Sandomierz. It supported the combat at Gorzyce (June 12) entering the village during the afternoon. There it lost: 60 men dead, 160 wounded and 50 prisoners. The 1st battalion (Szinkovics) participated in the attack against Sandomierz (June 14) (Brig. Geringer). After the second day of the combats it lost 30 men dead, 180 wounded, 29 prisoners and 18 missing. One battalion remained at Sandomierz as garrison after the capitulation (June 16). On June 30 the regiment had 121 men detached, 1137 ill, 121 unfit and 2525 men fit to duty at the Opatów camp (Brig. Pflacher, Div. Schauroth).

- at Wagram: in July the regiment retreated through Bochnia till Kety and there got the armistice news.

The Capital City's regiment

Budapest (became a single city occupying both banks of the river Danube with a unification only on 17 November 1873 of right (west)-bank Buda and Óbuda with left east-bank Pest). So, in that times, there were three different towns.

Buda (German: **Ofen**) was the western part of the current Hungarian capital on the west bank of the Danube. The name Buda takes its name from the name of Bleda, the Hun ruler, whose name is also Buda in Hungarian. The Roman name for Buda was Aquincum (waterish - "aqua" means "water" in Latin.). Buda was declared a free royal town in 1703, and became the Hungarian capital again in 1784, after Pressburg.

Óbuda has a name which means Old Buda in Hungarian (in German, **Alt-Ofen**). Óbuda's centre is Fő tér (Main Square).

Pest is the eastern, mostly flat part of Budapest, comprising about two thirds of Budapest's territory. It is divided from Buda, the other part of Budapest, by the Danube River. Pest was a separate independent city, references to which appear in writings dating back to 1148. In earlier centuries there were ancient Celtic and Roman settlements there. Pest became an important economic center during 11th–13th centuries. It was destroyed in the 1241 Mongol invasion of Hungary but rebuilt once again soon thereafter.

K.K. IR 32– FZM baron Nikolaus Esterházy de Galantha – 3 battalions
Recruitment: 2 Depot comp. Brig. Szörenyi in Pest under Alvinczy. moved from Pest to Hainburg (Austria) under brig, Carl Friedrich von Riese, Div. FML Friedrich von Kottulinsky, VI Corps archduke Louis.

Pest-Pilis	Pest	
Pest-Solt	Kiskőrös	
Árva	Alsókubin	
Liptó (Liptau)	Rózsahegy	32
Heves	Eger	
Jász-Nagy-Kun (Jazigien)	Jászberényi	
Nógrád (Neograd)	Losonc	
Depot Kader	Peterwardein, Pest	
Commander oberst	baron Ludwig Eckhardt	after Wagram – oberst Anton von Hirsch
Oberstlieutenant	Anton von Hirsch	
Majors	Pasquale D'Assante	Paul Lanyi
	Franz von Tittus	Petar von Radivojevich

before Aspern: it reached the Corps definitively assigned to the Brig. Ettinghausen Div. Jellachich, VI Corps. On April 16 the regiment marched toward Munich, where stood one battalion, whilst the other two went on the Isar banks. It did not take part to the bavarian battles and withdrew from Munich to the Salzach creek on April 24. On 29th it defended the Laufen bridge. The 2nd battalion fought at Salzburg where it lost: 15 dead, 22 wounded, 31 missing and 276 made prisoners. On May 3 two companies defended the Abtenau pass.
- between Aspern and Wagram: on May 25 the regiment was at Mautern. There the Division was engaged by the Eugène Behouarnais' army at St.Michael and the regiment was in the first line. It lost 32 dead, 104 wounded, 1122 prisoners with Oberstlieutenant von Hirsch, 35 missing. The remnants were some companies and the 1st batt. led by major D'Assante. They tried to defend the Leoben's bridge but they were overcome losing again 16 men dead, 6 wounded, 406 prisoners and 16 missing. Before the Raab battle it received 400 recruits from Pest (mainly for the 2nd batt.). It was in the Brig. Eckhardt, Div. Jellachich (Inner Austria Army), the 2nd batt. in reserve on the Martinsberg with major Tittus, the 1st and 3rd along the Panzia creek banks. After the battle they had 21 dead, 46 wounded, 87 missing, 115 prisoners.
Then the regiment marched toward the Pressburg fortress but …
- at Wagram: on July 5 it received orders to reach the Wagram's battlefield. Too late to be of some support.

WESTERN HUNGARY

Ergänzungsbezirks Kommando		Werb-bezirk	R army	other
HQ Recruitment District	**hungarian**	**recruitment area (Kreis)**	**IR**	
		Tolna		
Fünfkirchen	Pécs	Baranya	52	Somogyi (Sümegh) cavalry. Insurr. 8th batt. (Somogyi)
Kopisch	Kaposvár	Somogyi		
Gross-Kanisza	Nagykanisza	Zala		Insurr. 8th batt. Zala cavalry
Steinamanger	Szombathely	Vás (Eisenburg)	48	Insurr. 5th Eisenburg I batt. Eisenburg II batt. Zala cavalry Eisenburg cavalry
Ödenburg	Sopron	Sopron - Moson		Insurr. 6th Eisenburg II batt. Ödenburg cavalry

K.K. IR 52– FML Erzherzog Franz Carl – 3 battalions

Recruitment: 2 Depot comp. at Pecs (Fünfkirchen), Brig. baron Carl Weidenfeld (Ofen) under Alvinczy. The Staff at Görz (Gorizia) under brig. GM Anton von Gajoli (Klagenfurt), Div. FML marquis Friedrich von Bellegarde, IX Corps (Ban Ignaz Gyulai), army of Inner Austria.

Baranya	Pécs	52
Bács-Bodrog	Szabadka - Maria Theresiopel Zombor	
Tolna	Szekszárd	
Somogy	Kaposvár	
Depot Kader	Fünfkirchen (Pecs)	Görz (Gorizia) Agram (Zagreb)
2nd Owner	FML Mathias Rukavina von Bonyograd	
Commander oberst	Andreas von Gyurkovich	baron Gabriel Collenbach (after Wagram)
Oberstlieutenant	baron Gabriel von Collenbach	
Majors	Michail Ogrisovich	
	Franz von Csorich	Paul Toperczer

before Aspern: attached to Brig. Marziani, Div. Görupp, IX Corps. Advanced in Italy. The 1st battalion was in the Detachment Oberstlieutenant Volkmann (advance from Raibl till Venzone – April 11). The battalion lost at Venzone: 4 dead, 63 wounded, 32 prisoners and 30 missing men. Then it was sent to Osoppo in order to make a road blockade, remaining there till April 19. The 2nd battalion came from Gorizia with the Brig. GM Gavassini restoring and crossing the Isonzo bridge. The colonel commander Gyurkovich had order to form a detachment to cover the army flank; in it was the 2nd battalion. They went to Latisana on Aprl 15 (time of Sacile battle) and then drove towards north (Conegliano) in order to cut off the fremch units retreating from Sacile.

The 3rd batt. was attached to the avant-garde of the VIII Corps, Brig. GM von Wetzel, Div. Frimont and was at Pordenone (April 14). Advanced till Porcia it took part at the Sacile engagement. The 3rd batt. lost 20 dead, 70 wounded, 29 missing.

Detachment Gyurkovich was then sent to Venice from Treviso with the 2nd and 3rd batt. On April 30 they attacked Marghera bridgehead (called Malghera by austrians) and seized it (burnt it) after an hard combat. The 1st battalion had left Osoppo, having sent two detachments to the Malborghet and Predil forts, and had reached the main army. On April 29-30 they fought at Soave, with the Brig. Schmidt.

After the retreat orders, the regiment was attached to the rearguard division Frimont, but the Brig. Schmidt was sent to Bassano in order to link with the troops in Tirol, while Gyurkovics was recalled at Treviso, were they had an engagement on May 5. There the regiment lost: 22 dead, 50 wounded and 97 prisoners.

The regiment reunited at the Piave with all its three battalions in the rearguard division Frimont, under GM Splényi; the 1st batt. (Toperczer) at Vidor, the 2nd batt. (Ogrisovich) at Ponte di Piave and the 3rd batt. (Collenbach) at the Ponte della Priula bridge. From May 7 till 9 they fought at the Piave. The french breakthrough against the austrian Piave Cordon isolated the 1st and 2nd batt. from the main army. The 2nd batt. recovered to Portogruaro, while the 1st withdrew northwards through Ceneda and the Higher Piave valley. It was then attached to the Tirol's Corps Chasteler, brig. Fenner, at Innichen (on May 15 it had only 472 men under Toperczer). The 3rd batt. remained with the Inner Austria army in the Brig. GM Kálnássy, which formally would have had also the 2nd batt. It withdrew from Portogruaro till Palmanova, where it met the Zach Detachment and, with it, continued till Gorizia and the Isonzo, fighting at Sagrado with its 798 men. The retreat continued till Prewald (near Postojna) were the 2nd batt. found GM Munkácsy brigade , deploying with them behind some field fortifications.

On May 17 the 3rd batt. was engaged at Loitsch with its Kálnássy brigade. A division of the battalion was captured in the mountains together with its chief oberstlieutenant Collenbach, in total 396 men. At the same time the 2nd batt. was attacked at Prewald. They defended the fortification for 4 days (like a fort Alamo!) but finally they fell prisoners. On May 21 the remaining 4 companies (3rd batt.) withdrew till Neufstadtl.

- between Aspern and Wagram: in the meanwhile Chasteler with the 1st battalion withdrew in Carniola coming from the East Tirol. On June 6 they came in Klagenfurt (Carinthia). There was a combat in which the battalion lost 5 men dead and 137 prisoners. During the following retreat towards Croatia the 1st battalion met the rests of the 3rd in the rearguard Brig. Splényi. Finally on June 15 they reached Warasdin in Croatia with the IX Corps. At the Raab batle fought the Depot division of IR 52 in the Brigade Oberst Pétschy, Division FZM Davidovich while at the Graz battle (June 26) the 3rd batt. followed the Banus Gyulai (Div. Knezevich, Brig Kálnássy) and fought as support unit losing other 90 men. After the battle and after the advance of the French toward Wagram, the Banus returned at Graz, seizing the town on July 3. There thay had the communication of the armistice.

K.K. IR 48– FML baron Philipp Vukassovich – 3 battalions
Recruitment: 2 Depot comp. Brig. Daniel in Ödenburg under Alvinczy. Staff with Pflacher in Komarom, under Div. Dedovich, station Bátorkész.

Vas (Eisenburg)	Szombathely	
Zala	Zalaegerszeg	48
Sopron	Ödenburg	
Depot Kader	Steinamanger (Szombathely)	HQ Ofen – Leoben (Styria)
Commander oberst	baron Franz Ludwig Gabelkoven	baron Johann Rechemberg (from May)
Oberstlieutenant	baron Franz Ludwig Gabelkoven	
Majors	Wilhelm Dressery	
	Ferenc Papp de Vizahna	Joseph Klopstein

before Aspern: it began the campaign at Radom in the VII Corps avant-garde Brig. Anton von Mohr. On April 19 at Raszyn they were under the command of FML Schauroth. The regiment was ordered to seize the village of Falenty. It lost 24 dead, 201 wounded, 28 missing and 7 prisoners. The bravery of the Vukassovich regiment granted to the provisional commander Gabelkoven the rank of colonel. On April 21 the Brig. Mohr was sent south of Warsaw, on the left Vistula bank, at Gora. On April 25 it was attacked at Grochow (2 dead, 4 wounded and 31 prisoners).

In the meanwhile the Gora's bridgehead was lost (May 3). Brigade Mohr was directed toward Thorn. On May 15 they attacked the Thorn fortress with success. The losses were not heavy (8 dead and 58 wounded) but the Austrians lost the VII Corps General Staff Chief, colonel Brusch von Neuberg (former regiment's commander at Caldiero in 1805). The Poles' threat against Sandomierz forced archduke Ferdinand to retreat to rescue the Galician border. FML von Mondet was left back at Warsaw with the brigades Mohr and Civalart. In May the regiment had its new commander, Oberst baron von Rechemberg.

▲ Imperial grenadiers in 1805. Ottenfeld artwork

- between Aspern and Wagram: on June 1-2 they abandoned Warsaw. On June 9 they left Radom and were attacked, during the night, at Jedlinsko (June 9). Two days later the regiment fought again in the same location. Mondet was forced to leave Radom and detached the 1st and 2nd batt. IR 48 at Zarnowiec, while the 3rd, led by colonel Gabelkoven, drove to Pinkow, in order to link with the Div. Schauroth. The regiment fought at Zarnowiec on July 10, losing 26 dead, 68 wounded, 28 prisoners and 58 missing. On July 13 they reached Cracow where they got in touch with the 3rd battalion, but the day after they left the city. In August they camped at Myslenice and then Wadowice, under Brig. Civalart, and there they received the ceasefire orders. There they learnt also that the Owner of the regiment, baron Josef Phillip Vukassovich had found his death at Wagram.

The Reserve Depot division (874 men under hauptmann Jacope) defended the town of Raab during the June's battle in the FZM Davidovich Division, Brigade Oberst Pétschy. When Raab surrendered 767 men were made prisoners.Finally, in November, the regiment had his new Owner: baron Josef Simbschen.

ORGANIZATION OF THE HUNGARIAN TERRITORIAL DEFENCE

FM baron Jozséf ALVINCZY de Borberek (mispelled as Alvintzy, Allvintzi)

born: 1 February 1735, Alvinc (today Vinţu de Jos in Romania). dead: 25 September 1810, Ofen
Owner of IR19. Chief of the Corpskommando Ungarn then Commandant of the Reserve Truppen in Hungary. He will die on 1810, an year after the "disaster".

Freiherr Joseph Alvinczy de Borberek (or József Alvinczi Borbereky in the Hungarian spelling) was a Field-Marshal and Grand Cross of the Order of Maria Theresa. An ethnic Hungarian, he was born in Transylvania, which is now part of Romania, at a place now called Vintu de Jos. Lord of the estate in Vurpǎr (Burgberg-Walbersdorf), from which came "de Borberek" (from Burgberg). Alvinczy was the last of his family.

He became a soldier at the age of 15. He fought in the Seven Years War as a captain of grenadiers. He later became Colonel of IR 19, and became its "Inhaber" in 1786. He also fought in the War of the Bavarian Succession. He was the future Emperor Francis' military tutor, and instructed him in tactics. Commanded a division under Loudon during the Turkish wars. In 1790 he attacked Liège to bring it to obey its bishop. During the Revolutionary Wars he served in the Netherlands from 1792-4. He was at Neerwinden, where he won the Cross of Commander of the Maria Theresia Order. At Charleroi he won the Grand Cross of the Order. In 1795 he commanded on the Upper Rhine. In 1796 he took over command of the army in the Tyrol. He fought Bonaparte at Arcole on 15-17 November 1796. He also commanded at Rivoli, 14 January 97. Despite his defeat at Rivoli he was given the position of military governor of Hungary. He was promoted Feldmarschall in 1808.

ORGANIZATION 1809

The General Commando in Hungary (Croatia/Slavonia and Banat had own higher commands), subordinated to the Vienna's Hofkriegsrat, divided the territory into Brigade-areas, each led by a Generalmajor. They were generally formed by 2 infantry regiments, and were also regrouped into divisions led by a FML.

The General Headquarters were at Ofen (Buda), near the political hearth of Hungary (ungarischen Statthaltereirat), which helped in suggesting the military departments and provided to their supplies. The Militär Departement directed the army matters, the Ökonomie Departement directed the supplies partitions, with the Magazin-und Verpflegungswesen. There were also a Departement for the Justizwesens, with a special court called **Judicium delegatum militare mixtum**, which made trials, merging civilians and military personnel, under the supervision of the General commander. The Ökonomie Departement (administrative) had an Ober and a Feld Commissariate, which were divided among the land districts (Bezirke).

This were the rulers of 1809 Hungary (note the few or not-existing hungarian names among them)

Hungary General Commander at Ofen:
FM baron Jozséf Alvinczy (in 1810 with Ad Latus: GdK baron Michael Kienmayer)

Militär-Departement (abolished after the 1809 defeat):
Referent: General-Command Adjutant Oberstleutnant Radoshevich (IR Splenyi)
Ad latus: Rittmeister Hayden (Lothringen Cuirassiers)

Politisches Departement (same in 1810)
Referent: Hofkriegs-Secretaire Jüngling
Ad latus: Feldkriegs-Concipist Fastenberger

Ökonomisches Departement
Referent: Oberkriegs-Commissaire Leopold Mayer (Oeltl in 1810)
Ad latus: Feldkriegs-Commissaire Oeltl (Mottini in 1810)
Oberkriegs-Commissaires in the provinces:
Pressburg (Eipperg), Ödenburg (Meixner), Debrecen (Wachter), Kaschau (Männer), Fünfkirchen (Buchholz), Neusohl (Reinisch).
Feldkriegs-Commissaries of the provinces (by the Respicierung):
Ofen (Mottini, promoted in 1810), Pest (Baumgartner), Pressburg (Kiebast), Alt Ofen (Pachmann), Tyrnau (Weeber), Kaschau (Kuderna), Grosswardein (Richtenburg), Kaschau (Bargher), Temesvar (Pöltinger), Tyrnau (Schlossern), Ofen (Leitnitzgruber), Agram (Gerstl), Mezöhehyes (Kleber), Fünfkirchen (Jaswitz), Szombor (Korren).
Verpflegs-Departement
Referente:

Oberverpflegsverwalter Preitlochner
Oberverpflegsverwalter Hannold (Pogatschnigg and Gunsberg in 1810)

Justiz Departement (same in 1810)
Referent: General-Auditor-Lieutenant Lang
Ad latus: Stabs-auditor major Burian

Judicium Delegatum Militare
Präsident: FM Joszéf Alvinczy
Referent: General-auditor-lieutenant Lang
(in 1810 also Stabs-auditor major Burian)

Kriegs Cassa in Ofen (obviously it disappeared in 1810)
Cassa-Verwalter: Nuspicker
Controlor: Molitor

Hungary had also a circle of defensive fortresses, some of which were renowned since the past centuries (Peterwardein, Esseg and Temesvár); other fortress were in the inner lands, like Raab, but expecially the strong Komorn; they were hardly reinforced in 1809. The works were directed by the Festung-Commando in Ofen, Arad and Munkács.   In 1809 the mobilization moved away from Hungary almost all the troops. Any former military organization left place to another territorial subdivision. In the lands of Magyars remained only residential brigades under provisional division and brigade commanders like the actual closest "aides" of FM Alvinczy: FML baron Anton von Ellsnitz (Pest division) and FML baron Carl von Weidenfeld (Ofen division).
These residential brigades were formed by the depot companies and squadrons of the resident regiments. Note also that, while many Hussars regiments had their depots in Galicia, many other "german" cavalry had their own in Hungary (probably for the easy facilities when remounts were needed, in a land rich of horses).
The War of 1809 forced the Emperor to call to arms the Insurrectio. This special hungarian sort of Landwehr was organized in four Corps: the left Danube bank Corps, the right Danube bank Corps, the left Theiss (Tisza) Corps and the right Theiss Corps. Each Insurrectio Corps had its commander, some having been former divisional commander in Hungary, some being old "glories" of the austrian generalship. (see after: Insurrectio)

MOBILIZATION 1809
On Januar 8 this was the situation in Hungary: (resident brigades remained in Hungary after war beginning, some with the same area commanders)

OFEN – Divisionkommando FML barol Carl Philipp von Weidenfeld
resident brigades:
STUHLWEISSENBURG –K.K. IR 19 Alvinczy – 2 Depot companies
FÜNFKIRCHEN –K.K. IR 52 Erz. Franz Carl – 2 Depot companies
ESSEG (Croatia) –K.K. IR 53 Johann Jellacich - – 2 Depot companies
BROD and GRADISKA (Slavonia) – 2nd Garnison bataillon

PEST – Brigadekommando GM baron Andreas von Szörényi
OFEN -K.K. IR 31 Benjovszky (I and II batt. with 6 comp. – III batt. with 4 comp.) and 1 grenadier division
PEST –K.K. IR 51 Splényi (I and II batt. with 6 comp. – III batt. with 4 comp.) and 1 grenadier division
resident brigades:
PEST –K.K. IR 32 Esterházy – 2 Depot companies
PEST and OFEN – Grenzregiment Warasdiner Kreuzer – III battalion.
KOMORN fortress - Grenzregiment Warasdiner Sankt Georger – III battalion.

ERLAU – Brigadekommando GM Constantin von Ettingshausen
then GM and Brig. comm., Div. Jellachich, VI Corps
ERLAU -K.K. IR 58 Beaulieu 2 batt. (6 comp.) and 1 grenadier division

OFEN – Artilleriebrigade Kommando FML Josef von Vogelhuber
K.K. 3rd artillerie regiment Rouvroy – 2 artill.-techn. companies
K.K. 4th artillerie regiment Unterberger – 6 artill.-techn. companies
Miners – 2 companies and Sappers 1 company (on duty of fortresses build-up)
OFEN - Feldzeugamt Filiale

PEST – Divisionkommando FML barol Anton von Elsnitz
KASCHAU - resident brigade:
KASCHAU –K.K. IR 34 Davidovich - – 2 Depot companies
DEBRECEN -K.K. IR 39 Duka – 2 Depot companies
EPERJES –K.K. IR 60 Gyulai – 2 Depot companies
VESZPRÉM – Brigadekommando GM baron Josef Ferdinand Hager (Haager) von Altensteig
future commander of the Wolfskehl Dragoons brigade. (prisoner during the campaign)
KESZTHELY – K.K. 2nd Dragoner Hohenlohe – 6 sqns.
MOÓR – K.K. 5th Dragoner Savoyen – 6 sqns.
GYÖNGYŐS – Brigadekommando GM Andreas von Schneller
future commander of brigade (cuirassiers) in Div. St.Julien, III Corps, then II Res. Corps (cavalry). FML and
division commander after Wagram.
NAGYPATAK- K.K. 1st Cuirassiers Kaiser Franz – 6 sqns.
GYÖNGYŐS – K.K. 6th Cuirassiers Gottesheim – 6 sqns.

PRESSBURG – I Divisionkommando FML Fürst Ludwig Hohenlohe-Waldenburg-Bartenstein
Owner IR 26 –IV Corps division commander

TURNAU - Brigadekommando GM baron Leopold von Trauttenberg
TRENCSÉN -K.K. IR 24 Strauch 2 batt. (6 comp.) and 1 grenadier division
PRESSBURG -K.K. IR 46 Chasteler 2 batt. (6 comp.) and 1 grenadier division
TURNAU -K.K. IR 63 Baillet-Latour 2 batt. (6 comp.) and 1 grenadier division

PRESSBURG – II (cavalry) Divisionkommando FML baron Emmanuel von Schustekh
V Corps division commander

PRESSBURG - Brigadekommando GM baron Carl von Stutterheim
NAGYTAPOLCSÁN – K.K. 10th Hussars Stipsicz – 8 sqns.
St.GEORGEN – K.K. 4th Chevaulégers Vincent – 8 sqns.
KITTSEE - Brigadekommando GM baron Christian Wolfskehl von Reichenberg
Future division commander IX Corps.
SOMMEREIN – K.K. 4th Cuirassiers Kronprinz Ferdinand – 6 sqns.
KITTSEE – K.K. 8th Cuirassiers Hohenzollern – 6 sqns.
PRESSBURG Resident brigade GM Timothäus de Kérékes (sent to Brünn in January)
GROSS-SCHÜTZEN –K.K. Kaiser Hussars - 1 Depot squadron
EYBEL –K.K. Lothringen Cuirassiers – 1 Depot squadron
SKALITZ – K.K. Sommariva cuirassiers- – 2 Depot squadrons
SZENITZ – K.K. Hessen-Homburg Hussars - 1 Depot squadron
TAPOLCSÁN – K.K. Stipsicz Hussars - 1 Depot squadron
StGEORGEN – K.K. Vincent Chevaulégers - 1 Depot squadron
PRESSBURG - K.K. IR 2 Hiller – 2 Depot companies
ALTSOHL - K.K. IR 33 Sztáray – 2 Depot companies

ÖDENBURG – (Cavalry) Divisionskommando FML baron Michael von Kienmayer
Future commander of the 2nd Reserve Corps (Main Army).

ÖDENBURG - Brigadekommando GM Heinrich Bersina von Siegenthal
ÖDENBURG – K.K. 3rd Cuirassiers Herzog Albert – 6 sqns.
St. MARGARETHEN – K.K. 2nd Cuirassiers Erz. Franz – 6 sqns.
GÜNS - Brigadekommando GM Josef von Clary
GÜNS – K.K. 4th Dragoons Levenehr – 6 sqns.
SÁRVÁR – K.K. 3rd Dragoons Württemberg – 6 sqns.
ÖDENBURG – Resident Brigade GM Ludwig von Daniel (see Transylvania)
GÜNS – K.K. Kaiser Cuirassiers – 1 Depot squadron
GENSDORF – K.K. Savoyen Dragoner - 1 Depot squadron
TURGYL – K.K. Hohenlohe Dragoner - 1 Depot squadron
PETLAK – K.K. Hohenzollern Chevaulégers - 1 Depot squadron

KÖRMEND – K.K. Ott Hussars - 1 Depot squadron
KANISZA – K.K. Erz. Josef Hussars - 1 Depot squadron
HECKENMARKT – K.K. Liechtenstein Hussars - 1 Depot squadron
GOLS – K.K. Kienmayer Hussars - 1 Depot squadron
SARVÁR – K.K. Gottesheim Cuirassiers - 1 Depot squadron
STEINAMANGER – K.K. IR 48 Vukassovich - 2 Depot companies

FESTUNGPLATZ KOMAROM-KOMORN – Divisionkommando FML Josef von Dedovich

KOMORN- I Brigadekommando GM baron Franz Pflacher
future brigade comm. in Div. Denneberg VII Corps.
KOMORN -K.K. IR 37 Weidenfeld (I and II batt. with 6 comp. – III batt. with 4 comp.) and 1 grenadier division
BÁTORKÉSZ -K.K. IR 48 Vukassovich (I and II batt. with 6 comp. – III batt. with 4 comp.) and 1 grenadier division

KOMORN- II Brigadekommando GM baron Constantin d'Aspre
Future FML and Division commander in the Reserve Corps (grenadiers).
TÓVÁROS -K.K. IR 44 Bellegarde 2 batt. (6 comp.) and 1 grenadier division
LEOPOLDSTADT (Újvároska) K.K. Feldzeugamt klein Post

FÜNFKIRCHEN – Divisionskommando FML Franz Görupp von Besanez

TEMESVÁR -K.K. IR 62 Franz Jellacich (I and II batt. with 6 comp. – III batt. with 4 comp.) and 1 grenadier division
ESSEG – K.K. Feldzeugamt Filiale (Peterwardeiner)

FÜNFKIRCHEN - Brigadekommando GM Johann Frimont von Palota

PÉCSVÁRAD – K.K. 2nd Chevaulégers Hohenzollern – 8 sqns.
ESSEG – K.K. 5th Hussars Ott – 8 sqns.
BROD – 2nd Garnison batt. (6 comp.)

AGRAM – Brigadekommando GM Franz von Marziani

FIUME – 3rd Garnison batt. (6 comp.)
AGRAM - K.K. IR 19 Alvinczy (I and II batt. with 6 comp. – III batt. with 4 comp.) and 1 grenadier division
ZENGG – 4th Garnison batt. (6 comp.)

NEUSATZ – Brigadekommando GM Ludwig von Daniel sent to Ödenburg in January

ESSEG - K.K. IR 53 Johann Jellacich (I and II batt. with 6 comp. – III batt. with 4 comp.) and 1 grenadier division
NEUSATZ – K.K. 2nd Hussars Erzherzog Josef – 8 sqns.

NOTES:

1   In Balkan folkloric tradition, the hajduk (hajduci or haiduci in the plural) is a romanticised hero figure who steals from, and leads his fighters into battle against, the Ottoman oppressors. They are comparable to the English legend of Robin Hood and his merry men, who stole from the rich (which in the case of the "hajduci" happened to be also foreign occupants) and gave to the poor, while participating in a small guerrilla war against an unjust authority. **Hajdú**, formerly known as **Hajdúság**, is the name of a historic administrative county (comitatus-vármegye) of the Kingdom of Hungary.
2   German name of the twin town Buda (Óbuda). Pest-Ofen = Budapest.
3   Weissenbacher, Victor: Geschichte des k. u. k. Infanterie-Regimentes Nr. 19 Erzherzog Franz Ferdinand von der Errichtung 1734 bis 1896. Wien: 1896.
4   Ordered to other tasks before the beginning of the campaign.
5   Mayer, Ferdinand: Geschichte des k. und k. Infanterie-Regimentes Nr. 39 gegenwärtig Großfürst Alexis von Rußland von seiner Errichtung 1756 bis Ende 1875. Wien: 1875.
6   Finke, Edmund: (Geschichte des Infanterie-Regimentes Nr. 37) Wien: 18?
7   Seeliger, E.: Geschichte des k. u. k. Infanterie-Regimentes Nr. 32, für immerwährende Zeiten Kaisern und Königin Maria Theresia, von seiner Errichtung 1741 bis 1900. Budapest: 1900.
8   Geschichte des k. und k. 52. Linien-Infanterie-Regiments Erzherzog Franz Carl. Wien: 1871.
9   GM Munkácsy brigade (under FML Zach Corps) was formed by: 800 "green" recruits, 286 men of the Neustädt Landwehr, 3rd Garrison battalion (major baron Cazan), 430 men, a Cordon company of Braunitz and another Cordon unit, 236 men, 63 artillerymen and handlanger, 15 pioneers and 25 various troopers. The 2nd batt. IR 52 had 798 soldiers.
10   Hold, Alexander: Geschichte des k. k. 48. Linien-Infanterie-Regiments von seiner Errichtung im Jahre 1798 an.Wien: 1875. From November 1809 the regiment's Owner will be baron Joseph Simbschen.

THE AUSTRIAN MILITÄR GRENZE REGULAR HUNGARIAN MILITARY BORDER REGIMENTS

The MILITARY BORDER

From the Duchy of Bukowina (East) till the italian frontiers of Friuli (Küstenland) Austria had a group of militarized territories, which had the task to defend its borders mainly against the Turks. These lands, while being part of the geographical hungarian regions, were autonomous regions, not part of the hungarian Crown.

These Grenze (Gränze or Confinien) comprised lands of rumanian peoples (Walakians), hungarian (Széklers), german (Banat), serbian – slovenian and croatian (Vojna Granica). The Border consisted of Croatian (from 1578), slavonian (from 1702), german and hungarian Banat (from 1742) and Transylvanian (from 1764) military frontier. The military Border stood under own military administration for a whole area of 33.422 sq. kms (1.750 km in length). It was settled with free farmers (from Serbia, Croatia, Romania) who were, however, militarily ruled. The borderlands remained a military possession, however, territory was largely tax-free (Steuerfrei). In 1807 the border areas were divided in 4 Generalate and had parallel regular army commands for the nearby lands.

THE MILITÄR-GRENZE FROM 1800 TILL 1810

Uncomfortable conditions in the administration led to a drastic reorganization, by regulation of Nov. 1, 1800. Till 1800 the Leader had been the regimental commander (Leiter), while the Area Commander was merely a military employee or an administration chief. From 1800 also the administration was subordinated to the regimental commander. All became again an absolute dominion of the armed forces.

In 1807 was remitted a new "Grundgesetz" (basic law) for the military border and one of the most important regulations concerned the treatment of the Corps. Fundamentally the new regulation did not change so much the former rules. The Grenzers (military Border troopers) got countryland as a loan. This meant actually the military authority did not have more arbitrarily control over troops and lands, in contrast to early rules.

The long Cordon was divided in 17 regimental areas, one Székler Hussar district and one Danube boatmen district (the Czajkisten).

The Carlstädter Generalat was the closest to the Adriatic coasts and had four regiments. The Banal Gränzbezirk had two regimental areas, the Warasdiner Generalat had two regiments, the General Commando in Slawonien had three regiments, the General Commando of the Temes Banat had two regiments and the General Commando of Siebenbürgen had five regiments (2 Széklers, 2 Valachians and 1 Székler hussars). All these general Commandos were subordinated to the Hofkriegsrat in Vienna. The former separate military authorities, Militär Appellations Behörden of Agram, Peterwardein and Hermannstadt, from September 1, 1810, were merged into a one Militär Appellations Behörde in Peterwardein, which commanded also the boatmen Czajkisten (town of Titel) recruited in a territory of 5 companies (Kapitanate), around 19463 inhabitants.

Military border dwellers were spread in the countryland and were catalogued as having various degree of ground assignments, borrowing from regiment the property of cultivable terrain. Only men received land, so there were also, probably, the most "active" widows of the Empire; in effect they could mantain the property for two years, during which period they had to marry another man fit for service (Dienstfahig), or they risked the confiscation, with the forced restitution of the loan. So the properties were not heritables, if there were no heirs (they inherited the loan, not the lands), they also were not to be sold away, other than in special occurrences, whenever other Grenzers could buy them.

The Militär Grenze (without Siebenbürgen) had 777.406 inhabitants in 1807. After 1809 Austria did lose about 288.562 men (under French rule) . Counting one sixth of men (males) as fit for military Duty, the austrian Empire could have about 80.000 men ready for the army, even having lost six of its former regiments.

It was a respectable army , which did not cost anything in peacetime, in war feared nobody, sturdily suffering pain and lack of food, had no deserters, was not so worried by illnesses and had always ready its reserve of younger men, trained as soldiers since their teen-ages.

The austrian Border regiments in 1809 and beyond

After the 1805 campaign, Napoleon concluded peace with the Austrians signing the Treaty of Pressburg. This treaty ceded to France control of northern Italy as well as Friuli, Istria, Dalmatia and the Cattaro Islands. With this transfer of territory, a French administration was established on July 7, 1806 when General Marmont was assigned as Commander-in-Chief of Dalmatia.

This transfer of "Austrian" territory was amongst the most hated clauses of the treaty and one of the main causes of the 1809 campaign. Though the Austrians threatened this territory in 1809, it remained in French hands and the battle of Deutsch-Wagram eliminated any possibility of a military threat to the French possess on the area. When the dust of the 1809 campaign settled down, further territories were ceded to France, including the home districts of six of Austria's "Grenz" regiments.

When their territories were transferred to France, so were some of the grenz regiments too. These regiments were organized along Austrian lines. Each "French-Croatian" regiment had two battalions of six companies. There were no elite companies and, unlike regular Austrian infantry regiments, no grenadier companies. However, they did have regimental artillery companies.

K.K. MILITÄRGRENZE 1809

SIEBENBÜRGEN (Transylvania) commander FML Graf Vinzenz Kolowrat-Liebsteinsky
KARLSBURG **(**Gyulafehérvár**)** – KK Feldzeugamt klein Post
KARLSBURG **(**Gyulafehérvár**)** – KK 4th Artillerie regiment Unterberger – 1 company

Divisionskommando FML baron Wunibald von Löwenberg

Brigadekommando GM Johann von Branovacky
CSIKSZEREDA – 1st Székler Grenzer – 2 batt. (6 Comp.)
KÉZDIVÁSÁRHELY – 2nd Székler Grenzer – 2 batt. (6 Comp.)

Brigadekommando GM Ignaz von Novak
ORLÁTH – 1st Walachen Grenzer - 2 batt. (6 Comp.)
NASZÓD – 2nd Walachen Grenzer - 2 batt. (6 Comp.)

Divisionskommando FML baron Johann de Szent-Kereszty

Brigadekommando GM Gabriel Geringer von Ödenburg
SEPSI-SZENTGYÖRGYI – Székler Hussars n. 11 – 6 esc.

BANATER GRENZE FML Peter von Duka

Brigadekommando GM Paul von Radivojevich
PANCSOVA – Deutsch Banater Grenzer – 2 batt. (6 comp.)
KARÁNSEBES – Wallachisch Illyrische Grenzer – 2 batt. (6 comp.)

Resident brigade GM baron Lippe
TEMESVÁR –KK IR 62 Franz Jellacich - – 2 Depot companies
TEMESVÁR –KK IR 61 Saint Julien - – 2 Depot companies
GROSSWARDEIN – KK IR 37 Weidenfeld - – 2 Depot companies

BANAL-GRENZE – Ban (Banus) FML Graf Ignaz Gyulai

Brigadekommando GM Josef von Wetzl
GLINA – 1st Banal Grenzer reg. n. 10- 2 batt. (6 Comp.)
PETRINJA – 2nd Banal Grenzer reg. n. 11 - 2 batt. (6 Comp.)

SLAVONIAN GRENZE FML baron Johann von Simbschen

Divisionkommando FML baron Christoph von Lattermann
PETERWARDEIN FORTRESS – KK Feldzeugamt Haupt Post

Brigadekommando GM Peter von Lutz
VINKOVCE – 7th Grenzregiment Brod - 2 batt. (6 Comp.)
GRADISKA – 8th Grenzregiment Gradiska - 2 batt. (6 Comp.)

Brigadekommando GM Josef von Pfanzelter
MITROVITZ – 9th Grenzregiment Peterwardein - 2 batt. (6 Comp.)

CARLSTÄDTER – WARASDINER GRENZE FML baron Franz Jellacich de Buzim
CARLSTADT– KK Feldzeugamt klein Post

Warasdiner generalät Brigadekommando GM baron Gustav von Roschovsky
BELOVÁR – 5th Grenzregiment Warasdiner – Kreuzer - 2 batt. (6 Comp.) – to Pest
BELOVÁR – 6th Grenzregiment Warasdiner – StGeorger - 2 batt. (6 Comp.) – to Pest

Brigadekommando GM Johann Kálnássy von Kálnás
OGULIN – 3rd Grenzregiment Oguliner - 2 batt. (6 Comp.)
CARLSTADT - 4th Grenzregiment Szluiner- 2 batt. (6 Comp.)

Brigadekommando GM Andreas von Stojchevich
GOSPIĆ – 1st Grenzregiment Liccaner - 2 batt. (6 Comp.)
OTOČAC – 2nd Grenzregiment Otoschaner - 2 batt. (6 Comp.)

TRANSYLVANIA – Siebenbürgen 1809

Transylvania (Siebenbürgen, Hung. Erdely; Rumanian, Ardeal) in 1765 was raised to Grand Principality status (Großfürstentum) by the empress Maria Theresia, as one government quite independent from other crowns. The State had, sometimes incidentally in union with its Regions, the power to do laws and to raise taxes, while the Empire exercised only all other Imperial rights. The Landtag become Hermannstadt, a royal free city, (in addition with Cronstadt, Carlsburg, Clausenburg etc.).

Until 1848 the chief influence and privileges, as well as the only political rights, were divided among the three " privileged nations "of the Hungarians, Szeklers and Saxons". The first are the descendants of the Magyar conquerors. The Szeklers are of disputed origin, but closely akin to the Magyars (see after) The Saxons are the posterity of the German immigrants brought by King Geza II. (1141-1161) from Flanders and the lower Rhine to cultivate and repeople his desolated territories. However, by far, the most numerous element of dwellers, though long excluded from power and political equality, was formed by Rumanians. The efforts of the Rumanian inhabitants to secure recognition as a fourth "nation," and the opposition of the non-Magyar population to a closer union with Hungary, led to troubles early in the 19th century, culminating in 1848.

The bourgeois population of the main towns, mainly of german language, had, as "national" regiment the IR 31 Benjowski, rather than the n. 51 Splenyi, which was especially recruited in the rural outskirts.

Brassó (Ger. Kronstadt; Rumanian, Brasov) was one of the most populous town of Transylvania, and its population was composed in about equal numbers of Germans, Magyars and Rumanians.

Hermannstadt (Ung. Nagyszeben, Rum. Sibiu) for many years was the siege of the local Government (Landstag). The larger part of its inhabitants was of german origins and traditions.

Gyulafehérvár (Ger. Carlsburg, Rom. Alba Julia) After the reversion of Transylvania in 1713 to the Habsburg monarchy the actual strong fortress was built in 1716-1735 by the emperor Charles VI, whence the German name of the town.

Koloszvár (Ger. Klausenburg, Rum. Cluj) Kolozsvar is believed to occupy the site of a Roman settlement named Napoca. Colonized by Saxons in 1178, it then received its German name of Klausenburg, from the old word Klause, signifying a "mountain pass." Between the years 1545 and 1570 large numbers of the Saxon population left the town in consequence of the introduction of Unitarian doctrines. In 1798 the town was to a great extent destroyed by fire. From 1830 it became the capital of Transylvania and the seat of the Transylvanian diets.

Maros-Vásárhely (Ger. Neumarkt) was the ancient capital town of the Szeklers lands.

Main town	hungarian	Stuhl – Szék – (county)	IR Reg. army	Grenzregiment
Kronstadt	Brassó	Brassó-Haromszék		2nd Szekler
Hermannstadt	Nagyszeben	Szeben-Fogaras	31	1st Walachen
Carlsburg	Gyulafehérvár	Unter-Weissenburg		--
Klausenburg	Koloszvár	Kolosz-Szilagy		2nd Walachen
Neumarkt	Marosvásárhely	Máros-Torda		1st Szekler part 2nd Walachen
Bistritz	Beszterce	Beszterce-Naszod Szolnok-Doboka	51	2nd Walachen
Broos	Szászváros	Hunyad		1st Walachen
Odorhellen	Székely-Udvarhely	Csik-Udvarhely		1st – 2nd Szekler

1809 REGULAR INFANTRY K.K. (Kaiserliche königliche) Ungarischen Infanterie Regimenter

K.K. IR 31 – FML Johann Benjowski (Benjovszky) von Benjov – 3 battalions
der Siebenbürger Regiment

Recruitment: 1 Depot comp. at Ofen, Div. baron Karl Weidenfeld, Brig. baron András von Szörenyi.

Alsó-Fehér (Unt.Weissenburg)	Gyulafehérvár	31
Szeben	Nagyszeben	
Brassó	Kronstadt	
Fogaras	Zernest	
Háromszék	Kézdivásárhely	
Nagy-Küküllő	Segesvár	
Torda-Aranyos	Torda	
Depot Kader	Ofen	Peterwardein - Hermannstadt
Commander oberst	Franz Splényi von Mihaldy later GM	Anton Stephan Hirsch then Paul Maria Joseph Senitzer (after Aspern)
Oberstleutnant	count Georg Bánffy	Josef Odelga
Majors	Mathias von Ivanka	Adam Retsey von Retsee
	Johann Mécsey	Johann von Meiller

before Aspern: Assigned to the army of Germany, VI Corps FM von Hiller, Div. Jellacich then was in the Div. Vincent, Brig. Hofmeister.

At Abensberg 2 comp. were with the Détachement Rittmeister Spannagel, other 2 comp. with the Avant-garde brigade GM Armand von Nordmann, the regiment with Brigade GM Hoffmeister von Hoffeneck, Division FML comte Friedrich baron von Kottulinsky. During the retreat it returned in the Div. FML Vincent in the rearguard fighting at Rohr and finally at Landshut (April 21). At Landshut the 1st battalion was detached from the rearguard of baron Carl Vincent. During the two battles the regiment lost 41 dead, 60 wounded and 345 prisoners. At Neumarkt it was in the 3rd Column (Left), Brig. GM Josef Hofmeister von Hoffenegg.

At Ebelsberg the Brig. Hofmeister was always under Div. Vincent but in a rearguard sector led together with the Div. FML Emmanuel von Schustekh. Vincent deployed the Brig. Hofmeister with the Chevaulegers at Klein-München in order to support the extreme rearguard retreating under the French fire (Brig. Bianchi). The brigade Hofmeister found the new positions full of all sort of carriages and material. So was forced to deploy north of the village. They were attacked by the French cavalry and retreated till the bridge (Traun river) repulsing the advancing enemies with bravery. However when the French guns began to bombard the situation becam critical and they withdrew on the opposite river bank. There the regiment lost around 598 men in total, of which, it was referred, 189 sunk in the cold river waters.

It followed the retreat in Austria, the passage of Danube at Mautern (May 8) and the rest at Grafenwörth camp. The regiment was reorganized in the Division GM baron Carl Vincent under the provisional brigade oberst baron Franz Splényi de Miháldy.

at Aspern: Brig. Hoffmeister, Div. Vincent, VI Corps with 3 battalions (1130 men). The 1st battalion was ordered to do a flank attack against the Kirchhof positions (Aspern), under the command of General Staff-Oberleutnant Josef von Ehrenstein. The rest of the regiment supported the assault and lost, in total: 38 dead, 166 wounded, 5 prisoners.

between Aspern and Wagram: After the battle the weak 1st battalion was disbanded and the regiment remained only with the 2nd and 3rd batt. with the new colonel Stefan Hirsch. Meiller and Bánffy left the regiment and the new oberstleutnant was Mathias Ivanka. On June 22, however, Hirsch returned to IR 32, and the new colonel was Paul Maria Joseph Senitzer. Ivanka retreated from service and the new oberstleutnant was Josef Odelga (majors Johann Mécsey prisoner, Baumgartten and Déak).

at Wagram: the 2 batt. were with Brig. baron Franz Splényi de Miháldy, Div. FML baron Kottulinsky, VI corps Klenau. They followed the retreat of the VI Corps losing: 9 dead, 54 prisoners. During the retreat they fought at Korneuburg (3 dead, 23 wounded and 87 prisoners), Stockerau (1 dead and 10 wounded). Always acting as rearguard it was ordered by GM Mariássy to stop at Hollabrunn, together with the twin regiment Splényi and some companies of IR 60. They lost there (July 10) 46 dead and 543 wounded. It was not at Znaim.

K.K. IR 51 – FML baron Gabriel Splényi von Mihály – 3 battalions

Recruitment: the 1st Depot comp. at Carlsburg, the 2nd at Klausenburg. Later the 2 Depot Compagnien at Pest, Div. baron Carl Weidenfeld, brig. GM Andreas von Szörényi.

Kolosz	Koloszvár	
Szilágy	Zilah	
Hunyad	Déva	
Besztercze-Naszód	Besztercze	51
Udvárhely	Székelyudvarhely	
Szolnók-Doboka	Szamosújvár	
Depot Kader	Klausenburg (Koloszvár)	
Commander oberst	Michael von Scharlach	Franz von Scharlach
Oberstleutnant	baron Johann Rechenberg (transf.) Franz Seyringer (dead at Ebelsberg)	Franz von Scharlach Dimitri Rado-sevich von Radosch
Majors	Franz Seyringer Franz von Scharlach	Peter Businelli Johann Böhm

before Aspern: twin of IR 31, it was assigned to the army of Germany, VI Corps FM von Hiller, Div. Jellacich then Div. Vincent, Brig. Hofmeister.

At Abensberg the regiment was with Brigade GM Hoffmeister von Hoffeneck, Division FML comte Friedrich baron von Kottulinsky. Then returned in the Div. FML Vincent. During the retreat they fought some rearguard clashes losing 17 dead, 40 wounded and 12 prisoners. At Landshut the regiment was employed to delay the French cavalry. Its losses were severe: 22 dead, 66 wounded, 157 prisoners and 86 missing.

At Neumarkt it was in the 3rd Column GM Josef Hoffmeister von Hoffenegg with two companies in the avantgarde and the rest in the main column.

At Ebelsberg the Brig. Hofmeister was always under Div. Vincent but in a rearguard sector led by the Div. FML Emmanuel von Schustekh. Vincent deployed the Brig. Hofmeister with the Chevaulegers at Klein-München in order to support the extreme rearguard retreating under the French fire (Brig. Bianchi). The brigade Hofmeister found the new positions full of all sort of carriages and material. So was forced to deploy north of the village. They were attacked by the French cavalry and retreated till the bridge (Traun river) repulsing the advancing enemies with bravery. However when the French guns began to bombard the situation becam critical and they withdrew on the opposite river bank. Oberstleutnant Franz Seyringer was severely wounded and then died. The regiment lost 93 men dead, 236 wounded and prisoners, 102 prisoners not wounded, 425 missing men of which 236 surely drowned in the Traun waters.

It followed the retreat in Austria with only 799 men, the passage of Danube at Mautern (May 8) and the rest at Florisdorf camp.The regiment was reorganized in the Division GM baron Carl Vincent under the provisional brigade oberst baron Franz Splényi de Mihály. The regiment received there around 800 men from Transylvania (with 300 green recruits).

at Aspern: it was in the Brig. Hoffmeister, Div. Vincent, VI Corps with 2 battalions (938 men). During the second day of the battle the 2nd batt. had orders to support the attack against Aspern led by colonel Scharlach, soon followed also by the 1st battalion. There the regiment lost (grenadiers comp. included) 146 dead, 83 wounded, 38 prisoners and 32 missing.

at Wagram: the battalions were with Brig. baron Franz Splényi de Mihály, Div. FML baron Kottulinsky, VI corps Klenau with tasks to cover the Corps retreat. During the retreat the regiment met its new 3rd battalion at Hirschstetten. On July 7 they fought at Korneuburg (18 dead, 13 wounded, 112 prisoners and 12 missing), Stockerau with the Brig. Mariássy, Div. Wallmoden (2 batt.). One battalion was in the Brig. Vécsey. The Brig. Mariássy engaged the enemies at Hollabrunn (July 9) (69 dead, 92 wounded, 62 prisoners and 8 missing). Finally the 24 Officers and 719 men of IR Splényi withdrew to Leitomischl, without taking part at the Znaim battle.

Banat and Vojvodship (Vojvodschaft) of Serbia - (Vajdaság or Vojvodina)

The territory of the Banat is presently part of the Romanian counties Timiş, Caraş-Severin, Arad and Mehedinţi, the Serbian autonomous province of Vojvodina and Belgrade City District, and the Hungarian Csongrád County. In the 17th century, parts of the Banat were incorporated into the Habsburg Monarchy of Austria. In 1716, Prince Eugene of Savoy took the last parts of the Banat from the Ottomans. It remained a separate province in the Habsburg Monarchy under military administration until 1751, when Empress Maria Theresa of Austria introduced a civil administration. The Banat of Temeswar province was abolished in 1778. The southern part of the Banat region remained within the Military Frontier (Banat Krajina) until the Frontier was abolished in 1871. Maria Theresa also took a great interest in the Banat; she colonized the region with large numbers of German peasants, encouraged the exploitation of the mineral wealth of the country, and generally developed the measures introduced by Mercy. German settlers arrived from Swabia, Alsace and Bavaria, as well as people from Austria. The ethnic Germans in the Banat region became known as the Danube Swabians, or Donauschwaben. Some of them, coming from French-speaking or linguistically mixed communes in Lorraine, maintained the French language for several generations. Hungarians were not allowed to settle in the Banat during this colonization period. In 1779, the Banat region was incorporated back into Habsburg Kingdom of Hungary, and the three counties Torontál, Temes and Krassó were created.

The "german" speaking Banater served expecially in the Grenzregiment n. 12 with HQ in Pancsova, but the reference units of the Banat was the 61st regiment (actually St. Julien).

Main town	hungarian	Hung. Counties (Vármegye)	IR r. army	I. Grenzregiment
Neusatz	Újvidék	Bacs – Bodrog South		n. 9 Petrovaradin (Peterwardein)
Zombor	Zombor	Bacs-Bodrog center	62	
Maria-Theresiopel	Szabadka	Bacs-Bodrog north		--
Becskerek		Torontal		n. 12 Deutsch Banater
Temeschburg	Temesvár	Temes	61	n. 12 Deutsch Banater
Karansebes		Krassó-Szörény		n. 13 Wallachisch-Illyrisches

K.K. IR 61 – FML Graf Franz St Julien Waldsee – 3 battalions
Recruitment: 2 Depot Comp. Brig. baron Lippe in Temesvár under Alvinczy

Temes	Temesvár	61
Torontál	Nagybecskerek	
Arad-Zárand	Arad	
Krassó-Szörényi	Lugos	
Depot Kader	Temesvár	HQ Peterwardein - Graz
Commander oberst	Johann von Longueville	
Oberstlieutenant	Stephan Rétsey von Retsee	Anton Janusch
Majors	Johann Szent-Iványi	Anton Janusch (grenadier)
	Josef von Herdlizka	

before Aspern: assigned to Inner Austria army. In the VIII Armeekorps FML Marquis Chasteler, 1st Truppendivision FML count Albert Gyulai, Brig. GM count Colloredo-Mansfeld. After the advance in Italy the regiment was at Sacile, supporting the avant-garde. It assaulted the village of Porcia and lost 184 men dead or wounded (the wounded mainly made prisoners) and 61 prisoners. On April 28-29 they fought at Soave near Verona, the regiment engaged in the village defence. There were 26 men dead, 18 prisoners and 10 missing, with a larger number of wounded. At the Piave battle the regiment supported the austrian cavalry attempt to stop the French, but general Wolfskehl was overrun by enemy cavalry and they were forced to put the units in Squares losing still 182 men. Brigade Colloredo was sent till Venzone where it was attacked (May 12). In the defence of the village the regiment lost 312 men with its Oberstlieutenant Stephan Rétsey.

between Aspern and Wagram: when GM Colloredo had the divisional command the regiment came under Brig. De Vaux, Div. Colloredo, VIII Corps (Juni 7). At the battle of Raab the regiment was in first line, behing the village of Kis-Megyer with the Div. Colloredo and with 2 comp. detached on the Maierhof under Oberstleutnant Kummel. During the battle the whole 1st battalion was isolated near the Maierhof with Kummel. The regiment lost 604 men, the main part (wounded) fallen prisoner. The regiment Oberstlieutenant was now Anton Janusch, former grenadier commander.

After Raab the regiment took part in the Pressburg defence. There Colonel Longueville was severely wounded and the command passed to Janusch. Actually the regiment had only 500 men in total!

At Wagram: the regiment was in the Brig. De Vaux, Div. Colloredo. But they arrived too late to help the Emperor at Wagram. After the armistice the regiment camped in the Zala county and waited for the end of the war.

▲ Austro-Hungarian territorial and border troops 1798-1805 about. From Ottenfeld artwork

K.K. IR 62 – FML Baron Franz Jellachich de Buzim - 3 battalions

Recruitment: 2 Depot Comp. at Temesvár, Brig. Lippe under Alvinczy. It was assigned to Inner Austria army; in the VIII Armeekorps FML Marquis Chasteler, 1st Truppendivision FML count Albert Gyulai, Brig. GM von Gajoli.

Máros-Torda	Marosvásárhely	
Csik	Csikszereda	62
Kis-Küküllő	Dicsőszentmárton	
Bács-Bodrog. Szabadka	Maria Theresiopel	
Bács-Bodrog. Zombor	Zombor	
Depot Kader	Temesvár	HQ Temesvár
Commander oberst	Joseph Papp	
Oberstlieutenant	baron Franz Stutterheim	
Majors	Franz Ghequier de Melly-Nádasd	
	Johann De la Hamaide	

before Aspern: on April 15 they were at Pordenone with the 1st battalion in the GM Wetzel column. The day after (Sacile) Brig. Gajoli with the 2nd and the 3rd batt. were deployed on the right. The 1st batt. was at Porcia in skirmish order. In the two days the regiment lost 70 dead, 114 wounded. On April 29-30 the regiment attacked at Monte (Castel) Cerino against the div. Severoli, in the second line behind IR 53.

The regiment had there many losses, 3 officers dead and many soldiers, with over 200 wounded. At the Piave the regiment supported the Brig. Colloredo and had other hard fights at San Daniele and Venzone (May 12). From 16 till 17 May they defended the Tarvis pass fortifications under FM Gyulai command. The 1st batt. (only 200 men under Ghequier) was in a redoubt, the 2nd and 3rd battalions were defending the Schlitzbach bridges with Gajoli. The French attack was fierce and the regiment surrounded losing 8 Staff officers prisoners, among whom was colonel Papp; many died or were wounded and captured. Only two columns under majors Ghequier and De la Hamaide escaped.

- between Aspern and Wagram: the regiment was reorganized under the new interim commander Franz Stutterheim, who raised two new battalions with 840 recruits. It was attached to the Brig. GM Marziani, Div. Colloredo, VIII Corps. At Raab the two battalions deployed between Szabadhegy and Kis-Megyer in the second line. After the loss of Szabadhegy village the two battalions were ordered to counterattack. In the battle the regiment lost 442 men (57 dead, 159 wounded, 190 prisoners, 36 missing).

- at Wagram: the regiment marched with 1083 men marched with the column De Vaux, Div. Colloredo, Inner Austria army but arrived too late in oder to participate at the battle. The 1st battalion (De la Hamaide) was then order to reach Pressburg defences. The 2nd battalion and the staff retreated to Komorn.

Croatia and Slavonia

Croatian soldiers served in many European armies since the seventeenth century. So in the French army in the 17th century, during the reign of Louis XIII, there was a cavalry composed exclusively of the Croats, called Royal - Cravate, which existed in the period of 1664-1789. These soldiers gave the world something that is today unavoidable in fashion: the tie, called la cravate by the French and by the Germans die Krawatte - the expression was coined from the Croatian name, and mentioned for the first time in 1651.

The economic policies pursued by the Viennese administration under Maria Theresia (1740-1780) and Joseph II (1780-1790) had less of an impact on Croatia-Slavonia, because of their location on the fringe of the Habsburg possessions. The fact that Croatia-Slavonia was split in areas under civilian and areas under military administration provided another obstacle. The many new regulations passed by the Viennese administration frequently caused unrest. In 1715 the customs border separating Habsburg Croatia from Habsburg Inner Austria was lifted; in 1719 Fiume was declared a free port. Beginning in 1732, the river Sava was regulated, in order to facilitate river navigation. A road was constructed to connect Fiume with the Croatian and Hungarian interior, the Karolina (1726). The fortress city of Carlstadt developed into an important junction, attracted business and settlers.

Ethnic Germans immigrated into the cities of Croatia; German language gained in importance, in education as well as in the administration. In 1781 Joseph II decreed the Patent of Religious Toleration which permitted both protestants and Jews to permanently settle in Croatia, applied since 1783; it also permitted for the establishment of Orthodox communities in Croatia-Slavonia under civil administration. Serfdom was abolished in 1785.

In 1783 Joseph II decreed that Germans and other non-Croatians were to be admitted to public office (thus abolishing the indigenate). An administrative reform implemented in 1785 abolished Croatia-Slavonia as a territorial unit, replacing it by the districts of Pecs (Fünfkirchen) and Zagreb (Agram). In 1784 Joseph II decreed German to be introduced as the official language of administration, jurisdiction and education in 1786; judges, administrative officials etc. given a period of 3 years to learn the new language (German replaced Latin). This reform served to create national Croatian consciousness; the reform was rejected outside the German-speaking community. In 1789 Croatia-Slavonia and her Sabor were reestablished, most of the unpopular Josephinian reforms cancelled. The 1st and 2nd national Croatian regiments, the ownership of which was direct matter of the higher croatian authority, the Ban, were the two Banal Grenz (Gränz) regiments of Glina and Petrinja. The Ban was FML baron Ignjat (Ignatius) Ðulaj (Gyulai) de Maros-Nemeth and Nádaska, in command from 1806 till 1831. The third national regiment was the 53rd infantry, entitled to FML Jellacich (Jellačić od Buzim).

Main town	hungarian	Counties (Vármegye)	IR regular army	I. Grenzregiment
Belovar-Bjelovar	Belovár	Belovár-Körös	nn	n. 5 Warasdin-Kreuzer
Agram	Zágráb	Agram		--
Warasdin	Varasd	Warasdiner-St.Georger		n. 6 Warasdin-St.Georg
Esseg	Eszeg	Verőcze-Pozsega	53	
Peterwardein	Pétervárad	Szérem (Syrmia)		n. 9 Peterwardeiner
Carlstadt	Karlovac	Carlstadt-Modruš Fiume		
Fiume	Fiume	Modruš Fiume		Kriegsmarine
Grenze – Military Border				
Gospić	Gospics	Lika-Krbava		n. 1 Liccaner
Otočać	Otocsán	Lika-Krbava		n. 2 Otochaner
Ogulin	Ogulin	Carlstadt		n. 3 Oguliner
Slunj	Szluin	Carlstadt		n. 4 Szluiner
Glina	--	Banal Grenze	nn	n. 10 1st Banal
Petrinja	--	Banal Grenze		n. 11 2nd Banal
Brod	--	Slavonia		n. 7 Brooder
Gradiska		Slavonia		n. 8 Gradiscaner

K.K. IR 53 – FML –Johann Jellachich de Buzim (Jellačić de Buzim) 3 battalions
National Croatian regiment

Recruitment: 2 Depot Comp. in Esseg, Brig. Weidenfeld in Ofen unter Alvinczy – also Reserve Div. of Inner Austria army. Regiment in Temesvár with Fünfkirchen Div. FML Franz Görupp von Besanez, later in Brig. GM Ludwig von Daniel in Neusatz (Neusandec). One battalion was in Esseg.

Zágráb (Agram)	Agram	
Varasd	Varazdin	
Verőcze	Esseg (Osijek)	53
Szerém (Syrmien)	Vukovár	
Pozsega	Pozsega	
Depot Kader	Esseg (Osijek)	HQ Esseg
Commander oberst	Chev. Ludwig Papp de Vezprém	Anton von Volkmann
Oberstleutnant	Anton von Volkmann	Carl Van der Mühlen gren.
Majors	Emerich Marx	baron Franz Hundt
	Johann von Lutter	

before Aspern: assigned to Inner Austria army. In the VIII Armeekorps FML. Marquis Chasteler, 1st Truppendivision FML count Albert Gyulai, Brig. GM von Gajoli. On April 9 it was at Tarvis where Volkmann took command for an illness of colonel Papp. Gyulai ordered Volkmann to create a Mobile Column for the invasion of the Kingdom of Italy territories, avoiding the main road, driving through mountains toward Pontafel and Chiusa. On April 11 Volkmann reached the village of Venzone and the Tagliamento river, defended by French general Broussier. The Volkmann's attack was a true surprise and after some hard fire volley, the French abandoned their positions, having fear to be forced to engage an Austrian corps behind that vanguards. So 3 austrian battalions and 3 guns repulsed a French division. The IR 53 battalion lost only 17 men wounded and 2 prisoners during the affair. The other two battalions led by major Marx marched through Flitsch (It. Plezzo, Sl. Bovec) and touched

Karfreit (It. Caporetto, Sl. Kobarid), reachin on April 12 Udine.

On April 16 the Brig. Gajoli had orders to seize Vigonovo and to get a link with Volkmann. Having reunited the forces the 1st and 3rd batt. under Volkmann advanced to Fontanafredda, while the 2nd batt. (major Lutter) supported the attack. The assault was quick and bloody. It had success but the Austrians did penetrate too deeply into the enemy lines and were counterattacked by French cavalry. The regiment lost: 61 dead, 254 wounded (major Lutter had severe wounds), 265 prisoners. Volkmann was promoted to 2nd colonel and maintained the command till June 16 when colonel Papp returned from the period of recovery.

The new colonel was then ordered to cover the right army flank, trying the contact with the troops in Tirol with his Column (1st batt. IR 53, one batt. Banal, 4 sqns. Hohenzollern Chevaulegers and 2 brigade batteries). He marched through Asolo till Bassano, covering the hills of the valleys north of Vicenza. At Montebello Volkmann restituted the 1st batt. to Marx and took command of the other two battalions marching to Montorso and being now part of the avant-garde Div. Frimont. He engaged the French at Villanova near San Bonifacio. On April 29 the Viceroy Eugene counterattacked Frimont; Volkmann was in the right austrian wing at Soave. The 1st battalion was with Brig. Gajoli, Div. Colloredo, VIII Corps with support orders. The day after the French renewed the attack on the hills (monte Cerino). The croatian regiment was sent till Castel Cerino to help the defenders there deployed. In two days the regiment lost 17 men, 159 wounded and 51 prisoners.

Finally came the withdrawal order. On May 2 the regiment was attached to the brig. Schmidt and sent to Bassano to defend the valley of the Brenta river (road to Tirol). After an hard artillery bombardment against the town of Bassano, Schmidt retreated through Feltre and Belluno, reaching the Tirol. Ther the 1st battalion (Marx) remained with Brig. Schmidt, the 2nd batt. (Lutter) was sent to Sterzing (It. Vipiteno) and the 3rd battalion (Volkmann) to Trento; the colonel himself was made commander of South Tirol. The regiment was then under Corps Chasteler. Volkmann had to march till Bozen (It. Bolzano) and the same order was sent to the 2nd batt. The 1st battalion was with Schmidt in the defence of the Pustertal. On May 17 the 1st and 2nd battalions were in the Brig. Fenner, Corps Chasteler at Toblach (It. Dobbiaco) for the defence of the Pustertal; the 3rd remained at Bozen. On May 19 the two battalions returned under Schmidt at Sillian. The column Volkmann marched till Schabs.

at Aspern: on May 21 Chasteler charged GM Marschal with the task to gather the imperial troops at Lienz, in order to support the battered Inner Austria army. The 1st battalion remained in the Brig. Schmidt, the other two units in the Brig. Marschal. The regiment had some combats in Carinthia while trying to get in touch with the army (Div. Jellacich). The 1st division (comp. 1 and 2) under captain Vauquez remained in Tirol with the brig. Buol. The whole Corps Chasteler advanced and, on June 6, reached Klagenfurt and attacked the town. The combats lasted an complete day mainly in the Calvarienhöhe position. Volkmann was soon isolated from the rest of the Brig. Schmidt and remained in his position. Chasteler had given order to withdraw, but looking at the Calvarienhöhe, authorized a last assault, in order to try Volkmann's rescue. They surprised the French, who were sent back in the town and the regiment went out of the dangerous pocket.

- between Aspern and Wagram: on June 9 the retreating Corps Chasteler met the Banus Gyulai at Gonowitz and followed his way to Croatia. The regiment was at Varasdin on June 16.

- at and after Wagram: 2 comp. remained detached with the Brig. Buol in Tirol, while the regiment marched through southern-west Hungary in garrison duties.

Note: the Reserve division marched in May from Esseg till Raab where it stood as garrison till June (battle of Raab) Brigade Oberst Pétschy of Div. FZM Davidovich.

Notes:

1   The German word "grenz" means border and these "grenzers" were the border guards of Austria. They were formed into military colonies and were held in a constant state of military preparedness because they were the first line of defense against incursions of the dreaded Turks.

2   January 1807 Census:

Liccaner regiment 52734 souls; Ottochaner regiment: 46131; Oguliner regiment: 44940; Szluiner regiment: 45730 Zeng 2800; Carlopago 1600; 1st Banal 47313; 2nd Banal 43933; Petrinja 2853; Costanizza 1108

3   In the Europäischen Annalen St. 5, 1810, the strength of a Croatian-slavonian or Banat regiment was 2723 men, while a Transylvanian regiment had 2482 men. They had actually two fusiliers battalions and two Scharf-

schützen companies. The remaining 11 Grenz regiments had a strength of 28989 soldiers (without the Csajkisten battalion, which had 1068 men).

4   About the name and its origin there is no yet agreement: some wanted it to derive from the Seven Castles of the Saxon nation, or Johanniter in Burzelland; others believe that this word did come only after the arrival of the Saxons in the countryland.

5   Blazekovich von, K. : Chronik des K. K. 31. LinienInfanterie Regimentes. Wien: 1867/69.

6   Maendl, Maximilian : Geschichte des K. und K. Infanterie-Regiments Nr. 51. Klausenburg: 1897-99.

7   Hoffmann von Donnersberg, August: Geschichte des k. u. k. Infanterie-Regiments Nr. 61. 1798 -1892. Wien: 1892.

8   Bichlmann Wilhelm: Chronik des Infanterie-Regimentes Nr. 62 dermalen Ludwig Prinz von Bayern von seiner Errichtung 1798 bis 1880. Wien: 1880.

9   Gebauer, Karl Edler von; Ulrich, Heinrich: Geschichte des k. k. 53. Infanterie-Regimentes Erzherzog Leopold Ludwig. Tulln: 1881

10   Gruppe Volkmann was formed by: IR 53 3rd battalion under Volkmann himself, one battalion of the 2nd Banal regiment, 2 squadrons of n. 5 Ott Hussars and half brigade battery. Practically it served as the army avantgarde. During the advance Volkmann got also the 1st batt. of IR 52 Franz Carl.

IR 61 FML St Julien   **IR 62 FML Franz Jellachich**   **IR 63 FZM Baillet de Merlemont**

▲ Austrian Infantry uniforms regiments nr. 61, 62 & 63

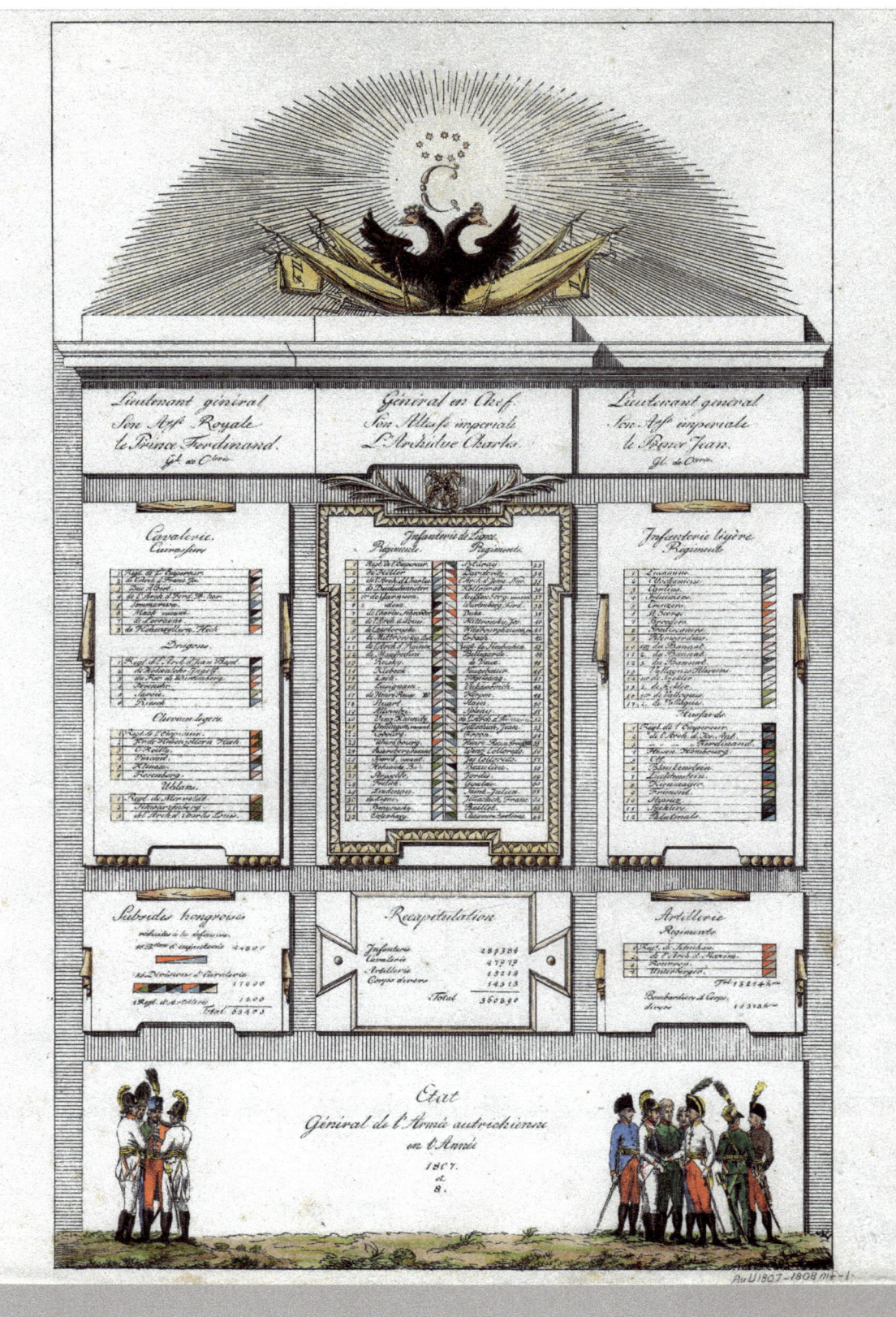

▲ Austrian army scheme 1807–1809.

TITOLI PUBBLICATI - ALREADY PUBLISHING

SOLDIERS&WEAPONS 029